TRIG
The voice of m

The**inspirational**series™
Overcoming adversity and thriving

Sex, Suicide, and Serotonin

Taking Myself Apart,
Putting Myself Back Together

BY DEBBIE HAMPTON

We are proud to introduce The**inspirational**series™. Part of the Trigger family of innovative mental health books, The**inspirational**series™ tells the stories of the people who have battled and beaten mental health issues. For more information visit: www.triggerpublishing.com

THE AUTHOR

Debbie Hampton is from Greensboro, NC. She has recovered from decades of depression, a suicide attempt, and resulting brain injury to become an inspirational writer, a leading blogger in the brain-health arena, and well-known voice in the mental health community.

Debbie's lifestyle work been featured on MindBodyGreen, TinyBuddha, and The Huffington Post, and she has attracted an enthusiastic fan base on social media. She writes about behaviour and thought modifications, along with the mental health practices and alternative therapies she used to rebuild her brain in order to find joy and thrive.

First published in Great Britain 2018 by Trigger

Trigger is a trading style of Shaw Callaghan Ltd & Shaw Callaghan 23 USA, INC.

The Foundation Centre

Navigation House, 48 Millgate, Newark

Nottinghamshire NG24 4TS UK

www.triggerpublishing.com

British Library Cataloguing in Publication Data

A CIP catalogue record for this book is available upon request
from the British Library

ISBN: 978-1-912478-26-2

This book is also available in the following e-Book formats:

MOBI: 978-1-912478-29-3
EPUB: 978-1-912478-27-9
PDF: 978-1-912478-28-6
AUDIO: 978-1-78956-000-8

Debbie Hampton has asserted her right under the Copyright,
Design and Patents Act 1988 to be identified as the author of this work

Cover design and typeset by Fusion Graphic Design Ltd

Project Management by Out of House Publishing

Printed and bound in Great Britain by Clays Ltd, Elcograf S.p.A.

Paper from responsible sources

www.triggerpublishing.com

Thank you for purchasing this book.
You are making an incredible difference.

Proceeds from all Trigger books go directly to
The Shaw Mind Foundation, a global charity that focuses
entirely on mental health. To find out more about
The Shaw Mind Foundation visit,
www.shawmindfoundation.org

MISSION STATEMENT

Our goal is to make help and support available for every
single person in society, from all walks of life.
We will never stop offering hope. These are our promises.

Trigger and The Shaw Mind Foundation

AUTHOR'S NOTE

This book is based on my personal experiences and opinions. Many names and identifying characteristics have been changed, characters combined, and events expanded and / or altered. Happenings have been portrayed as recorded in personal and legal documentation, medical records, and from memory. Memory is subjective. I acknowledge that others' recollections of the circumstances described in this book may be different from my own. Imaginative re-creation has been applied to certain episodes, and they are not intended to portray actual events.

Please visit the author's website: **thebestbrainpossible.com**

To Chris
Love ya, miss ya, mean it

Trigger Warning: The book contains references to suicidal ideation.

Disclaimer: Some names and identifying details have been changed to protect the privacy of individuals.

CHAPTER 1

Still Alive, Dammit!

I woke up in a hospital bed. My arms and legs, secured with cloth restraints to the bedrails, could only move about a foot in any direction before they snapped back like an overstretched rubber band. Tied down like an animal. Normally, being treated this way would make me cussing mad, but, at the time, I didn't have the energy or clarity of mind to even care.

A bored-looking male orderly in aqua blue scrubs sat to the right of the bed in what must have been a very uncomfortable chair.

Machines in the room blipped, whirred, and hummed, like the "Oompa Loompa" song in *Charlie and the Chocolate Factory*; however, there were no dancing munchkins to be seen anywhere.

It was the middle of June 2007, but I didn't know this. Like a foggy dream, some distant notions of the past and future existed in my mind, but had no bearing on my present world. All that I knew was the right here and right now.

Surprisingly, I wasn't experiencing any angst due to my condition and the circumstances. Usually, I'd be freaking out about now, but because my mind had no concept of normal for comparison, the situation didn't bother me. All I could do was subsist on a physical level in the present moment, a challenging task requiring every bit of my energy. Breathe. Sleep. Wake up. Back to sleep.

In an attempt to end it all, a kaleidoscope of pills had slid down my throat seven days earlier. I was gradually emerging from the coma that I'd been in for the past week. But the attractive 43-year-old woman, who on the outside seemed to have everything going for her, but felt empty and inadequate on the inside, remained locked in the darkness along with the details of the life she had known. In my injured mind, the troublesome ex-husband, the on-again-off-again boyfriend, and the terrified mess of a woman, and poor excuse for a mother that I'd become, ceased to exist.

Mentally, I was barely there, maybe a 20 on a scale of zero to 100, if even that. Before learning that it was gasp-worthy politically incorrect, I used to tell people that I was retarded. The closest thing I can compare my state of mind to was being shit-faced, out-of-your-mind bombed when it's way past the point of being anything close to fun anymore. Stumbling around, room spinning, can't think or function, drunk. But in this case, there was no sobering up in a couple of hours.

Whenever I'd been under the influence in the past, there was still some rational part of me that would pop up intermittently, watching the bombed me like a responsible parent making "tsk" noises and shaking her head disapprovingly. This clear-headed persona never really controlled my decision-making or behavior – unfortunately because she could have saved me from plenty of bad decisions – but she was always there, lurking and judging in the background. This time was different. The higher me had defected and was nowhere to be found.

Within a few days, the panicky, "Oh shit, shit, shit ... how am I ever going to begin to fix this mess?" thoughts began to surface as I came more into consciousness. I started to become cognizant of the fact that I needed to perform for all the people poking me and asking questions.

"What's this?" asked a fleshy-faced older man in a white coat, holding an object right in front of my face.

"A pen."

"Follow the pen with only your eyes," he said, bringing it to my nose, making me go cross-eyed, moving it away and then to the right and left. He used the pen to scribble on the chart and continued with his exam. It seemed like a fun little game to me.

As the mental fog continued to lift, I became increasingly aware of the seriousness of my situation. Without having a clear idea of how much of my messed up mental state was discernible to those around me, I attempted to do what damage control I could. Instinctively, I started to "play the game", like I had my entire life, which wasn't very good at this point. Like a child incapable of telling a convincing lie, my damaged brain couldn't spin information to put me in the best light, like I thought everyone wanted to hear, and to make what I had done seem not so heinous. For the first time in my life, I was blatantly honest because I couldn't be anything else.

My ego started to kick back in, and I began to feel embarrassed about how I must look in the ugly faded hospital gown with my shoulder-length hair, usually an auburn crown of curls and waves, now like me: limp and lifeless, and with no make-up. I usually never went anywhere without my face on, not even to bed if my boyfriend was sleeping over.

I couldn't focus on anything for more than a few seconds. It was as if someone had commandeered the remote control and was flipping through the channels inside my head. Before I could make sense of what was in front of me, like changing acts of a play, new props and characters would invade the scene I was looking at. A blurry haze of fragmented thoughts and disjointed images whizzed through my mind, and everyone and everything grabbed my attention and turned my head. My brain couldn't filter out extraneous information and stimuli nor prioritize what was incoming in any kind of sensible order.

I didn't automatically decipher what I was seeing or what was happening anymore. My brain knew a chair was a chair, a bed was a bed, and that kind of thing, but the process of visually taking in information and giving it contextual meaning eluded me. Understanding what I was seeing and hearing required making a conscious effort to try to assimilate, organize, and join the disparate parts. Most of the time, I simply couldn't piece together what I was looking at.

In addition to my broken brain, my mouth couldn't make comprehensible sounds to correspond with what I wanted to say. To my surprise, garbled noises and mutilated words spewed from my lips when I tried to speak. It sounded like my jaw was wired shut and my mouth crammed full of marbles. If you're old enough to remember *Gilligan's Island*, I sounded something like a drunk Thurston Howell. What came out was disturbingly slow, flat, and mangled, and didn't sound anything like the voice I heard in my head. The sluggishness of my speech was an indication of how quickly my brain was working: s-l-o-w. I couldn't control the volume of my voice, and I either spoke way too loud or in an inaudible whisper.

*

Most of my time in the hospital was spent sleeping, not only because I couldn't have stayed awake even if I had wanted to, but also because it was preferable to the reality that I was beginning to understand when I was awake. Sleep also made it easy for me to be a good patient and not rip out my IVs and explore the hospital. Like losing power during a thunderstorm, the lights would go out, and I would seamlessly slip in and out of consciousness whether I wanted to or not. I found comfort in the darkness and nothingness of sleep because while I was asleep, I didn't have to think, feel, or even exist.

Sleep was like the red, fuzzy blanket I kept folded up on the back of the couch. At any time, I could pull it over my head and disappear. In slumber, I could escape the consequences of my actions and the harshness of the real world, with its intrusive people, grating sounds, and head-hurting lights. Realizing what I had done made me cringe. It gave me that heavy feeling of dread in the pit of my stomach and made me want to turn away and cover my eyes, like I was watching a horror movie. Only, this wasn't a movie. This was my life.

In what seemed like forever, but was really only two weeks, that I spent lying there flat on my back, I can only remember one dream I had. In the dream, the sky was pitch black in the farthest corners behind the moon. The moonlight was so bright that the tall, scrawny, pine trees cast spooky shadows on the ground.

A single lane road ran through a group of buildings, looking like a hastily constructed military base – with identical, white aluminum buildings, arranged in symmetrical rows. Red dirt and patches of crab grass formed rectangles between the cement walkways connecting the buildings.

The trunk of a large pine tree stood so close to the building that wooden steps, like those leading to a child's tree house, had been nailed onto it.

Climbing the steps swiftly, I spotted a three-sided room, like a loft, with the open side towards me jutting up in the middle of the otherwise flat roof. Sitting in the loft drinking from little ceramic cups were my two older brothers, Chris and Ken. The white cups with no handles were the kind in which the warm Japanese wine, sake, is served. Maybe they were drinking sake. It wouldn't have been out of character for them.

I hugged both of my brothers tightly, inhaling their scents deeply. I've always been extremely sensitive to smells, especially people's signature, innate odor. Recognizing Chris and Ken on a primal level, I was comforted by the familiarity of their scents. The air was charged with a tingly yellow glow.

Ken looked as he had ten years ago in his mid-30s with his thick, brown hair in tousled waves falling just below his shoulders without any of the gray that's there now. A youthful, happy energy emanated from his face, and he smirked as if he had a juicy secret.

Chris, who had died 11 years earlier, appeared as he had in his late 20s. His small frame was defined and muscular just like he had liked it, and there was a devilish sparkle dancing in his eyes. His picture could have appeared beside the word "robust" in the dictionary. As he often did in life, he looked like he was ready to have a good time. The gaunt, haggard frame, resembling a skeleton, and flat, lifeless stare that haunted his sunken eyes during the latter part of his sickness were gone. The ashen, stubbly face with the protruding cheekbones that I'd become accustomed to at the end of his life had been replaced with his handsome, healthy pink, clean-shaven face.

As we caught up, little wrinkles formed at the corners of our eyes to make room for our smiles.

The reunion had the feeling of coming home on Thanksgiving Day, after a long absence, to the welcoming hugs of family and the smell of roasting turkey and baking pumpkin pie. Our love for each other hung thickly in the air with a tangible texture, like honey that you could reach your hand right out and grab a fistful of.

Bursting at the seams with happiness and totally at ease, I felt completely accepted and loved in the company of my brothers. I could have picked my nose, and it wouldn't have mattered one bit to them. This was the elusive, million dollar feeling I was always searching for in my life but could never seem to find anywhere with anyone. Little did I know that this sought-after place of love and acceptance didn't exist only in my dream. As I would find out, this treasure had been buried deep inside of me all along, and now, perhaps because I was so cracked and broken, maybe it could start leaking out. While I don't remember anything else about the dream, I will never forget that wonderful feeling.

*

My first week in the hospital was spent flat on my back, unconscious, and hooked up to a respirator. For the next week, I was conscious in varying degrees, stabilizing, and trying to learn how to perform the basics of living again: breathing, swallowing, eating, controlling my bladder, and communicating.

While many concerned people came to visit, all I really wanted to do was sleep. Being in the presence of others was mentally exhausting, and I couldn't carry on a conversation or recognize most of the people.

Because I'd already been informed, I knew who my family members were and their relationships to me. Other visitors were introduced to me, but even then, my messed-up brain didn't understand who they were or how I knew them. The pity and disappointment the visitors felt upon seeing me in my damaged condition showed on their faces, and I could sense their wanting me to be something else, to be better, to be the Debbie they knew. Feeling embarrassed for us both, I just wanted everyone to leave me the hell alone.

In retrospect, I can only imagine how distressed everyone must have been in the hospital around me during the ordeal. I'm sure that they were doing the best they could under the circumstances and while I can empathize with friends and family now and the hell they must have gone through, at the time this didn't even register with me.

When I first regained consciousness, I believed that I was still married to Jimmie, even though we had divorced three years earlier. I thought Chris was still alive, and my second son, Gabe, who was nine at the time, hadn't been born. I'd gone back to a period in life before my most painful memories occurred, before the comfy bubble in which I lived had so many holes poked in it that it finally burst. The medical staff directed my family to play along, to tell me, "He's not here right now," and make up other excuses whenever I asked about my husband.

With her arm intertwined in mine for support, my mother, who is five inches shorter than I am, would walk me, in my hospital gown and no-slip socks with the rubber strips on the bottom, down the hospital halls drawing my attention to each piece of mass-produced art on the walls. She would animatedly talk about each picture as though it were an exquisite painting hanging in a museum as I stared blankly at it.

"Oh, look at the beautiful purple hydrangeas in this one. They remind me of your grandmother and her bushes she loved so much."

Dad, whose olive skin and height I inherited, would keep the tone lighthearted during his visits, and was always good for a few treats off of the hospital menu.

"Why, Deborah Lynn, you're looking well today, but I bet you'd look even better after some orange sherbet."

Having been fed intravenously for a week, I'd lost 13 pounds and, having been thin to begin with, I now looked emaciated. Like when I was a kid, Jell-O or ice cream always made things better. Because I couldn't coordinate the acts of swallowing and breathing anymore, even these old favorites proved challenging.

A girlfriend, Julie, took it upon herself to shave my legs and armpits during a visit because she knew that the old Debbie wouldn't like being hairy. I sat in a chair in my room hugging a large pink, stuffed bunny, with orange inside his ears and green whiskers, that someone had given me, while Julie cleaned the stubble off of my legs.

Reaching down and cradling her cheek with my hand, I told her, "I love you."

With tears in her eyes, she looked back up at me and said, "I love you, too."

For the rest of her stay, I curled up on the bed clutching my bunny.

Ken flew across the country for an emergency visit when he received the news of my suicide attempt, and I slipped in and out of consciousness as he sat by my bed. In a brief moment of lucidity, I sat straight up and looked at him and said, "We love each other: why don't we act like it?" I lay back down and closed my eyes.

At this point, a light began to dimly flicker in the attic of my mind. As I became more alert, I started to recall chunks of my past and remember the words for common items that had previously remained nameless. The world began to make a little bit of sense again.

There were some visitors who were obviously missing. My sons, who were nine and twelve at the time, had been hurriedly shuttled to their father's care in the same city and were never brought to visit me in the hospital. In retrospect, this was probably for the best. I can only imagine how upsetting and confusing it would have been for them to see their mother in such a messed-up condition.

The other person conspicuously missing was the man with whom I had had a relationship for the previous three years, Steve, who had moved to a nearby city weeks earlier and called us quits. I'm told that he came to the hospital one time to see me and even brought a bouquet of flowers. On the way up to my room, he shared the elevator with my girlfriend, Karen.

Karen, a fiery redhead, blasted him. "You sure have some kind of nerve showing up here," she said. "Haven't you done enough damage already?"

Steve retreated to his car without seeing me. If he, the person I thought life wasn't worth living without, had shown up in my hospital room, would I have even recognized him?

CHAPTER 2

I Have a House?

I improved physically and played the game well enough mentally, telling the white coats what they needed to hear regardless of what I was actually thinking or feeling, to be able to get out of the hospital after two weeks. This was a good thing, but what followed wasn't so good. Without my or my family's consent, the doctors committed me to an institution for monitoring and rehabilitation because of my mental instability.

An ambulance deposited me at the hospital's inpatient rehabilitation facility a few miles away in the same city. The hospital was a spa compared to this place, which, populated mostly with drug addicts, was just plain scary. I watched nervously as patients lined up three times a day at the pharmacy window to get their hands on prescription drug substitutes to ease their withdrawals. The brain damaged woman who was so messed up that she tried to kill herself was afraid of them. I wonder if they were afraid of me?

I'd sustained a global, acquired brain injury, medically labelled encephalopathy, a non-specific term meaning disorder of the brain. In my case, it meant that I was seriously cognitively impaired. Lack of oxygen, high body temperature, drug overdose, or a combination of all of these and more were among the possible causes. No one could really say what my prognosis was, and it was wait and see, as is the case with all brain injuries.

The staff at the rehabilitation facility didn't know how to make anything better for me nor did they try. According to what I know now, this place was not the environment my freshly injured brain needed. One strategy in treating a new brain injury is to let the brain rest by simulating a coma with darkness, quiet, and as little stimulation as possible. With stark fluorescent light bouncing off of every surface, ceaseless commotion, and the constant hum of a beehive, the rehab facility was anything but restful for my brain.

Many brain injury patients wrongly end up in nursing homes or in psychiatric units because of a lack of better alternatives. Regulations are changing, but care and insurance are often denied unless some diagnosable physical condition or psychiatric condition other than the brain injury exists. Once the initial medical crisis is over that might have caused or accompanied the brain injury, all too often assistance abruptly stops. For a brain injury, recovery and rehabilitation literally take years. The real work is just beginning when the immediate medical emergency is resolved. When I sustained my injury, the healthcare system had no idea what to do with brain injury cases as they didn't fit neatly anywhere into the medical and insurance systems. I hope things have changed.

No one realized how extensively brain impaired I was, and it didn't help that I kept quiet with my head down, eyes glued to the floor to minimize my obvious impairments and to avoid interaction with others. Being in damage control mode big time, I desperately tried to hide what was going on or, rather, not going on, inside my head as much as possible. I also suffered from a general lack of awareness and was in denial about my own deficiencies.

While I do have an appreciation for the rehab facility staff and like to think that they were doing the best they could, even in my impaired condition, I thought they were a bunch of buffoons. In this one-size-fits-all rehabilitation program, no one bothered to learn what was going on with me specifically nor did they try to meet my unique needs, which were very different from those of a drug addict – not even close.

Because I was a suicide risk, upon admittance, the facility staff confiscated my razor, my hairbrush, and anything that could potentially cause bodily harm to me or someone else. I guess a hairbrush with the good boar bristles could do some major damage in the wrong hands.

I was allowed to keep three changes of clothes and a pair of pajamas, which was uncharacteristically fine with me. Fashion wasn't a pressing concern at the time. All of my possessions had to be kept in open cubicles, like the ones you find in a kindergarten classroom, making it difficult for people to hide drugs or forbidden items, like hairbrushes.

Sharing a room with a stranger made me antsy. Growing up with two brothers, I had always had the privilege of having my own room. I hadn't had a roommate since college, and even then, I didn't like it. "Great!" I thought, "Here I am, a grown woman in some kind of sicko camp with a roommate, a bunch of druggies, bad food, and plastic sheets."

Anxiety, feelings of insecurity, mood swings, impulsiveness, and an inability to control emotions are common following a brain injury. The conditions at the rehab facility would have made me nervous before the brain injury and now my anxiety was through the roof. I repeatedly told myself, "Just get through it."

As part of the rehabilitation program, I was expected to attend several meetings and group discussion sessions daily, which was a good idea in theory. However, I couldn't talk, stay awake, nor follow a discussion, much less add anything intelligent to it.

A mental health professional on staff assessed me every morning, and because it wasn't the same person each time,

I had to recite my history all over again at the beginning of each counseling session.

"So, tell me about yourself and how you come to find yourself here," was the usual opening line.

In stalled, slurred speech, I'd convey the bullet points of my story as best I could, trying to sound remorseful and rehabilitated. How can a complete stranger who knows nothing about me or my past evaluate my mental health in a 30 minute session? Even then, as impaired as I was, I knew that these sessions were just a matter of protocol. The conveyor belt approach doesn't work with mental health issues.

Because my brain and internal clock were scrambled, I didn't sleep well at night. After slipping as quietly as possible out of the crinkly pink plastic sheets – which was impossible – so as not to wake the roomie, I'd shuffle down the hall of my wing, past the nurses' station, down the other wing and back for hours when everyone else was sleeping. I'll bet that I wore the shine off the linoleum floor along my path. Although I would imagine the third-shift nurses probably grew very tired of seeing me pass by a hundred times, if they even noticed, they never did anything to try to help me.

I didn't know much at this point, but I did know that this place wasn't helping me. Feeling like a tea kettle just before the steam escapes in a shrill whistle, I screamed mostly unintelligible sounds at my parents, making it clear that I wanted out of there. It was incredibly frustrating and infuriating to have all of these emotions and thoughts percolating to the surface without being able to adequately express them. By using sounds, body language, hand gestures, and facial expressions, I managed to get my point across loud and clear.

My mother, a pint-sized dynamo, who built a successful career in commission sales, took charge of the situation. After making a few phone calls to her acquaintances in the local medical community, I was released from the rehab facility after only four days.

As a child, I'd squirm like a suspect sweating under the bright lights in a police interrogation when my mother targeted her assertiveness at me, or someone in front of me. I witnessed waiters being humbled, my dad acquiescing, and my brothers being cut down to size, and winced when I was unfortunate enough to wear the bulls-eye on my chest. Like an archer fine-tuning her skill, over the years my mother has learned to wield her weapon with kindness and respect, and I've developed an appreciation for her assertiveness. While I've come a long way in becoming more assertive myself, I can definitely recognize where I could have used a lot more of this kind of gumption throughout my life in the past.

*

After the longest four days of my life, Dad checked me out of the rehab facility.

"We'll make a quick run by her house, pick up a few things, feed the dog and cat, and make sure everything's OK," he said to his wife sitting in the passenger seat of the car.

Listening to this exchange from the back seat, I had one question: "I have a house?"

Being mentally impaired with the "here and now" being all that existed in my mind, I'd never considered where I lived or what would happen upon leaving the rehab center.

After spending the weekend with Dad, he took me home to my house. He and my mother alternated staying with me around the clock for weeks. Having to get back to their lives, they hired a Certified Nursing Assistant to stay with me during the day while they continued to take turns covering the nights. The nursing assistant was well paid with my money to sit on my sofa, watch my TV, eat my food, and make me feel uncomfortable in my own home. A pretty cushy job if you ask me, and having her there made me mad as hell. Although, I understand and agree with the need for constant surveillance now, at the time I seethed, feeling like I, a grown woman, was being babysat – well, because I was.

The brakes that used to restrain my mouth, emotions, and behavior were broken, and I had little control over these things. Much to my surprise and those around me, the nice Debbie who had avoided conflict at all cost was gone and had been replaced with somebody who looked just like her but said whatever she felt like whenever she felt like it. I remember thinking more than once, "Did I just say that out loud?"

My mother overcame a lonely, difficult childhood as the only child of two alcoholic parents. She attended a strict, Catholic school with cruel nuns, and even though she had three children by the time she reached the age of 20, she went on to own her own business and earn a master's degree. I have benefited from her example of strength, determination, and tenacity, and our relationship has healed and grown as life forced both of us to evolve individually over the years during my recovery from the brain injury and her battle with breast cancer. I have tremendous respect and compassion for her and would say we're good friends – uh, now.

This wasn't always the case. While she was staying with me one night, the dog pooped in the house, and Mom stepped in it. After the brain injury, it didn't occur to me to take the pup outside to do his business. Apparently, it didn't occur to anyone else either (I did replace the carpet). Coming out of the guest bedroom, Mom rounded the corner into the hall on the way to the bathroom and stepped in the fresh pile of dog shit.

"Well, hell! I guess Bandit decided the hallway was as good a place as any to go to the bathroom." She scrunched up her nose, took off her black patent flat which had poop smeared across the bottom, and held it at arm's length.

"This is Bandit's house. He lives here; you don't. If you don't like it, you can leave." I told her loudly in my slurred speech.

"Do you think I've enjoyed spending every minute of my free time day and night over here, young lady? I've done absolutely nothing for weeks but go to work, go home and do the bare necessities, and then come over here. I have a life too, you know, or at least I used to. I was supposed to go to the mountains last weekend. I was supposed to go the beach next month. Your little suicide stunt has ruined my summer."

"Your summer? Your summer? Really? I may have ruined my whole life," I thought, but managed to have the good sense not to say.

Bluntly speaking to her like this was not the norm for me and was the start of my beginning to emotionally emancipate myself from my mother – which most people accomplish in their 20s. Like my mother, I eventually learned to temper the blunt honesty brought about by the brain injury with gentleness.

During this exchange, Dad and his wife were still downstairs getting packed up to go back to their house after spending the night with me as it was the weekend "shift change". Fired up and on a roll, I stomped down the steps, pointed my finger at them, and ordered them to leave as well.

"You're just going to have to trust me at some point whether you like it or not. You can't watch me around the clock for the rest of my life. If I want to find a way to kill myself, I will."

They all left in tears.

*

Each brain injury is unique with no way to adequately predict or prepare loved ones and friends for the drastic changes that may occur in the injured person's personality and behavior. My family wasn't warned of this fact and having me explode like a loose cannon ten times a day was bewildering and upsetting for them.

I've read accounts of brain-injured persons sliding down banisters naked. If I did that, I don't remember it, and everyone has, thankfully, been kind enough not to tell me. Altered behavior is common with a brain injury, because when the frontal lobe, which is essentially our humanness, isn't functioning properly, all the "shoulds" can go out the window. From the moment we're born, we absorb cues and learn the unspoken rules of our species about what's appropriate, like how far you stand from someone when talking, or how much eye contact is polite, or what's inappropriate, such as walking around in your underwear in front of your preteen sons.

Forty-three years of societal conditioning had carefully carved socially acceptable pathways in my frontal lobe, politely reining in my behaviors. With all that wiped out, my brain was frolicking buck-naked through a field of daisies, which wasn't altogether a bad thing after being held prisoner for so long.

My lifelong practices of people-pleasing and avoiding conflict were long gone. I sulked, yelled, and was a rude bitch at times. I wanted everybody to get out of my house and leave me alone. Thinking that it was selfish of my parents to keep me alive, I was particularly mad at them and at everyone else for wanting me to be happy about surviving. "Why don't they mind their own damn business?" I thought. "I'm supposed to be happy about living like this? LIKE THIS?"

The anger I flung at others was nothing compared to the hatred festering inside me for myself. The self-loathing I felt for botching the suicide was a colossal weight sitting on my shoulders, threatening to crush me at any minute. If I could've spontaneously combusted, leaving nothing behind but a little pile of smoldering ashes, I gladly would have. My "suicide stunt" had ruined my mother's summer and had made things worse for me. Much worse.

During my recovery, I learned that significant personality and behavioral changes frequently accompany a brain injury. For the family, it's often as if a death has occurred. While the body of the injured person is still there physically, the same being doesn't inhabit it. For a spouse, a husband or wife may become a total stranger, and parents may no longer recognize their child. Friends and siblings may not be able to locate any part of the person they knew. The people around the brain injury often have to mourn the loss of the person they loved as well as the loss of hopes and dreams they had for and with that person. It's as if there has been a death, but there aren't any acknowledgement rituals or casserole brigades organized to deal with such an event, like when someone actually dies.

As was certainly true in my case, anger and brain injury are common companions. When the frontal lobe, which largely controls emotions and personality, isn't functioning optimally, impulsiveness, impatience, anger, and speaking out inappropriately may happen. Hostility can also stem from frustration caused by the brain-injured person not being able to function in their own life, follow simple conversations, multi-task, or cope with crowds, noise, and other everyday things. Extreme frustration also comes from all of the major life changes, loss of independence, and privacy, and the many "can'ts" and "don'ts" that become part of life after brain injury.

*

Thankfully, for myself and others on the road, I wasn't operating an automobile immediately after my injury. A family friend drove me to my occupational therapy and doctors' appointments and assisted me at home during part of the day for the remainder of the summer after a few weeks with the nursing assistant. At night and in between the friend's visits, I was left on my own at home – finally. I relished this alone time, which I spent sleeping, resting, and allowing myself to just be brain damaged because keeping up the act of trying to appear as normal as possible around other people was literally exhausting.

In the presence of others, I spent what little mental energy I had trying to conceal how messed up I was because I had to put on a good show to seem well enough for my sons to come home. When I was by myself, I could exhale, let down my guard, and just be me – mangled speech, broken brain, hand tremors, and all.

One evening, while lying on the couch in the den of my big, too-quiet house, I looked out of the windows to the wooded back yard, and I remember my eyes interpreting the trees, their leaves just beginning to display autumn colors, swirling and swaying unnaturally, almost as if dancing. After squeezing my eyes shut, I opened them to find the trees still thrashing around. However, there were moments when the trees were still and the whole scene seemed unremarkably typical, as if I was just lying on the couch watching TV on any normal evening. As rare as these moments were, they gave me hope that my brain was healing and that my life could be normal – unremarkable and boring even – again someday.

Over the summer, I participated in three months of occupational and speech rehabilitation therapy on an outpatient basis. Three times per week for one-hour sessions, I said nursery rhymes, read out loud, performed simple math, science, and word challenge worksheets, learned how to cook a grilled cheese sandwich and heat up soup, played computer games, put pegs in holes, grabbed items with tweezers, and pedaled a stationary bike. One regular rehab exercise had me dribbling a ball while going from room to room in the center and saying the names of animals starting with each letter of the alphabet. This was teaching my brain to perform motor skills and cognitive functions at the same time again. After running through the exercise a couple of times, I had the animal names figured out.

"Alligator, bat, cat, dog, elephant, frog, gorilla ..."

I never could come up with an animal that began with the letter "u". The staff always let me slide with "unicorn".

Speaking, understandably, was by far the most frustrating and challenging task, as my mouth just didn't operate how it was supposed to anymore. Working with a speech therapist, I learned to roll into sounds, exaggerate articulation, and speak slowly. Because my speech was already halted and punctuated with unnatural pauses to breathe, and because slowing down further sounded even more impaired, I intentionally tried to talk quicker, which still wasn't at a normal pace. I usually just ended up slurring everything into a breathy, incomprehensible babble. Slowing down was unacceptable to me because the last thing I wanted to do was draw more attention to my impaired speech. Because it didn't happen naturally anymore, I had to learn to coordinate the acts of breathing and talking. How could something I used to do automatically, without a thought – that babies are born knowing how to do – be so damned impossible now?

Again, I do have gratitude for the staff at the rehabilitation center because in the bad shape that I was in, the exercises they had me execute were beneficial; however, I now know that there was so much more that could have been done for me. I worked with whatever random staff member happened to be available at the time of my appointment, which prevented me from developing a relationship with any one person who might have become familiar with my challenges or progress. It also would have been tremendously helpful if I'd been more forthcoming about my condition because it was hard for anyone to really help me when I wasn't honest about my deficits in the first place. I was still in the "don't let them see how messed up you are" mode because of my ego and denial, but these same traits also fueled my motivation to improve.

Ideally, one professional would have been overseeing my rehabilitation, at home and at appointments; however, no one was. Even though I had what was considered "good insurance", after three months of outpatient rehabilitation therapy, my provider stopped paying for services, and I graduated. I was too impaired to be my own advocate or to inquire about continuing therapy that I could do on-site or at home, which would have been ideal. To paraphrase, the medical advice I was given by the neurologist and therapists at the time was, "Go home and cross your fingers."

In late August 2007, three months after the suicide attempt, my children were still living with their father, and I was finally left on my own day and night. All summer, I'd been working hard at rehab and hoping to recover enough for my boys to come back and live with me in time to return to school. I wanted to see their dirty socks tossed about the den floor, and hear their little-boy feet run up the stairs, and feel their skinny arms wrap around me. These images fueled my efforts in rehab classes and were the reason I woke up every morning to a lonely, brain-injured life. Reluctantly admitting to myself that I wasn't improving fast enough to be able to take care of them, I began to realize that their homecoming wasn't going to happen by the start of school.

It was terribly strange and sad being without my sons. For more than a decade, my primary concern in life had been one, and then two, little boys. Now they were nowhere to be found. The house, which usually oozed the smells of sweaty clothes and sneakers, the whimsical sounds of SpongeBob SquarePants, and the incessant squabbling and giggling of brothers and friends, was now cavernous and eerily quiet.

I felt as if my arms had been amputated. Missing my boys was a constant throbbing pain in my heart, my gut, and my head. Without them, I didn't have any idea who I was. I wasn't a wife or girlfriend anymore. Now, I wasn't even a mother. Who the hell was I?

Despite having low self-esteem for most of my life, I had always been fortunate (or unfortunate as the case may be because I didn't get to learn from failure) to accomplish whatever I set out to do. As Mary Tyler Moore said, "You can't be brave if you've only had wonderful things happen to you." No, I didn't get the gold medal in the 50 meter butterfly at the city swim meet when I was 13. I got the bronze. However, I did go to a prestigious college, which happened to be my first choice, on scholarship, graduated with honors, married my handsome high school sweetheart, and had two picture-perfect babies. Suffering from a kind of "princess syndrome" and still having the naïve sense of invincibility that comes with youth, I had expected this time would be no different. In a rude awakening, I was beginning to understand that this injury was serious; I wasn't getting over it any time soon, and I wasn't going to just go back to my life as if nothing had happened.

While the solitude without my boys was excruciatingly painful, it did provide the optimal conditions for recovery. I have to admit that I was often relieved not to have anybody else to worry about because it was all I could do to take care of myself. Being alone pushed me to remember or relearn the everyday minutia of life and to nurture my reasoning and problem-solving skills, which forced my brain to stretch and grow, re-establishing old neuronal pathways, and making new connections. Unknowingly, through performing the mundane activities of life, just the routine everyday stuff you do to make it from one day to the next – doing laundry, sweeping the floor, making the bed, feeding yourself, loading the dishwasher, and walking the dog – I was learning to live again, even if I wasn't sure that I wanted to.

CHAPTER 3

Pulling The Trigger

It was a sunny Wednesday morning, June 6, 2007, but I wasn't looking so bright-eyed. A walking zombie, I could count the number of hours I'd slept in the last week on my fingers. I didn't even need my toes. After dragging my wine-soaked ass out of bed, I sent the kids off to school, showered, got dressed, and numbly went through the morning routine. So far, so good.

While walking the dog around the block, I saw my neighbor and friend, George. We had gone to high school together and were pleasantly surprised to find that 20 years later, we ended up living in the same neighborhood and running in the same social circle. Our group celebrated birthdays with lots of wine, the Super Bowl with cold beers, and the Kentucky Derby with mint juleps. I never knew which horse raced across the finish line first, nor did I care, but it was a good excuse for a party.

"That was some blow-out at Kristie and Charles', huh? Bet your head hurt Sunday morning," he said, referring to a little get-together that past weekend.

"I felt like shit, but that's not anything unusual for me these days."

Knowing that Steve had just broken up with me, George asked, "How ya doing?"

"Not good. I can't sleep or eat. All I want to do is smoke cigarettes and drink wine, but I'm surviving."

"Broken up." That sounds so high school-ish, but what else do you say? The man whose natural scent I found so intoxicating that I wanted to roll in it like a dog wallows on his back in a good smell, the man with whom I enjoyed the most mind-blowing sex, the man I thought I was planning a future with had given me the "it's not you, it's me" speech again.

Out of genuine concern and with the best intentions, George went in his house and returned with an envelope containing five Xanax to help me. Right then and there, I started hatching a plan.

Minutes later, another neighbor, Mike, a friend in the same social group with whom I was closer, backed out of his driveway behind me and the dog, and proceeded to whiz right on by. No wave or "Hi, how's it going?" or anything. I threw up my arms and dropped them in the universal gesture for "What the ...?" Feeling lower than low already, this small indignation felt like a wounding blow.

While the notion of killing myself had been lurking in the back of my mind for some time, on the walk home, I hatched a real plan. My girlfriend, Julie, had all kinds of problems because of a car wreck, had recently undergone surgery on her neck, and had a smorgasbord of pills. I knew that I didn't have the strong enough stuff.

I even had a key to her house, and she had a key to mine. It was a single mom thing for safety and emergencies. If I locked my keys in the car, I could call her to bring me the spare set. If she had to go to the emergency room with one of her boys, as she often did, I could let her dog out to pee while she was gone.

She had called earlier that morning to tell me that she was going to run some errands and would stop by my house early afternoon to pick up her son's Nintendo, which he'd left after spending the night with Gabe over the weekend. I drove the short distance to her house, let myself in the front door, and helped myself to her stash of pills. Lucky for me, she had just refilled her prescriptions, and the bottles were almost full. I also found a crumpled paper bag in her nightstand drawer with a buffet of old prescriptions. Jackpot! Being the considerate friend that I was, I did leave her a couple of pills in each of her current medications to give her time to get more refills.

I knew that I was going to have to get drunk to take my life. Even though it was only a little after 10.00am, I started swigging my favorite cheap Shiraz right out of the bottle. The room temperature liquid glided smoothly down my throat until I had drained that bottle and started chugging another. This was no time to worry about looking like a wino. Besides, I rather liked the pathetic image that drinking right out of the bottle evoked. In my mind, it was most fitting for the occasion.

I added a bottle of my antidepressants and a bottle of Tylenol PM to the assortment I'd taken from Julie. With my heart thundering in my chest, I wondered if I could really do it. Cramming a handful of pills in my mouth, I quickly spit them back out. Once. Twice. A third time.

While tears rolled down my cheeks, dripped off of my chin, and made little dark spots on my shirt, I felt crushed that it had come to this point. I didn't want to do it, but at the same time, I did. I knew that if I did it, I'd regret it, but I also knew that if I didn't do it I'd regret it.

My mind raced. The boys will be better off without me. I'm no good for them. I'm a sad excuse for a mother. I can't even handle them now. It's only going to get worse. I don't earn any money. Never have. I never did anything with my college degree. How will I support them? What kind of pitiful example am I? My marriage ended in a hellacious mess that never stops. They deserve better than this. Now, I can't even keep a boyfriend. What's the point? I'm so tired of it all.

Washing them down with gulps of wine, I quickly swallowed handful after handful of the happy-colored pills. They looked like candy, but there was no sweet taste. I knew that you weren't supposed to mix meds with alcohol, but in this case, it didn't matter.

That should do it. I felt calmer, triumphant, and proud even for having had the guts to actually pull the trigger. Once the deed was done, the snarly bitch in my mind finally shut up. The mental movie of the hideous past and dreaded future reached the end of the reel, and it was eerily quiet inside my head for the first time in a long time.

Peace and quiet. That's what I really wanted. A break from the non-stop chatter, all the "should haves" and "what ifs". My inner voice never shut up long enough to even let me sleep. Like the Energizer Bunny after a Starbucks Grande, my brain hopped tirelessly from panic-inducing thoughts to harsh self-criticisms to an endless supply of regrets, even though it knew I had to get up early, get the kids to school, and go to real estate sales training all day the next day. Stressing about being too stressed to sleep only made me more anxious and more unable to go to sleep.

*

It took years of wrong turns, things not working out, and being flat-out disappointed and disgusted with life to get to this point. My life was like a pile of laundry that never got washed and had grown to an overwhelming heap, as more dirty clothes kept being thrown on the top of the stack. Growing deep within the mountain of fabric were bacteria, mold, and God-only-knows what else. The soiled mound reeked with a sour, foul odor that stung my nostrils. I didn't know where to begin to sort it, and I didn't have the energy to even begin to try. I was way too young to feel this old and tired. Mentally and emotionally exhausted, I was just plain worn out and had nothing left.

My ex-husband, Jimmie, and I had divorced three years earlier. We'd been high school sweethearts since I was 16. With a few break-ups here and there, we dated on and off in college and got married right after graduation. After 18 years of marriage,

11 moves, and two sons, he went to one state, and the kids and I went to another.

With all the moves and 70-hour workweeks, Jimmie rapidly climbed the corporate ladder to achieve executive status. After a decade of following his career and putting my business degree to use in low-paying jobs with titles like "Marketing Assistant", I was more than happy to stay at home when the kids came along.

Upon divorcing, we divided the proceeds from the sale of our elegant home in Florida, complete with marble countertops, a laundry chute, a swimming pool in the backyard, and a Porsche in the three-car garage. The Porsche was a two-seater convertible. We had a family of four. Guess whose car it was?

After a grueling trial lasting a week, I was awarded a generous alimony settlement for 15 years. In the deposition, Jimmie's lawyer, intent on humiliating me, grilled me about the intimate details of my sex life since the split. How was whether I had engaged in sodomy at all relevant to an alimony decision? I'm just curious. Does a woman get less money if she answers "Yes"? Regardless, the judge declared me the poster child for alimony because of our lives revolving exclusively around Jimmie's career from which he benefited handsomely, and me having little earning potential at that point.

The legal proceedings didn't stop there, as every issue, no matter how minor, became the grounds for a full legal assault. We even had to have lawyers oversee the division of the five paper bags of family photographs. Over the years to come, I became well acquainted with my lawyer's office and the local courthouse. Naïvely, I'd thought a divorce was supposed to put an end to all the bickering. Separating had only made fighting more formal and costly because now we had to launch attacks through lawyers and couldn't just scream insults directly to each other's faces.

Out of the blue, the day before that sunny Wednesday in June, I'd received yet another stapled packet of papers in the mail from my lawyer informing me that Jimmie had filed a cohabitation lawsuit against me. In the action, he alleged that Steve and I had lived together.

Here we go, again. Is this madness ever going to stop? I'd initiated and had been in negotiations with Jimmie to phase out the alimony over the next five years. Guess that wasn't quick enough for him. The thought of ending the alimony prematurely scared the shit out of me, but his financial obligations to me gave him way too much power to intrude in my life. In an effort to get some peace of mind, I was genuinely willing to end his financial support.

Steve and I hadn't cohabitated, and Jimmie knew it, but that didn't matter to him. The lawsuit gave him a shot at ending his payments to me. Steve had stayed with me on and off for days at a time while having extensive renovations done to his house. If the court decided that what we did met the legal requirements of cohabitation, the alimony would stop immediately, and I'd be obligated to pay back any money that I'd received from the time the order was filed until the matter was resolved, which could be years in a court system that didn't do anything in a timely manner.

Having just acquired my realtor's license and in training with a local real estate company, I was anticipating earning straight commission, not a stable income. The thought of losing the court ordered money, my security blanket, gave me that choking, can't-breathe, bug-eyed feeling. No matter which way I fast-forwarded the visions of my future, I couldn't come up with a convincing enough scenario of me as the competent breadwinner to make the panicky feelings subside.

The fact that Steve and I were no longer dating only added insult to injury. I felt so stupid, so used because in my mind, Steve and I had been building a future together. A couple of months earlier, I'd purchased the vacant lot adjacent to his house from him. Together, we interviewed contractors and poured over house plans searching for a home to build on the land for me. The two properties even shared a driveway. How perfect was that? I would own and finance the new house exclusively which were important legal distinctions. The alimony prohibited me from cohabiting or getting married, so I figured living next door to Steve was the next best thing. This arrangement would be even better than living together because Steve could have his own space to escape to when needed, which would be a lot, while the kids and I could have free reign over our place. He and I would be close enough to watch movies together, cuddled up on the couch, late into the night, and I could stumble back to my house and bed to be there to get the kids up and out the door in the morning.

I had every feature of my fantasy world painted. Now, it was more like a water-color on which somebody had flung a bucket of water. The happy images in my make-believe scenes were now disturbingly distorted with the colors running down the canvas and forming little mud colored puddles on the floor. What was once a beautiful vision was now a garish mess.

About a month after his remodeling project was completed and he didn't need a place to stay anymore, Steve broke up with me.

"I'm sorry, but I really just don't think I can do the whole kids, houses beside each other, marriage-like thing. I don't want to write a check I can't cash."

Over three years of dating, we'd become pros at the on-again off-again thing. "Why should this time be any different?" I told myself in my most grown up voice.

Having married my high school sweetheart, I was an amateur at the nuances of adult relationships and had the emotional maturity of a teenager. The perplexing dynamics between a man and a woman that most people understand by their late 20s was unfamiliar territory to me at 43. I manufactured the believable appearance of keeping my shit together, but inside I was crushed and felt like my world was crumbling down around me.

Two days earlier, I'd driven to Steve's house to surprise him, to talk. I did surprise him. I surprised him while he was having dinner with a woman and another couple.

Before I could close the distance between my car in the driveway and his front door, he came out of the garage, blocking me from getting any closer to the house.

"What the fuck?" I shouted, "On the phone this morning, you said you missed me and that we'd talk soon, and you have another woman at your house tonight?"

"Whoa. I'm not doing anything wrong here. We're broken up."

"You're such a lying piece of shit," I said. Knocking him flat on his ass, I stormed past him, through the garage, and into the house. Steve called this side of me "Bad Debbie". Bad Debbie is strong! He later told me that his dinner guests were cowering in the hall closet, peeking out of a crack in the door.

Technically, he wasn't doing anything wrong, but the scene made everything all too real for me. Feeling like I'd been hit in the face with a two by four, my illusory bubble had burst with a loud bang. I couldn't live in my fantasy world anymore, and I didn't know how to live in the real one.

*

After downing the pills, I considered making myself throw up. Being bulimic in college, I could have stuck my fingers down my throat and done it easily, but I didn't.

Going to the computer, I composed several suicide notes. To my children, I wrote: "My little angels. You have been the best things that have ever happened to me. I love you both with all my heart, but my heart is broken." Telling them to grow up to be good people, I ended with, "I will always watch over you."

Addressing my parents and Ken, I dramatically proclaimed: "I've screwed up this life so bad that there is no place here for me and nothing I could contribute. I don't know who I am, what I am doing here, or how I am supposed to go on."

My sentiments to Jimmie conceded that, after years of emotional torment in the marriage and since leaving him, he'd finally won. I gave up. He wouldn't have to bother with me any longer or part with another penny of his precious money.

In Steve's note, I told him that he'd pulverized my heart beyond repair despite how hard I had tried to be the perfect girlfriend to him in every way. I had made him my top priority at the expense of everyone and everything else in my life and had almost achieved "perfect girlfriend" status in my mind, and that I regretted it like hell. How could I have been so stupid and gullible? I had bet on the wrong horse again.

As if I was already a corpse, I lay down on my bed to die, but I kept jumping up, dashing down the hall to the computer, adding to the suicide notes. I might have been leaving, but I was going to have the last word, dammit!

I don't remember anything after that. But apparently my body was still functioning while my mind was unraveling, because I left some interesting handiwork on the computer. I composed the following poem, and it was even in an old typeface.

Be Not Nobody

Have you ever felt like no one ever pays any attention to you?
Well I'm here to tell you all about it.
I'm Lizzy, but my friends call me Elly, Elizabeth Cornington.
I grew up in a small, sweet town called Birmingham, Alabama.
On a farm for 13 years with my mother, Sarah, my father, George,
my three brothers: George 2nd, Henderson, Phillip,
and my baby sister Arian. My parents thought Eunice was a chaotic
name, so we went with Arian.
Back to the attention topic, I have four best friends:
Katherine, Anna Maria, Emilliana, and Ty.
Ty's one of my guy friends just so you don't get confused.
He's really cool, we've all been friends since we were three years old.
Oh I almost forgot, Katherine and Ty are brother and sister.

On the computer, I also found this letter I'd written in my drug-induced state:

Dear Family,

I write this as tears fall from my eyes. I fear that I will never see any of you again. I have been captured by the white men, and I am on a slave ship headed to a faraway land. I will try to tell you how it all happened. First, I was at Manhood Camp, and everything seemed to be going really well. I wrestled a good but very strong teacher and lost. He was the strongest man I have ever known. My next assignment was to catch a bird in the wild. While I was trying to catch a bird, I accidentally ran through a young woman's dinner. The young woman's name was Fanta. After running into the girl, I saw the foreign white men leading some of our own tribesmen around in chains. I was so scared by this sight that I ran back to camp and told the leader what I had seen. The leader told us to stay away from the white men. The next day I came home. I saw you all and put my things into my hut. Next, when I ventured outside around the village, I saw the same people who had been leading our men around in chains. They began to chase me too, but I took off running very fast and escaped them for a short while. Eventually, they caught up with me as I tired. I managed to stab one of my captors with my machete, but the other three overpowered me in the end. They chained my arms. I thrashed around and fought the chains for what seemed like hours until I finally fell down. The people then dragged me onto what I now know is this slave ship. I don't know how long I have been on this ship, but it seems like forever. The ship is crowded and nasty and we are packed in like animals. People are dying every day and they don't even remove the dead bodies. This is the worst treatment of men I have ever witnessed. It is very sad and bleak. While on this ship, I have seen my same strong wrestling teacher from camp being captured, which causes me to give up all hope of ever getting off of this ship and of ever seeing you, my family, again. Goodbye forever and be careful not to get caught as I did.

Kunta Kinte

In 1977, as a 14-year-old girl, I camped out on the couch in our den, with the dark wood-paneling and rust colored carpet, with my family, night after night, watching the miniseries, *Roots*[1], on the television. The drama portrayed Alex Haley's novel, which was loosely based on the oral history of his family as told by his grandmother and the factual history as he could confirm it.

The hero of the story, Kunte Kinte, was a 17-year-old Mandinka warrior when he was captured from his village in Gambia, West Africa, transported to Annapolis, Maryland, and sold as a slave. *Roots* traced the lives of Kinte and his descendants down to Haley himself, who is Kinte's great-great-great-great-grandson.

*

I don't know what happened from the time I took the pills around 11.00 that morning until around 3.00 that afternoon when my blond-haired, blue-eyed son, Gabe, who'd just celebrated his tenth birthday two weeks earlier, came home from school. Upon trying to enter the house through the kitchen door in the garage, as usual, he found it locked. Thinking it strange that the garage door was down with my car inside, he walked to the back of the house and retrieved a key hidden in the belly of one of those ceramic turtles – that everyone knows houses a key – on the deck. Instead of going back around to the door in the garage, he entered the kitchen through the patio door off of the deck. Looking through the glass door as he unlocked it, he saw me sprawled out on the kitchen floor.

Quickly opening the door and frantically yelling, "Mom! Mom!" Gabe grabbed me and shook my shoulders. Without opening my eyes, I mumbled something incoherently. In sheer panic, Gabe sprinted to his friend's home, three houses up the street, and alerted his friend's mother, who was a nurse. After they all raced back to me, she called 911. The paramedics roused me enough to help me stagger into the adjacent den onto the couch where I passed out again.

While the ambulance was at the top of my driveway, the neighbor that I'd seen that morning, George, drove by and stopped to find out what the commotion was. The ambulance rushed me to the hospital, the neighbor who called 911 took Gabe home with her, and George was left at the house alone.

George called our mutual friend, Karen, who also lived in the neighborhood, and they swept the house, removing anything they thought could potentially be damaging to me including the suicide notes and empty wine and medicine bottles. Thinking that this was going to be a minor incident, they were attempting to spare me the embarrassment and scandalous gossip that was sure to follow. With the same intention, they didn't alert anyone. Hours later at the hospital, George and Karen realized that I wasn't leaving there any time soon, if I did leave alive, and called my father who then notified my mother.

Back at the house, my older son, Collin, an olive-skinned, lanky 13-year-old with brown eyes and hair, stepped off the school bus, as usual, a little after 4.00pm with his good friend, Nathan, in tow. For more than an hour, they played electronic games, watched TV, munched on chips, and downed soda, as usual, with no reason to believe anything out of the ordinary had occurred until the neighbor returned with Gabe. Collin reached his father on his cell phone, and Jimmie, who was about to get on a plane for a business trip, immediately abandoned his travel plans and retrieved the boys.

Julie, whose pills I had swiped, didn't stop by that afternoon as she had planned, and called my cell phone to explain her no show. Karen, who had claimed my purse for safe keeping from the house earlier, heard the phone chiming and answered it.

Thinking it very strange for Karen to be answering my cell phone, Julie quizzed her, "Why are you answering Debbie's phone? Where's Debbie?"

"Debbie's had a little problem," Karen assured her calmly. "Don't worry. Nothing major. She and the kids are fine, but she left her purse with me." Although this lame answer seemed really odd to Julie, she didn't press further.

Later that night, upon going to take her medication, Julie was bewildered to find only a few pills rattling around in the bottles of her just-filled prescriptions. After digging in her nightstand, she discovered that her old medications were gone as well. Connecting the disappearance of her pills with the strange phone call to Karen, Julie figured out what must have happened. Immediately phoning Karen again, Julie demanded to know exactly what had taken place with me, explaining that she may have some crucial information. Disclosing the details of my suicide attempt, Karen noted the medications I'd taken from Julie and phoned my mother at the hospital with the information. By now, it was after 10.00pm, more than 12 hours since the pills had slid down my throat.

CHAPTER 4

Born To Die?

The paramedics burst through the doors of the ER with me on the stretcher at 4.10pm. Coded as a "triage acuity level one", the worst category a person can be labeled and still be alive, I was in acute respiratory failure with a breathing tube forced into my windpipe. I wasn't responding to anything – even pain – and had an abnormal heartbeat. Knowing that I'd attempted suicide, but not knowing whether I'd eaten Drano or something like it, and not wanting to do more harm than good, the medical personnel didn't pump my stomach. Instead, they pushed sodium bicarbonate intravenously in the hopes of neutralizing any substance that had already invaded my bloodstream.

Not until 10.30pm, when Karen called my mother with the list of pills I'd swiped from Julie, were the medical staff able to administer specific agents to counteract the effects of the now known drugs. It was too late to use charcoal to absorb them. The pills I'd swallowed, originally intended to help a body, were toxic poisons surging through my body, leaving destruction in their path.

The medical records indicated that it was believed I ingested over 90 pills, ten different prescription drugs, including sleeping pills, muscle relaxers, antidepressants, and more. Stabilizing on the respirator, I achieved passable vital signs, but remained in a coma, and after a barrage of tests, I was moved from the ER to the ICU. The story becomes sketchy at this point, and I've pieced it together from the hospital's medical records and people's first-hand accounts. Although I know the medical records don't tell the whole story, I also know that each individual's recollection is colored by their emotions, perceptions, and beliefs, both then and now.

It was a hectic night in the ER, and gurneys filled with bodies needing attention lined the hallway. Hours after my arrival, when my initial medical crisis appeared to be over, Dad and his wife, Karen, her husband, and George left the hospital, and my mother stayed behind to spend the night with me.

According to Mom, I received top-notch, attentive medical care until the nursing shift changed at 11.00pm. Personal opinions may have then entered into the picture as some people have strong, negative judgments about suicide. Perhaps the nurse assigned to me thought, "She tried to kill herself. I'm not going to help her now." Perhaps she was extremely busy, thought I was going to die, and spent her time helping patients with better odds of survival.

For whatever reason, no one took my temperature or checked my vital signs for hours. Because Mom could feel my temperature climbing higher and higher with the touch of her hand and no one was monitoring me over that time, she finally went and found the nurse, who immediately paged the doctor on duty. Before a doctor arrived, I began jerking spastically with myoclonic seizures, episodes during which muscles rapidly contract then relax, alternating with periods of catatonia. The fits turned into one long non-stop seizure during which I sat straight up in the bed with my arms flailing wildly and legs twitching violently on and off for over an hour. Having no recollection of this first-hand (for which I'm very thankful), an image of Linda Blair in the movie *The Exorcist* minus the spinning head and green vomit comes to my mind.

Mom, I apologize profusely for making you witness that horrific scene. I can only imagine how horrible it must be to see your child go through something like that.

At this point, my mother, frantic to find help, went to the nurse's station and told the woman behind the desk, "If you don't get a doctor in there right this minute, I'm going to go grab one and drag them in there." As it turned out, the doctor wasn't even on-site.

Right after that exchange, the nurse marched into my room, slammed down the medical charts, and began frantically scribbling notes to cover the hours during which she hadn't been checking on me during her rounds. At 2.45am, my rectal temperature was recorded as 107.3.

Materializing from another floor in the hospital, at 3.00am a doctor ordered treatment to begin for serotonin syndrome and a cooling blanket for hyperthermia, both life-threatening conditions. While the fever receded and the seizures eased, I lay comatose hooked up to a ventilator, with my pupils not even reacting to light. But I was still alive.

The medical records the next morning, June 7, at 8.25am stated: "The patient is critically ill with circulatory failure, respiratory failure, and severe/multiple traumas, and requires high-complexity decision-making for assessment and support ..."

The records also indicate that I had sepsis, a severe condition in which bacteria overwhelm the bloodstream, was in septic shock, and had life-threatening low blood pressure. During the night, I'd also aspirated, inhaled fluid into my lungs, and developed pneumonia. Things weren't looking too good for me at this point.

The next day, I was conscious at times, but mostly "somnolent", sleeping heavily with response to pain. The notes indicate that I could follow simple commands with feeble motor control and strength, and that my hands shook with uncontrollable tremors.

By June 9, I was taken off the ventilator only to be re-intubated shortly thereafter as the pneumonia worsened. For the next day, I was heavily sedated to allow my body to rest and fight the pneumonia.

After five days in the hospital, on Tuesday, June 12, I was weaned off the ventilator and was easily aroused and able to mouth words. The next day, speaking slurred gibberish, and extremely confused and disoriented, I could name common objects in the room, but was at times combative, ripping out my IVs, and launching out of the bed. To avoid the risk of me hurting myself, soft restraints and a waist bolt were applied.

Someone wrote on my chart, "She is alert, but quite agitated. She does not know the time, the date, the place, or the situation. She does recognize family members."

Makes sense. At this point, I think I was operating out of my primitive brain, the subconscious part that ensures our survival, with little higher-level functioning going on. The executive hadn't reported back to the office yet. My brain was only concerned with, and could only handle, the basic bodily functions: pumping blood, breathing in and out, and regulating temperature. I couldn't make sense of all the disconcerting machines around me, the tubes trespassing on and in my body, or the abrupt people with ID badges.

My mind began to hold onto hazy memories, like torn pieces of paper with ragged edges, around this time. By Friday, June 15, I had calmed down, was more clear-eyed and alert, noticeably watched the staff, interacted at times, and earned the removal of the cloth restraints. I could wobble to the bathroom and down the hall with assistance and openly wept, repeatedly declaring, "I'm a bad mother." I begged to see my children.

Over the next three days, the delirium began to dissipate like a rain puddle evaporating in the warmth of the sun, and I began to become cognizant that I needed to make an effort to "play the game" with the hospital staff and everybody else.

"Do you have suicidal thoughts?" an official-looking woman wearing street clothes and a badge asked me while holding my chart in one hand and a pen poised to write in the other.

"No."

"Are you remorseful about what you did?"

"Yes." I shook my head to look extra convincing.

The medical records show that I was intermittently combative and ambivalent about being alive. At times, I think I reverted to operating from my caveman brain, but when my frontal lobe was in charge, I was the good patient, saying and doing all the right things. Someone noted on my chart that they thought I was "minimizing". They were right.

Looking back on this ordeal, I have an incredible amount of respect for my physical body, its strength, and innate wisdom. Little did I know that my physical fitness, born out of pure vanity, would come to serve me so well. I can guarantee you that I wouldn't have survived had I not been in such good shape. I also like to think that I had some otherworldly help from my late brother, Chris.

*

While my circumstances were unique, unfortunately, attempting to take one's life isn't unique at all. According to the CDC as of this writing, suicide is the tenth leading cause of death for all ages and takes the lives of over 38,000 Americans every year. There is one death by suicide every 13 minutes, and an estimated quarter of a million people each year become suicide survivors. There is one suicide for every 25 tries.

This wasn't my first suicide attempt. While I consider the initial one more of a dramatic stunt than a real effort to take my life, I downed a bunch of aspirin when I was a junior in high school. Although I don't recall the exact details, I'm sure my despondency had something to do with Jimmie: a break-up, fight, or some other event of histrionic proportion that rocked my teenage world. I was taken to the ER, and my stomach pumped. Suffering no physical repercussions, I cheered at a football game later that night.

The second attempt was more serious. In 2001, after 16 years of marriage and having recently moved to an impressive home in a city located in the panhandle of Florida, Jimmie informed me that he wanted a divorce. With three-year-old and six-year-old sons, I was a busy stay-at-home mom running kids to schools, Gymboree, and Kindermusik. Jimmie had risen to big shot status, a managerial position in computer operations for a large, national corporation. This most recent change of address was the eleventh leap during our marriage in our quest for the "good life", our third move to the state of Florida, and the third relocation to a different state in the previous four years. Somewhere while we were busy chasing the dream job and the illusion of a better life, Jimmie and I had become hostile strangers with conflicting priorities, living in completely different worlds most of the time, and in different states for long stretches at a time.

My world included enough sand in the floorboard of my van to fill a sand box, eight guinea pigs, Thomas The Tank Engine and all of his cheeky roundhouse friends, and more chicken nuggets than I'm proud to admit. Jimmie's world included crisply starched shirts and dry cleaned suits, phone conversations where he wasn't interrupted five times, a sports car with leather seats and that oh-so-yummy new car smell, and meals where you actually had to use utensils.

After relentless campaigning on my part, Jimmie begrudgingly agreed to go to marriage counseling, which did seem to help for a little while, until I confessed in a session that I had had a brief affair outside the marriage nine years earlier. Mistakenly, I thought you were supposed to be completely honest in couples' therapy. However, I learned the hard way that you're not actually supposed to spill your guts, and found myself being called a whore, sleeping in the guest bedroom, and asking neighbors for the name of a good divorce lawyer.

One evening not too long after that, Jimmie innocently called for me to come to the front door, and I was shocked to see, through the side glass panels, a uniformed courier standing there ready to serve me an envelope which I assumed contained divorce papers. Instead of going to the front door and accepting the delivery, I grabbed my purse, hurriedly snuck out of the kitchen door leading into the garage, and sped away with my heart pounding in my throat.

"Ha! I'll show him!" I thought in a fleeting moment of triumph, as if escaping in my metallic green mommy van meant I could run away from the circumstances of my life.

After buying a six-pack of mixed berry wine coolers at a convenience store, I found a 24-hour Wal-Mart and positioned the van at the edge of the parking lot, facing some scrubby bushes, palm trees, and a retention pond. Not a bad last view, and no one would notice a car parked here for a while.

Inside the Wal-Mart, I purchased four bottles of extra-strength acetaminophen and two bottles of the green, liquid night-time-so-you-can-rest medicine. After washing the pills down with the wine coolers, I chugged the bottles of green stuff. Playing my favorite CD by Dido on repeat, I sang with growing passion and despondency as I melted into an alcohol and drug-induced numbness. Isn't it funny how you think you sing so fabulous when you're drunk?

As the sun sank into the pond and the frogs began their evening chorus, I stretched out in the back seat to die, and promptly passed out. Two hours later, I woke up in a panic. "Oh, shit!" I thought, "I've got to get home."

Although I have no memory of it, I managed to drive the ten miles to my neighborhood unscathed, where I proceeded to plow the van over the curb onto the grass on the opposite side of the road, hang out of the car door throwing up bright green goo, and fall to the ground unconscious. Someone driving by witnessing the scene called 911, and after being rushed to the nearest ER and having my stomach pumped, I suffered no physical consequences again.

Florida had a statute that required someone who had attempted suicide to be automatically involuntarily committed for 24 hours, and I was sent to the psychiatric ward of a state hospital. Like a prison, the windows in my room had that wire mesh built into the middle of the glass, and the room and bathroom doors had no locks on them. With nothing to do, and too scared to even take my glasses off or shut my eyes, I curled up in a fetal position on the hard single bed and fixated on footsteps going back and forth out in the hall. That night, the hospital admitted a screaming woman, put her in a straitjacket, and locked her in a padded room no bigger than a walk-in closet on the ward. As if inspecting a specimen under a microscope, the other patients and I took turns gawking at her through the little wire-reinforced square window in the top of the door. Her screams continued to pierce the silence of the psych hall until she finally exhausted herself and fell asleep. Feeling like I'd been reluctantly cast in a low-budget horror flick, I desperately wanted to play the lead role in my normal life again.

I didn't make a conscious effort to "play the game" to be released from the hospital that time as I did after the later attempt. Feeling genuinely remorseful and happy to be alive, I couldn't wait to get home to my kids.

*

The factors that contribute to suicide are as varied, on the surface, as the individuals committing the acts, but a common bottom line, in my opinion, is an inability to recognize alternate options and lacking the faith or energy to pursue them. It's simply emotional exhaustion.

Several of my relatives have committed suicide. My paternal grandfather shot himself in the head one night in 1976, in the back bedroom of his home, at the age of 64. I remember the eerie and confusing feelings the shocking event evoked in my preteen self.

49

How was it possible that Pawpaw, as I called him, was just here one day and gone the next? Upon entering the bedroom where he killed himself, my imagination went into overdrive, concocting gruesome images. Were his brains splattered all over the walls? How long did his body lie there? Who cleaned it up?

His brother shot himself in the head in 1967 at the age of 59. Their father killed himself when he was 68. One evening in May of 1945, my great-grandfather went behind his garage, propped the rifle butt up on some stacked boards, positioned the barrel against his temple, and squeezed the trigger. A cousin on that side of the family also shot himself in the head at the ripe old age of 18.

Science has known for a while that suicide runs in families without knowing why. While there is scientific evidence suggesting that some genetic tendencies do exist, it is most likely that suicidality is determined by multiple genes and heavily influenced by environmental factors.[1] Studies on twins have suggested that suicidal behavior is between 30 and 50 percent due to heritable factors[2] and that a first-degree relative (parent, sibling, or child) of a person who has committed suicide is four to six times more likely to attempt or complete a suicide.[3]

Similarly, scientists have pinpointed evidence of a gene that predisposes a person to depression and believe that around 40 percent of those with depression can trace it to a genetic link.[4] Genes aren't destiny by any means, and no one simply inherits suicidal behavior or depression. Each person gets a unique combination of genes from their mother and father, and certain combinations can predispose them to a particular illness. Whether you actually ever develop depression or suicidal tendencies depends on the events of your life.

The fast growing field of epigenetics is proving that who we are is the product of what happens to us, which causes genes to actually switch on or off. In other words, you're born with certain genes, but your life determines which genes get expressed and which genes don't. Hence, our environments are expressed through our genes.

Your brain also changes its structure and function over your lifetime due to your experiences, behaviors, emotions, and even thoughts, a capability known as neuroplasticity. Every brain has depressive tendencies in addition to wellness tendencies. At the most basic level, depression is just the routine activation of certain brain circuits, which we all have, in specific patterns that result in depression in that person.

Depression is unique and complex, varying greatly among individuals and even within the same individual. In my case, I believe too many traumatic and stressful life events turned on my suicide and depression genes, and carved depressive patterns in my brain. Although I didn't have chronic, debilitating depression, I took antidepressants for more than a decade as life just kept getting harder and harder for me to handle, and the black dog of depression, which was originally only an occasional visitor, became my full time companion.

I believe my depression was the combination of a learned way of reacting, coupled with anxiety and life just sucking the happy right out of me. Research has shown that depression coupled with anxiety has a much higher suicide rate than depression alone. Although my prescribed antidepressant didn't really do much to help me after a while, I kept taking the prescription because it was preferable to me than digging in my heels and doing the hard work of making the real changes needed to turn me and my life around. Even when life was going pretty smoothly, I practiced unhealthy thought patterns, such as black and white thinking, catastrophizing, and personalizing, and had a habit of focusing – more like obsessing – on what was wrong instead of what was right.

When confronted with tough life challenges, I did the internal equivalent of throwing my hands in the air, shrieking like a little girl, and running away as fast as I could, yelling for my Mommy.

Outwardly, I put on a brave face, and I really did want to be strong. Doesn't that count for something? But, I wasn't. Inside, I was scared shitless and doubted my ability to handle it. Whatever "it" was. Anyone around me was probably blind to my crippling fear and self-doubt because I hid it so well. I was used to existing in the emotional chasm between looking brave and being brave. When I was younger, I used to be strong. Although I would feel the nervous butterflies, I'd stuff the feelings and barrel on, but after years of weathering one emotional storm after another, my knees buckled.

While I do think there was certainly a genetic predisposition for depression and suicidal tendency in my case, I also believe the power of suggestion and learned behavior came into play for me. Taking my life was always a viable option on the list of possibilities beside others that seem much more reasonable now.

I don't doubt that chemical imbalances in the brain contribute to most suicides, whether the disparity is caused by alcohol, or drugs, or is natural in origin. Two weeks before my last suicide attempt, I started taking a new SSRI (selective serotonin reuptake inhibitor) antidepressant. Although prescriptions for antidepressants aren't hard to get your hands on, these medications are powerful substances that alter the neurochemical balance in the brain. In 2004, the FDA directed manufacturers to print a warning on the box of increased risk of suicidal thoughts and behavior in children and adolescents, and emphasizing the need for close monitoring of patients. Antidepressants do work to relieve depressive symptoms for some people, but in many cases they don't, and sometimes they even make symptoms worse. The bottom line is that these are serious drugs, people!

Having revealed my previous suicide attempts to the prescribing psychiatrist, I would think monitoring me closely would be paramount, but it wasn't. Although I do realize that I had a responsibility to tell her about my suicidal thoughts,

I wasn't about to let anyone know when I was actually suicidal because they would try to stop me. See how that works? For this reason, it's not enough to rely on self-reporting in the case of suicidal ideation. The strategy may prove successful when a person is well enough to reach out for help, but there was a point at which I wasn't going to tattle on myself and thwart my plans.

*

Mental illness and suicide are touchy issues that aren't generally the topic of dinner party conversations, although this is beginning to change. These taboo subjects can make people squirm and want to talk about the weather really quickly. Surprisingly, very few people have asked me about my mental state at the time of my suicide attempt and usually apologize profusely for asking probing questions which lead me to reveal attempted suicide as the cause of my brain injury. Avoidance of the issues only contributes to the shame and stigma surrounding them.

In March 2010, Marie Osmond's 18-year-old son, Michael Blosil, leaped from his downtown Los Angeles eighth floor apartment to his death. Upon reading about the incident on Facebook, knowing tears filled my eyes. Of the 14 comments after the post, extending condolences to the family, not one of them expressed compassion for the deceased son. Although my heart certainly went out to those he left behind, I could sense the suffocating darkness of the pit he must have been trapped in that made him want to take his life.

In both of my suicide attempts, the fact that my brother Chris was dead was a huge compelling factor for me. I didn't have a well-defined notion of where I thought he was, but I wanted to be with him, wherever that was. If neither of us had been deserving of a halo or horns, surely we would end up in the same place, and it had to be better than where I was at the time. Although my therapist assured me that this doesn't make my suicide attempts more understandable to her, I still believe it does somehow.

Desperately craving a break from my own thoughts, I longed to not exist in a constant state of fear and anxiety anymore, with my mind broadcasting non-stop pathetic scenarios of the future and the hideous scenes from the past. But I don't know that I would have found the relief I sought by killing myself.

In almost every religion, suicide is considered a sin or seriously frowned upon. My brother, Ken, believes in the Buddhist teaching of "bardo", which portrays an intermediate state of transition between this life and the next. The spirit of the person who committed suicide remains in bardo, not progressing on to peace or the next life, and faces their karma for a time equal to what they would have experienced in the physical form. That doesn't sound like any fun.

I would never think of suicide as an option today. This self-destruction is the desperate act of a person who is in excruciating pain and cannot fathom any other way out. Suicide is inherently selfish because it demands that a person think only of themselves and not the destruction they leave behind, but they are not capable of seeing this at the time. For me, killing myself masqueraded as a benevolent gesture that I viewed as a favor to my kids and everybody else. I seriously believed that the world would be better off without me. I now understand how warped this sounds, but that's exactly the type of thinking that leads someone to end their life.

By trying to find an easy way out, I'd unknowingly positioned myself squarely in the starting block for the hardest race of my life.

CHAPTER 5

Learning To Live Again

I was alive, but my life as I had known it was over.

Because my brain didn't recognize the physical sensation of having to pee anymore, I'd race to the bathroom whenever it dawned on me that that's what that feeling down there meant, and rip my pants down to around my ankles. Occasionally, I didn't make it in time, but never in public, thank goodness. Potty training went much faster the second time around.

Something as simple as eating now proved to be challenging, as I couldn't eat without chomping down on my cheek or tongue. Raw, chewed up places dotted the inside of my mouth, but by chewing gum, I trained my tongue, teeth, and jaw to play nicely together again. For the longest time, a wad of gum would go flying out of my mouth whenever I would try to blow a bubble, and I was prouder than a six-year-old when I could finally produce one without sending the gum shooting across the room.

Table manners vanished with the brain injury. Holding a fork and getting the food into my mouth was physically not a problem, but I had to learn to eat in a socially acceptable manner all over again, like a toddler. Because cutting the food simply didn't occur to me, I would shove whopping forkfuls into my mouth.

Eating a salad with oily Italian salad dressing could ruin a shirt really quickly and maybe even a pair of pants. In retrospect, I should have figured out to match what I was wearing to the color of whatever I was eating. As tomato soup was easy to fix and a favorite, I would have been sporting a lot of red.

Dining alone most of the time only encouraged my vulgar eating habits. "Manners schmanners, who cares?" I would think, but when I did share a meal with someone, my face would flush with embarrassment when food hung out of my mouth or dropped in my lap, because I realized that it did indeed matter to me. "How am I ever going to go on a date again eating like a pig?" As with most everything, I watched others intently and copied them to re-learn the art of polite eating.

Like a little old lady, my hands shook with a constant tremor for months, probably because of the toxic level of serotonin still in my system from all the antidepressants I ate. While the shakiness eventually subsided, my fine motor skills took much longer to come back and are still less than normal. The first time I tried to wear my contacts, I stood in front of the mirror poking myself in the eyes for 15 minutes trying to get the damn things in, but I was determined and vain, and finally succeeded.

Pushing the itty-bitty buttons on a phone or remote was infuriatingly difficult. At the time cell phones didn't have keyboards like they do now and sending text messages required pushing the same number key multiple times for a particular letter. Because I had to start over so many times, one text message could take me ten minutes to compose, if I ever got it complete and accurate enough to press send. I'd taken these seemingly insignificant things for granted before and didn't notice them in the background of my daily life because they were so mindless and routine. Now, I was discovering that they weren't so trivial and punctuated almost every day numerous times.

Muscle tension and contracted, frozen muscles are a common side effect of a brain injury. When typing on a computer keyboard, my hands resembled a claw as I stiffly hunted and pecked with my index finger for the longest time. One email message might take me an hour to compose, but because I couldn't talk understandably on the phone and absolutely hated using it, I persevered in my time-consuming pecking, which only helped to rewire the connections in my brain needed to type. I found instructional typing websites and practiced for months until I could use all of my fingers on the keyboard again, but not with anywhere near the fluidity or speed that I used to enjoy. My hands are still stiff, with the last two fingers on my left hand tightly curled when I type, but I'll take it. It's amazing what you appreciate when the alternative is worse or not at all.

My handwriting looked like chicken scratch, but by meticulously tracing the ABCs printed on a dry-erase board meant for a first-grader, I taught myself to write again. Like a youngster, I practiced writing my name, numbers, and primary words over and over within the lines of the board and then I graduated to filling up my sons' spiral notebooks. I have to say that their handwriting looked much better than mine at that point. Borrowing their tubs of broken crayons, I bought assorted coloring books and rediscovered one of my favorite childhood activities. I'm pleased to report that coloring is just as much fun as an adult as it was when I was younger; however, staying in the lines was easier back then. There's been information all over the web saying that coloring isn't just for kids and has therapeutic, stress relieving brain benefits for all ages.

Three years post-injury, I was fiercely determined to improve my handwriting, and I wrote longhand a sheet of notebook paper of copied text every day for months. Although my script did become more legible, I still wouldn't call it pretty, and I don't know that it will ever get anywhere near attractive again.

Immediately after the injury, my arms hung limply by my sides without swinging when I walked, and I didn't know what to do with them. I never had to actually think about what to do with my arms when I walked before. Because having my arms just hanging there like lifeless noodles looked and felt awkward, I would bend them at the elbows, waist high, make fists, and kind of chug them. (I did manage to refrain from making choo choo noises.)

This is the kind of thing you never even think about normally. Your arms just know what to do when you walk, but when your brain doesn't work right, nothing is natural anymore. I used to like to think of myself as being this graceful gazelle-like creature, especially after a few glasses of wine. Now, I was more like a baby giraffe.

*

Because I lived alone, it was up to me to figure out what to do if the cable, internet, or phone went on the fritz. In my isolated post brain injury world, these services were often my only links to the outside world on a daily basis, and any little glitch with them was enough to send me into a tearful tirade. Before dialing the service provider, I'd exhaust every possibility that I could think of, which was a short list, because talking on the phone was a dreaded, last resort. I could barely talk, and the stupid automated systems couldn't understand what I was trying to say. After ten minutes of wending my way through telephone hell, punctuated with bad music and a synthesized voice repeatedly telling me, "We appreciate your patience and value you as a customer," I'd inevitably press the two button instead of the three, and have to start the whole process all over again.

If I did successfully make my way through the maze and get a live person on the phone, they couldn't understand what I was saying. "Do they think I'm drunk?" I wondered and took comfort in believing that they probably thought I was a computer illiterate little old lady, which wasn't too far from the truth.

I'd always prided myself on maintaining a yard that never hinted at the fact that a single woman resided in the house. No one probably ever even noticed, but it was just one of those quirky little things that always meant something to me.

As I'd begrudgingly done many times before, I sweated in the North Carolina sun maintaining a respectable looking yard. Prior to the brain injury, keeping the yard up was no big deal, just one of those pain-in-the-ass chores. After the injury, the lawn certainly wouldn't have won the yard of the month award, but mowing, weed eating, trimming the bushes, and planting a few flowers became triumphant accomplishments, which made me feel normal.

At three months post-brain injury, I resumed managing my finances. My father, who had been paying my bills up until that point and who still wrote and mailed his checks, was astonished when I actually somehow remembered the password to access online banking and was able to use it. I guess I had had so much anxiety around finances before the brain injury that the stuff was seared permanently into my brain.

"I can't believe you can figure out how to do that. I don't even want to deal with that stuff, and I don't have a brain injury," Dad exclaimed.

Quite often at first, I would just simply forget to pay bills, so I learned to scribble a reminder on the calendar on my built-in desk in the kitchen, which became scheduling central, until paying bills every Monday became a habit again.

When I had to shop for two growing boys, going to the grocery store was an annoying task I'd done a million times. Now, it was a daunting challenge requiring me to summon all my courage and take a nap after. Making a list was an absolute must because, if I didn't, I might come home from the store without what I went for in the first place. I got in the habit of jotting down items as I became aware that I needed them, which was a good idea in theory. I would diligently keep a running list, only to arrive at the store and realize that I'd walked out of the house without it.

Standing in the checkout line at the grocery store, I'd start to get nervous at the thought of having to unload the cart, put the items on the moving belt quick enough (those cashiers are fast!), produce the rewards card on my key ring, retrieve the plastic from my wallet, swipe it, and cram it all quickly back into my purse. By watching the people ahead of me, I figured out how to pay with my card, although a few of the questions that popped up on the keypad stumped me. You aren't actually supposed to thoroughly read each question and thoughtfully contemplate your answer, I discovered. The cashier was inevitably through ringing up my order and shoving the receipt at me while I was still trying to stuff everything back into my purse. Because I found the whole experience about as enjoyable as a root canal, I would avoid shopping as long as I could – until I was out of tomato soup.

I watched other people and learned, in this situation and others, not so much out of a motivation to recover, but as an attempt to appear normal. I now realize that it would have been perfectly fine for me to take a little longer to check out, but at the time, doing anything that might draw attention to myself was not OK. Had I taken the extra time, I wouldn't have been behaving out of the ordinary, and even if I did, "So what?" It wouldn't have mattered one bit to anyone but me, I now realize. After the brain injury, this kind of skewed perception and self-consciousness was crippling. I felt like there was a red, neon sign over my head, reading "brain damaged idiot", with an arrow pointing right at me.

At the time of the injury, I lived in a 3,000 square foot, four-bedroom house that was perfect for me and my two sons. I used to wear myself out keeping the house looking like it came straight out of the pages of a magazine, complete with the clean sparkle and fresh smell. After, I lived in that big house by myself with a cat and a dog.

With no children in it, the house didn't suffer from muddy sneakers on the floors, greasy hand prints on the walls, or markers burrowing into the carpet anymore. Instead, the house got dirty from sitting and not being used. A thick layer of dust covered every surface.

On one visit, Gabe, not being used to the new cleaning standards, scrunched up his face and told me, "Mom, the toilet has a gross, black ring in it." I never used the toilet in their bathroom, and apparently the bacteria had liked that.

Keeping a clean, attractive home had always been one of the notches on my scorecard of life, but my priorities had drastically changed. The things that used to define me – an immaculate house, a manicured yard, and an enviable appearance at all times – weren't even on my radar anymore. Taking care of me and resting were more important than collecting dust bunnies, planting flowers, or looking flawless. It took me a ridiculously long time to accomplish the minimum daily requirements just to make it from one day to the next, and these things weren't done to anywhere near the level of perfection that they had been. Much to my amazement, the world didn't stop spinning.

Self-absorption, sometimes to the point of insensitivity and lack of empathy towards others, is common in people with brain injuries. After my injury, I only possessed the mental capacity to think about and take care of myself, and frankly, it just didn't occur to me to think of others most of the time. For someone who had always been more concerned with the feelings and needs of other people, this was radically different but not altogether a bad thing.

While re-learning almost everything was necessary after the brain injury, it wasn't as if I had to start from scratch. Becoming proficient in most things again was more like I needed to take the refresher "how to" course. Most often, the information was still in my brain somewhere, and an "Oh yeah!" light bulb would click on with a little coaxing, usually by seeing, hearing, or reading. It was as if my brain just had to be nudged to find and recognize information that was already in there and re-establish the connections to it. My kids thought it was hilarious that I didn't know whether the North or South had won the Civil War.

I became adept at observing the world and watching others. I was never one to ask for help even before the injury, so I wouldn't explain that I had a brain injury to people because doing so would mean that I would actually have to speak to someone. Being stubborn and self-conscious, I opted to endure the frustration of trying to figure everything out for myself. Although borne from my ego, this hard-headedness was beneficial because it forced me to have to learn. For the wrong reasons, I was determined, but determined nonetheless, and in doing so, I retrained my brain.

It's my guess that many of the peripheral connections and pathways in my brain were wiped out in the chemical bath, high fever, or lack of oxygen during the suicide attempt. The mere acts of seeing or doing must have allowed for reconnection. Somehow, I instinctively knew that the more I did for myself, the better I'd get.

*

With the same patience he showed when I was a nervous 15-year-old who couldn't wait to get my driver's license, my father bravely took me to parking lots and isolated roads to let me brush up on my driving skills. I had to reacquaint myself with the feel of the brakes, the gas pedal, the steering wheel, and get a spatial sense of the car. All of the elements of driving a car, which just feel normal and automatic after you've been doing it for a while, were new again to me. Remember how strange it all felt at first?

"OK. Just ease the car forward slowly and go around to the back of the church."

Taking a deep breath, I gently pressed on the gas, and the car began to move.

"That's it. Just keep going. You've got it."

I was happy to find that my motor memory of the physical skills came back rather quickly. Dad didn't make me parallel park, thank goodness. I couldn't do that even before the brain injury and still can't to this day.

The mental and emotional aspects of driving a car took longer to get comfortable with because driving scared the shit out of me. Instead of not even noticing or perceiving the other vehicles on the road as minding their own business, staying in their designated lanes, and obeying the rules, it felt as if the other cars were 4,000-pound metal weapons that could come hurling at me at any minute. I realized something that I'd never considered before: driving requires an enormous amount of trust. As a driver, you have to believe that the other drivers will all do what they're supposed to do and won't come barreling at you because they accidentally whizzed through a red light or swerved into the wrong lane.

My solution to this paralyzing anxiety was to argue with myself using counter-logic whenever the paranoid thoughts popped up and refuse to buy into them. If I hadn't, I wouldn't have been able to leave the driveway. Despite my fears, I desperately wanted to drive and knew that regaining this skill was essential to getting back to anything close to resembling a normal life.

In the past, I'd never been a very cautious driver or an avid seatbelt wearer. I became both. Admittedly, I wasn't the most confident or skilled driver on the road, which was why I was more cautious. Dad said that I actually became a safer, better driver after my brain injury.

At first, I didn't know all of the rules of the road anymore. Although I learned by observing, I also studied and passed the written and on-the-road driving tests. "When not sure, don't move" was a golden rule that I followed religiously that worked every time. I did get a few horns honked at me, but I never had any accidents.

*

Living with a brain injury is like having a bad day every day, but my messed up brain did bring some unexpected gifts. Seeing life through unjaded, childlike eyes, I was a blank page.

All the former "shoulds" and opinions were erased from my head. Hardly anything was a given with me anymore. The underlying belief system and perceptual foundation upon which I'd built my reality withered away along with my brain cells. This emotional and mental groundlessness was both frightening and freeing at the same time. Letting go of preexisting assumptions and beliefs and remaining open, or having a "beginner's mind", is a basic premise of the practice of mindfulness. I accomplished this, courtesy of the brain injury, and lived in the present moment, without even having to try.

I developed a new level of appreciation for the simplest things, which I hadn't noticed before. The sleek silkiness of a cat's fur under my fingers as I scratched her rumbling chin would cause my eyes to fill with tears. While walking the dog on a chilly morning, the rays of sunlight warming my upturned face had me smiling. I know it sounds corny, but I found it amazing that the sky could be so crystal clear and brilliantly blue with mounds of clouds looking like cotton balls glued into place. Why had I never noticed these wonderful things before?

While I wasn't consciously aware of this shift in attitude taking place, I was living it day by day and experiencing these little snippets of joy in an otherwise flat existence. Not being particularly happy or sad, I lived almost entirely in the present moment without question or judgment because my brain didn't have the capacity for it, which was the mindfulness practice of awareness.

With my speech still very slow and difficult to understand, it was a taxing effort to speak, physically and mentally. Roger Ebert, the movie critic who lost the ability to speak, eat, and drink as the result of surgeries for salivary cancer, summed it up appropriately when he said through Alex, his virtual Macintosh voice that translates written words into speech, "For most of my life I never gave a second thought to my ability to speak. It was like breathing. In those days, I was living in a fool's paradise."[1]

He also expressed how the act of speaking or not speaking is tied indelibly to one's identity because your voice defines you to yourself and others. A commanding, baritone voice yields a very different impression than a high-pitched, whiney voice. He pointed out that not being able to speak creates a disconnect between him and others, and a separation from the human mainstream. He also noted that people have little patience for speaking difficulties. I can attest to all of it.

When I did talk, I often got puzzled looks accompanied by "Whaaat?" from others. I guess because they grew impatient with me, or embarrassed for me struggling to speak, people would finish my sentences, or act like they understood me, when it would become clear that they hadn't. Finding this treatment insulting and figuring it was better to deal with the elephant in the room up front, I began telling people, "If you don't understand me, just ask me to repeat myself. It won't hurt my feelings" to put both them and myself at ease.

While I was living independently and functioning adequately on a daily basis, my thinking processes were still impaired and slow. My attention span was defunct, and like a butterfly flitting from flower to flower, my mind constantly jumped from one thing to the next. I couldn't finish one task before a thought would pop into my head, and I would have to stop what I was doing to go attend to whatever I had thought of. The strong urge of a new thought versus the pull of continuing with an existing thought or activity felt as if two entities were having a tug-o-war in my head. Although I knew I should ignore these compulsions and continue with what I was doing, I couldn't resist them at first. However, by holding out a little longer each time, I reached the point where I could curtail the intruding impulses, and with time and repetition, the practice of not giving in shaped pathways in my brain.

*

My short-term memory was almost non-existent while my long-term memory was tenuous and fuzzy. Initially, I couldn't remember the basics of my life, such as my sons' ages and their grades in school, the name of the road I lived on, or that I'd resumed using my maiden name when I got divorced. I couldn't even recall my phone number. While I'd usually get the digits right, they'd be in the wrong order. To remedy this, I would hear my voice on the answering machine: "You have reached ..." The information that used to be readily available in my brain wasn't there anymore and had to be consciously committed to memory again.

Life was a perplexing puzzle, with the pieces scattered all around and some remaining hidden, no matter how tenaciously I hunted. I'd discover an essential link only to have it fade back into oblivion because of my lack of memory and awareness, and then I would have go rummaging for it all over again.

I couldn't determine any rhyme or reason to the miscellaneous bits of information that survived the storm in my head. For some stupid reason, I could recall the lyrics for random songs – like I really needed to know the words to "Crocodile Rock". I could see the creepy shadows, looking like gnarled fingers, made by the tree branches outside my childhood bedroom window on the sheer white curtains with little purple flowers. I vividly remembered the sting of my ex-husband calling me a bitch when I was in the hospital, in labor with our second son. However, I couldn't remember something as precious as the actual experiences of giving birth to my sons. It made absolutely no sense. Pictures of events jogged my memory, and the snapshots became my memories.

When I went to the neurologist, he'd conduct a cursory assessment of my memory and cognitive skills each visit.

"I'm going to tell you three things, and I want you to remember them: ball, tree, and flag," he said at the beginning of the exam.

"OK. Got it."

Later, when he asked, "What were the three things I asked you to remember?" I could only recall one.

On my next visit I knew this test was coming, made an effort to remember the items when he told them to me, and was able to tell him two words later when he asked. On subsequent visits, I had learned some memory tricks and envisioned a ball and a flag in a tree, and aced the question.

When the neurologist asked me the name of the governor of my state, the first time I was stumped. Anticipating a similar question in later visits, I'd make sure that I knew the names of the people holding the top three state offices, but he outsmarted me by asking the name of the Vice President of the US and other things I hadn't prepared for ahead of time. Darn it!

"How many nickels are in $1.35?" he quizzed.

"Uh, 25?" I answered, after a long pause.

Drawing a clock face with only hands and no numbers, he asked me to tell him the time as he penciled in the arrows in different positions. Boy, that was a hard one. Early on, my pitiful performance on these tests hinted at how damaged my brain was, but I steadily improved.

Before the brain injury, upon opening my eyes first thing every morning, I just instinctively knew what day it was and what was required of me: get the kids up for school or roll over and go back to sleep because it was the weekend. Now, upon waking, much like a page loading on a computer screen with the text, links, and graphics filling in sequentially while the wheel spins in the tool bar, my mind would have to retrieve the information for what day it was and what was going on that day.

Oftentimes, my brain couldn't come up with the word I wanted to say, a condition known as aphasia. Although I knew that I knew the word and had a distinct sense of it on the tip of my tongue, I couldn't utter the word to save my life. I'm sure you know the feeling, but this happened to me all the damn time. The harder

I would try to locate the missing word, the more frustrated I would become, which only made it that much more impossible to remember. I learned to work around and cover up these brain blips by substituting a different word or rephrasing the thought. Later, the lost word would inevitably pop into my head out of the blue.

Similarly, I'd often use the wrong word in the wrong place without realizing it, which could be quite humorous when someone would point it out. For example, I started blogging three years after the brain injury when I was still experiencing some cognitive impairments. In one blog about Bikram yoga, I said that I did a good impression of an ostrich in the one legged poses.

After the injury, I figured out one solution to everything I needed to do, and if I was forced away from my familiar routine, I panicked because I couldn't rely on my brain to adapt to or problem solve in a new situation. When I had to venture out of my comfort zone, I was in trouble, but unbeknownst to me, these instances were growing my brain because new experiences meant new brain connections.

When driving home after having dinner with my father one night, I turned prematurely into the neighborhood next to mine. I frantically drove around the maze of cul-de-sacs and stop signs for ten minutes before finally escaping back to the main road from which I had turned and recognized. The entire time, I was only blocks from my house, as the neighborhoods were internally connected by cross streets, but I only knew my one way home.

I had to get gas at the same station every single time. Figuring out how to put gas in the car at that one was an accomplishment in itself, and an unfamiliar gas pump was like a Sudoku puzzle. Many times I drove away disgusted without filling the tank because I couldn't figure out how to work the damn things. Where do you swipe your card? Does it go this way or that way? How do you turn the pump on so it starts sending the gas?

*

Because translating thoughts to words and speaking were difficult, the computer became my primary means of communication and link to the outside world. Although Twitter and Facebook were beyond me at this point, I became the email queen. I fired off at least one message a day to the kids and became one of those annoying people who forwarded emails warning, "Send this to ten people or else!"

Roger Ebert wrote about the age of the internet:

... because of it, I can communicate as well as I ever could. We are born into a box of time and space. We use words and communication to break out of it and to reach out to others. The internet began as a useful tool, and, now, has become something I rely on for my actual daily existence ... [O]nline everybody speaks at the same speed.[2]

The computer allowed me to stay connected to the world. Without it, I would have been tragically isolated and don't know that I would have recovered as fully.

As we all know, computers have hiccups, are moody, and don't always work like they should. If my system didn't respond to the exact sequence of commands I knew, I was screwed. Not being able to open my email account, or discovering that the internet was down was cause for hysterical tears. Knowing that I probably could figure out a solution if my fried brain worked like it was supposed to only added to my frustration. Most often, the glitches probably could have been easily solved in a few minutes by my preteen kids, but I only knew my one routine and was unable to come up with workarounds.

*

Originally a time delay existed between thinking a thought and getting the signals to my mouth to speak. Like a video where the audio is out of sync, I found myself living in a confusing world where speaking and thinking weren't instantaneous and simultaneous anymore.

My thoughts raced ahead of my mouth, which made me seem more impaired than I was because I'd become flustered and lose my train of thought when speaking. So, I kept my thoughts to myself, only speaking when spoken to, and making my answers as brief as possible. For the first time in my life, someone actually described me as quiet.

When passing a neighbor while walking the dog, I kept my eyes glued to the ground, prayed that they were a stranger, and that the dogs wouldn't do the sniff the butt thing. I hoped that the grocery store cashier would just ring me up without spouting sunshine and chit-chat. Easy questions like "How's your day going?" were much appreciated. I could answer with a simple, "Fine," no further discussion needed.

A world filled with silence was new to me. In elementary school, teachers' handwritten notes on my report cards always mentioned my talent for talking incessantly. I was amazed at how much my eyes could see and my ears could hear, and what I could feel and experience when my mouth was shut. So much of my focus and energy thus far in my life had been directed outward into speech, and interacting with others and the world. Inward-focused energy, silent contemplation, and introspection are central components of almost all religions and of the practice of mindfulness for good reasons. When I was quiet, I began to be able to actually hear my inner voice and became more aware of the world around me.

Adding to my cocoon of silence, I wouldn't answer the telephone or return calls unless it was absolutely necessary because, besides not being able to speak comprehensibly, I couldn't get the hang of talking on the phone. Having face-to-face conversations wasn't completely fluid and natural, but speaking on the phone was infuriatingly difficult. Not being able to see the other person and read their physical cues threw me off. When chatting on the phone, I spoke at the same time as the other person, rudely talking over them. Although I would patiently wait for pauses in the conversation for my turn to speak, the breaks never seemed to come. Plus, I was so hypercritical and self-conscious about how I must have sounded on the other end, with nothing but a messed up, disembodied voice representing me, that I would rather just not bother.

Around this time, I became aware of some part of me, my spirit, higher self, or whatever you want to call it, objectively and compassionately watching the impaired me and her life unfold as if viewing a movie. "What in the heck? What part of me is observing me?" I thought.

While this other me witnessed the existing me squirm in many situations with empathy and understanding, she didn't intervene or have any influence yet. While the existing me was still a pro at negative self-talk, criticizing, and second guessing my every move, the other me extended kindness and grace, which was confusing yet comforting at the same time.

Even though huge chunks of my personality had vanished and my mental processes were sketchy, my soul remained whole and undamaged. In fact, it grew stronger and emerged more clearly defined, as my ego and physical self became less imposing.

Around this time, I read Eckhart Tolle's book, *A New Earth*, in which he takes issue with French philosopher Rene Descartes's well known assertion, "I think; therefore, I am." Descartes equated thinking with being, but what he had really discovered was the ego. Jean-Paul Sartre later disputed Descartes's logic also, writing, "The consciousness that says 'I am' isn't the consciousness that thinks," because the awareness of thinking is separate from the thinking.

Personally, I knew that Descartes had to be wrong because my logical mind was nowhere near normal, but "I" still existed somehow unaffected. In this new consciousness, I was both the observer and the observed.

I saw a video in which Deepak Chopra discusses the brain with Rudolph Tanzi, a Harvard Professor of Neurology, whom

GQ Magazine called a "Rock Star of Science". In the video, Tanzi explains his belief that a person isn't their brain any more than they are their stomach or gall bladder. The brain is a tool used by the mind for expression and function much like a computer. We exist as entities separate from our minds.

A newfound spiritual dimension of consciousness was rising in me, since my ego, which had always taken center stage in life, wasn't up to starring in *The Debbie Show* anymore. Eckhart Tolle writes in *A New Earth*:

When forms that you had identified with, that gave you your sense of self, collapse or are taken away, it can lead to a collapse of the ego, since ego is identification with form. When there is nothing to identify with anymore, who are you? When forms around you die or death approaches, your sense of Beingness, of I Am, is freed from its entanglement with form: Spirit is released from its imprisonment with matter. You realize your essential identity as formless, as an all-pervasive Presence, of Being prior to all forms, all identifications. You realize your true identity as consciousness itself, rather than what the consciousness has identified with.[3]

As this fresh persona began to take shape, the habits and perceptions of the old Debbie didn't feel right anymore. It was as if my favorite pair of comfy jeans, threadbare at the knees and worn-in in all the right places, had become too tight in the thighs and snug at the waist. With some distress, I said goodbye to a familiar part of myself that had been both an old friend and a formidable enemy.

CHAPTER 6

Old Habits Die Hard

Like a rebellious teenager sneaking out of the house, before I was supposed to be operating a car I drove to a convenience store right outside of the neighborhood and bought a pack of cigarettes. "The car's sitting in the garage. I have the keys and a license. I'm a grown adult," I reasoned. "Why not?" I've always thought of rules as general guidelines more than hard and fast verdicts.

Growing up in North Carolina in the 70s, smoking was common, the norm. I smoked my first cigarette when I was 15 with some other girls in a barn with horses and lots of hay. How smart were we? With the flagrancy and ignorance of youth, I lit up all through college and my 20s, but as I got older and began to feel my mortality a little more, I tried to relegate this bad habit to strictly a social activity, which really meant that I became a closet smoker, who was always trying to quit.

I didn't want to smoke. I knew better, which only made me feel worse and binge smoke when I did. Sometimes, I did good and wouldn't touch the things for weeks, but once I caved, I puffed like a chimney. After I divorced and moved to North Carolina with the kids, at night after they were in bed, it became my routine to sit on the deck behind the house with a glass of red wine in one hand and cigarette in the other. I would have a smokeathon and talkathon on the phone to Steve, if he and I were speaking at the time, or whoever the guy-du-jour was at the time.

To justify buying a pack, I'd promise myself that I was only going to smoke one, but like Lay's potato chips, I couldn't stop at just one. If I could have done that, I could have quit the damn things years before. After lighting one cigarette, I'd run water over the rest of the pack to make them un-smokable and to keep me true to my promise. I became an expert at drying out soggy cigarettes in the microwave and on top of the toaster. They did have a strong twang, but they could be smoked.

Although I hadn't had a cigarette during the two weeks in the hospital, days in rehab, or month since I'd been supervised at home, I desperately missed my cigarettes and their frequent night-time companion, red wine. So, I finally went and bought me some cigs, but inhaling one was surprisingly and disappointingly like licking the bottom of an ashtray. Like a newbie, the fumes burned my throat, made me cough, and didn't even satisfy the intense craving I had.

It was like having an annoying as hell bug bite at that hard-to-get-at spot at the top middle of my back, and it was driving me absolutely crazy. I craved the way smoking used to feel, not how it actually felt now. Lighting up didn't scratch the itch, so I didn't smoke.

*

After the divorce and before the suicide attempt in my swinging single phase, I'd picked up the habit of sipping a perfectly acceptable glass or two of wine, often at night. However, in the month before the suicide attempt after Steve left, my wine habit turned into three or four glasses or the whole bottle every night. I missed the liquid warmth and companionship wine had offered me. With the first few swallows of a glass of wine, I could feel it working its magic, slowly spreading relaxation throughout my body and mind. Although I wouldn't go as far as to say that

I was ever physically dependent on alcohol, I sure craved that "aah" feeling.

New research has shown that alcohol actually increases your brain's neuroplasticity, the ability of the brain to learn or change, which results in subconscious conditioning.[1] This is what causes alcohol to be highly addictive, which isn't new information. However, research has also discovered that the activities that often accompany drinking, such as food, music, friendships, open conversations, laughter, risks, thrills, and sex, cause the brain to swim in dopamine, the feel-good, learning, and habit-forming neurochemical. A person becomes addicted to those squirts of dopamine and the activities that cause them, not just the alcohol. I missed every last bit of it.

Having always exhibited a very low tolerance for alcohol, I had a dreadful track record when drinking. That and the fact that alcoholism ran in my family never stopped me from partaking though. Not surprisingly, bad things tended to happen when I drank.

I recently read that Finnish researchers identified a genetic mutation that affects a serotonin receptor and literally renders a person not able to hold their drink. It also makes them more impulsive when sober and more likely to struggle with self-control or mood disorders. (Sounds about right for me, but I doubt I can use this explanation as the mutation is only found in two percent of the population.)

In my third week at college, my first venture into the world away from home, I was trying to avoid the "freshman 15" weight gain and had been surviving on salads, saltines, and not much else. So, the rum and cokes that I downed during the steak dinner I cooked for my then boyfriend, Jimmie, at his apartment went straight to my head. After dinner, we met up with some friends, checked out a couple of frat parties close to campus, and then bar hopped along the college's main drag, where I proceeded to get even more blitzed. Because Jimmie and I were arguing,

I left him with the friends and headed out, staggering across campus back to my dorm room alone. A guy followed me from the last bar I had been in with Jimmie, jumped me, dragged me behind some bushes, and raped me. After he saw me crawling around in the decorative plants at the bar in my drunkenness, I guess he figured I was an easy target.

In my 20s, I was a young wife already married to Jimmie and drank moderately within the safe context of being with my husband and our friends on the weekends, but nothing too excessive. In my 30s, I was busy trying to be the perfect little wife and mother, and rarely indulged. (I probably should have had a drink every once in a while to loosen up. It might have helped the bitch in me unwind.) After the divorce, alcohol became part of my single lifestyle. It felt grown up, glamorous, and very different from my married housewife persona. While I drank only socially at first, I joined Steve, who partook daily, much too often when we were dating, and then it became a habit for me when we weren't.

Upon returning from taking the babysitter home one night after dinner and drinks with Steve, I failed to turn the van sharp enough to make the right hand L-turn into my garage and clipped the edge of the brick wall of the house and garage. Big oopsie! In the kitchen just off of the garage at the time of the collision, Steve jumped out of his skin upon hearing the explosion of crunching metal and smashing bricks.

On another rainy night after dinner and drinks, Steve dropped me at my house to get my car and a few things, and after grabbing my overnight bag, I raced to his house in eager anticipation of some hot sex. Flying around a curve so sharp that it has one of those yellow caution signs every few feet, I lost control of the van, took out one of the yellow signs, smashed into a huge boulder on the side of the road at the end of someone's driveway, and came to a stop sideways in the ditch. After calling Steve from my cell phone, he came and got me, and we went to sleep and dealt with the accident the next morning. The van was totaled. Needless to say, the events killed the mood for any hot sex that night. (I'm sorry that it met such a violent ending, but I can't say that I was sorry to see the mommy van go.)

Early in our relationship, right after we met and were still in that honeymoon, can't-get-enough-of-each-other phase, Steve and I took a romantic trip to San Francisco and met up with a girlfriend of mine and her husband, who I'd known in Pennsylvania. She and I had lived across the street from each other and had become quick friends, both having two young sons, being recent transplants, and corporate widows. I reveled in the rush of getting decked out and dining at a trendy San Francisco restaurant. "This is the life! This is why I got divorced," I thought.

At dinner, the conversation and wine were flowing. In the pictures from that night, I have my head pressed adoringly on Steve's shoulder with a big purple smile, from the red wine, on my lips. My teeth even had a purple tint. After the meal, we continued the party at a fashionable dance club where I did what I thought was a rather Madonna-esque dance with a guy who I thought was gay. Steve, however, didn't agree with my assessment of my dance partner's sexuality, took my display as a serious insult to his manhood, and grabbed a taxi back to the hotel. With the help of my girlfriend, I made it back to the hotel via a taxi. When I got up to the hotel room, Steve tells me that I proceeded to squat in the corner of the room, pee on the carpet, and rip a few healthy farts. The rest of the trip wasn't so romantic.

After my brain injury, one glass of wine made me loopy, and two made me almost unable to speak or function. I was working diligently to rehabilitate my brain to try to feel normal again, as if I wasn't drunk, every waking moment of every day. The last thing I wanted to do was to indulge and feel more impaired than I already was.

Damn! I couldn't smoke or drink. How was I going to cope in this hellacious mess I'd created?

*

I began to gain a sincere appreciation for all of the seemingly insignificant things I'd taken for granted before, and cigarettes and wine didn't even make the list. The simple act of speaking clearly was at the top. Walking with some coordination and grace also made the list. So did being able to run. Typing. Writing. Thinking straight. Remembering. Being with my kids. Laughing with friends. I'd just gotten my real estate license and started work with a company before I tried to kill myself. All gone. What had I done?

To my horror, I realized I'd brought this predicament all on myself and couldn't blame anyone else no matter how much I wanted to. Sure, other people had done things that contributed to my suicidal anxiety, but I alone had masterminded this mess. And I thought things were bad before. I had no idea how good I had it. Why had I not realized this?

Three months after the suicide attempt, at the end of the summer, I was finally left alone full time and started to allow myself to sleep as much as my body wanted to. Staying horizontal for as many as 16 hours a day, I hid my slumber from family members because the neurologist had told them not to let me sleep more than ten hours a day. This was the first time that I heeded my body's innate wisdom in the recovery process, and giving myself permission to snooze was a turning point for me. Since then, I've read that sleep, and lots of it, is absolutely necessary after a brain injury because it's when the brain heals.

I'd still be in the bed at 2.00 in the afternoon when Dad would call to check on me.

Making the usual chit-chat, "Whatcha doing?" he'd ask.

"Oh, nothing much." Well, I wasn't exactly lying, was I?

For all that time spent staring at the back of my eyelids, I never really felt rested because my sleep wasn't deep or contiguous, and I woke often and couldn't go back to sleep. I would lie in the bed for hours in that half-asleep, half-awake twilight zone with thoughts whizzing through my head. What if I stay this way forever? Will I ever have sex again? Why did I get married at 21? What's that spot on the ceiling?

When I tired of the mental whirlwind, I'd get up in exasperation and take a bath. Some nights, I know I took as many as five baths. Although soaking in the hot water was soothing and temporarily gave my mind something to focus on for a little while, it would eventually return to its endless churning, and I'd crawl back into bed with wrinkly fingers.

When I couldn't sleep, I'd often try to read a book. Before the brain injury, reading was a favorite pastime, but immediately after, I couldn't maintain the focus required to read a chapter, much less a whole book. When I tried to read, my mind flitted from wondering what my boys were doing at that moment, to kicking myself in the ass for screwing my life up so bad, to fretting about the latest astronomical hospital bill. After staring at the words on one page for 15 minutes, I wouldn't have any idea what they said. My mind had always kept itself busy with this kind of chatter, but not like this. Previously, I could at least muzzle it long enough to read a book. Now, the noise in my head was imposing, insistent, and downright rude.

Several times a day, a debilitating mental fatigue would stop me dead in my tracks and demand that I lie down right that minute, no matter what I was in the middle of doing. Similar to a cell phone battery dying, my brain would just shut down, and I was unable to do anything until I recharged it with a nap. I usually nodded off quickly and only for 15 minutes or so, but that was all I needed to continue on, until the next time my battery died.

In between naps, I tended to the necessities of daily life. Just keeping up with the laundry was a challenge, and I was always shocked to find the laundry basket full again. Didn't I just do it – last week? As with most everything, out of sight meant out of mind. When two little boys were in the house, I used to wash a load or two every day and thought nothing of it. I realized that I used to do so much. Laundry, cooking, cleaning, mothering. How in the world did I manage it all? With a newfound respect for the old me, I recognized that I accomplished an impressive amount and had been pretty darn amazing, but had never seen it.

When putting away my laundry, I'd get lost for hours in my closets and drawers because I couldn't put a T-shirt in without having to compulsively refold and restack all the shirts in the drawer. With its hundreds of small assorted pieces, the underwear drawer could eat up a whole afternoon. When hanging clothes in the closets, I had to straighten and reorganize everything by the type of article of clothing and color. Because all of the clothes were new to me, each time I opened my closet doors was like going shopping. I had all three closets in the master bedroom filled to the brim. Where did all of these clothes come from? Apparently, I used to like to shop.

I added the old familiar habit of exercise to my daily routine as soon as I was able to, at about two months' post injury, and although it was a much healthier habit than drinking or smoking, working out wouldn't prove to be so easy to pick back up. Out of vanity, I'd consistently exercised over the years. In my late 20s, I huffed and puffed to step aerobics tapes in my leg warmers at home after work. When the children came along, I joined female-only gyms with childcare to get a break and a workout.

In the year following the brain injury, my girlfriend Julie and I went to the nearby YMCA frequently. Although I'd dropped 15 pounds during the brain injury ordeal and certainly didn't need to lose any more, exercise was second nature for me. Breaking a sweat was like visiting an old friend and allowed me to feel somewhat normal. On the treadmill, wearing my headphones, I looked just like everybody else, except when attempting to run, my arms and legs got tangled up. "Why can't I do this? I know how," I would think. My deficiencies never ceased to surprise me.

The elliptical machine, requiring that my hands and feet move in opposite directions simultaneously, proved extremely challenging. On the Stairmaster, I'd "thunk" my foot into the next step because judging the distance and rhythm of the moving steps was difficult. When lifting weights, the left side of my body was visibly weaker and trembled. I gulped mouthfuls of chlorinated water instead of air when swimming laps. Even though I wasn't trying to lose pounds, I couldn't abandon my efforts until I had burned so many calories, or worked out for a certain amount of time, usually an hour. Little did I know, cardiovascular exercise is the single best thing a person can do to promote the growth of new brain cells. The cross-lateral movement required in many of the exercises is also prime rehabilitative therapy for the brain. Hooray for vanity!

I'd been a regular at the local Y before the brain injury, and several of my neighbors were members there too. Hoping that I wouldn't see anyone I knew, I kept my eyes glued to the floor. When I spotted an acquaintance while lifting weights, I scurried to the furthest machine on the other side of the room or dashed to the bathroom. When conversation couldn't be avoided, I wasn't the friendly, chatty Debbie I'd been before, and it became clear to me that most people weren't aware of the suicide attempt and brain injury. Making my exit as quickly as possible, I didn't tell them either.

Every interaction with another person sent my heart racing and left me spent. I only ventured out when I absolutely had to or wanted to very badly. On the few occasions I did try to socialize, feeling stiff and inept, I'd cling to one person with whom I felt comfortable the whole time and probably ruined their evening, as they ended up babysitting me. While my speech had improved a little, it was still difficult to carry on a conversation physically as well as mentally. Being in the company of others wasn't the happy, rewarding experience it was supposed to be, but rather, had me on edge wanting to escape the entire time.

On one occasion when I did get up the guts to go to a singles hangout restaurant and bar with Julie, a guy that we had been chatting with turned to her and asked, "How much has she had to drink?" It was much easier just to stay at home, because alone, I didn't have to try to talk and feel completely inadequate. Well, I still felt inadequate, but at least I wasn't on display.

I rarely had anything interesting to say anyway. I could sum up a week's worth of activity in a few sentences that would include not-so-fascinating details about the dishwasher, the pets, and going to the grocery store. When I knew I was going to be with others, I would make a mental go-to list of things to talk about beforehand because I couldn't rely on my brain to come up with topics in real time. My conversations were punctuated with long pauses of dead air. Trying to be vicariously cool, I recounted others' happenings figuring that it had to be more interesting than my boring life, and I just ended up coming off as awkward and trying too hard. It felt like it too.

I withdrew from everyone and everything, not returning calls or answering the door till people just stopped phoning or coming around. While I took refuge in my isolation, at the same time I chided myself for hiding from the world. However, being by myself was teaching me to like my own company and allowing me to invest what limited energy I had into healing, although I wasn't consciously doing it for these reasons.

So, here I was alone, all day every day for the first time in my life. My knee-jerk instinct was to fill up the time and space with TV, emails to the kids, activities on the computer, yard work, housework, exercise, and any other general busyness to avoid the deafening quietness of solitude. I tried to find solace in the outlets that had worked in the past. Before the injury, I had just taken up painting and had gotten into the bead working, jewelry making craze, but like the cigarettes and alcohol, the frustrating juxtaposition between the old Debbie and the new Debbie was at play again. These hobbies just didn't work anymore with my shaky hands and zero attention span.

Pema Chodron, an American Buddhist nun, says in a teaching video:

Until your world falls apart in some way or another, and you have at least a glimpse of nothing working to get it back together ... when the ground has completely fallen out and going to a movie, smoking a cigarette, eating, drinking or taking drugs, overworking or whatever your exit is, isn't touching the extent of the pain that you're feeling ... To the degree that the old ways are not working, you start to look for answers of a different kind. I don't think anyone whose life is completely together and completely cozy and has never had the ground fall out, except maybe in the most minor of ways, would be even slightly interested in this path. We equate the bubble of false security with comfort and security and with certainty and with a sense that your stomach can relax and your jaw can relax.[2]

What had been comfortable was now uncomfortable. I desperately groped around to find a new comfort zone.

CHAPTER 7

A Mom Is Born

"Put your head between your knees, Debbie," my mother instructed.

The air grew thin as I sat outside the courtroom in the hallway on the hard wooden bench looking at the little brown flecks on the too-shiny floor through my tears, which were dripping onto my wrinkled linen blouse. Like the cry of a wounded animal, a whimpering sound that was something in between a wail and a moan emanated from deep inside of me. The display was partly for show as I had performed like this my whole life – not consciously, but instinctually – and partly because I had no control over my emotions.

Learning how to emote for effect early in life, I remember being ten years old when my mother was pulled over for speeding. Quickly turning to me in the passenger's seat as the police officer approached her car window, she instructed me to cry in an effort to convince him not to issue her a ticket. It didn't work.

Like a gag reflex, I couldn't stop the pitiful sounds from heaving up and out of me. It was like when you don't want to throw up and try really hard not to, but the warm, sour contents of your stomach hit the back of your throat no matter how you try to suppress the urge. A heavy queasiness, similar to the hollow, inside-out feeling I'd have the morning after drinking too much, spread through my abdomen.

After days of testimony and legal wrangling, the judge announced his decision to take custody of my two sons away from me, award it to their father, and allow him to move out of state with the children. It was late August 2007, three months after I'd tried to commit suicide, and the boys had been under their father's care since the attempt.

For the three full days of court, I'd made the monumental effort just to stay awake and alert sitting at the imposing wooden table next to my attorney. As severely brain injured as I was, I had no business appearing in a courtroom. Just trying to look presentable, like someone capable of taking care of two kids, was a formidable task, which I don't think I accomplished very convincingly.

Having lost 15 pounds, I was skin and bones. My clothes literally hung on me, and I had to roll over the waistband of my pants several times under my blouse to get them to stay up. Around this same time, a mental health professional refused to treat me because I wouldn't admit that I was anorexic.

Hanging halfway down my back, my auburn hair, lush and full of natural curls before the suicide attempt, was now, like me, limp and lifeless. My guess is that the drugs that I ingested changed the texture of my hair. Because I couldn't tell right from left when looking in the mirror and due to poor manual dexterity, trying to fashion the mess into anything resembling a hairstyle was an impossibility, and I ended up pulling it back in a ponytail every day for court. Over the months that followed, I progressively got my hair cut shorter and shorter until it required only a shake and some gel after showering.

With an unsteady and awkward gait, I made the long walk across the courtroom from the table to the witness stand when the other side called me for questioning. Having no oomph to my voice, I couldn't speak loud enough to be heard and what did come out was slurred and not easily understood. Although he was sitting right beside me to the left, the judge kept saying, "I'm sorry. Could you repeat that?"

Figuring it was better to be truthful than to blindly stab at answers, I often replied, "I don't remember," when cross-examined by the opposing attorney. If I guessed, I knew that I'd get tripped up, Jimmie's attorney would jump on my error, and capitalize the inconsistencies to humiliate and discredit me. That was her job: to make me look stupid. I made her job all too easy as it was.

Not being able to think quickly enough to respond cleverly, I was doing well just to mumble something appropriate and halfway intelligent. In the past, I'd learned to answer strategically without revealing too much information that would lead the other side to follow up with questions whose answers I didn't want to divulge. My goal this time was just to piece together a coherent reply, spit it out, and survive the ordeal.

Totaling the number of times I said, "I don't know," 13 to be exact, Jimmie's attorney used this as ammunition against me in her closing argument. In my testimony, like a kid proud of doing his homework, I rattled off my many rehabilitative activities, such as dribbling balls, stacking coins, jumping rope, and learning to juggle, to which Jimmie's attorney wisecracked, "I'd like to see you juggle!"

Having little impulse control, I dramatically pointed at Jimmie during the proceedings declaring him an absentee dad. While such theatrics work well on TV, they don't really help a person in court in real life. In the past, I'd known to keep such emotion out of the courtroom. Looking back, I have so much compassion for myself because being judged in a court of law three months after a serious brain injury was unreasonably cruel and sad.

I'd vacillated between agreeing to give Jimmie custody and fighting to keep custody of the children. By the end of the summer, I'd begun to admit to myself that I wasn't going to be able to take care of my sons on my own, and with my limited mental stamina, I was also beginning to accept that I couldn't devote the energy to the kids that they deserved, and have any left over for healing. Because of these realizations, I initially leaned towards letting the boys go with their father. However, at the last minute, I chose to fight to retain custody, and my mother offered to move in with us to make a plausible argument to the court.

In retrospect, this was a solid decision because, even though I lost, the visitation I was awarded was generous, and spelled out in a legal order that could be enforced. Such generous access to the boys wouldn't have been provided had I just agreed to let them go. The judge allowed Jimmie to move from North Carolina to Virginia, where he'd accepted a new job, with the boys, but made him responsible for transporting the children to visit me one three-day weekend a month during the school year. The visitation also entitled me to one weekend each month with the kids in Virginia, six weeks with them in the summer at my home, and divided holidays. All of their time with me had to be supervised, and I wasn't allowed to drive them until the court felt more assured of my ability to operate a vehicle.

At the time, I didn't view this decision as fair or generous at all. To award their dad custody and sanction a move out of state with them was unbelievable to me. How can the court take kids away from their mother? They're my life. We're a team. They barely even know their dad.

Feeling like my heart had been ripped out of my chest and crying inconsolably, I wrangled free and ran away whenever my lawyer or parents tried to comfort me after the judge announced his decision. I didn't want to hear their bullshit words. Nothing they had to say could make this better. I wanted to wake up to realize that the past three months had been a bad dream. I wanted to disappear and would have, if I could have figured out how. After an hour of hysterical antics, Dad coaxed me, swollen eyed, runny nosed, and emotionally exhausted, into his car and took me home.

If I had had any possible way, I would've killed myself that night, but my parents made sure someone was with me at all times. Feeling like my skin had been turned inside out, I couldn't run away or blunt the painful reality this time. I was actually going to have to stand by and watch Jimmie pack up my boys and move them to another state.

Angry thoughts tore through my mind. This is the same man who hasn't even been around for most of their lives. The same man that was perfectly OK living halfway across the country since we've been divorced, only seeing them for a few days a month and a couple of weeks in the summer. What in hell does he know about being a dad?

I realize now that I hadn't given the legal system many good options and had thrown the boys' lives into utter chaos. When I tried to end my life, I tossed their worlds into a blender and pressed the ice crush button. Having to go to live with a man they had spent very little time with, his significant other and her son in a different state, they were ripped away from everything familiar, which was ironically what I'd opposed in all the moving around with Jimmie. But this time, I was the one responsible.

Now, I think of how distressing these events were for them, but at the time my only focus was how this upheaval devastated my world. My head was spinning in shock as they were leaving in just two weeks before school started.

*

My sons, Gabe, who was ten, and Collin, who was 13 at the time, had lived with me since their dad and I split three years earlier. Upon separating, the boys and I moved to North Carolina, and Jimmie moved to Boise, Idaho to start yet another job. He had wanted the whole family to go. That relocation would have been the twelfth move in 18 years of marriage and the fourth since having children. Collin, in fourth grade at the time, had already attended four schools.

This wasn't the life that I'd envisioned for my boys. Moving around so much was hard on them and me. They couldn't make friends at school, in the neighborhoods, or at activities, and I became more isolated with every relocation. As soon as I met a few mothers, found a gym, established a care network for the boys, and figured out where the grocery store and Target were, it was time to go again. The page in my address book with my crossed-out home addresses ran out of space long before the book wore out. Although each relocation took us to a new place with new people to meet and new areas to explore, my world shrunk with each move.

When Jimmie and I had been married nine years, our first son, Collin, was born in Raleigh, North Carolina. Until then, I followed Jimmie's career in computer programming, which progressed quickly, while I had little success with my business degree. Hitting the pinnacle of my career there, I was employed as the Public Relations Manager for a start-up software company. With the CEO in his early 20s and most of the staff right out of college, I was an old timer at 30 and more experienced than most at the company.

I didn't know the first thing about being a "Public Relations Manager"; however, the firm was willing to let me try, and thankful for the opportunity, I gave it a determined effort and had surprising success. By that time, I'd worked stints in retail sales behind a cosmetics counter, as a ladies' accessories department manager at Macy's, and as an assistant in the marketing department of two hotels, a commercial real estate company, a commercial builder, and a medical records software company. Although it didn't make for an especially impressive resume, I picked up various skills at each job along the way.

My brief employment at the software start-up was one of the few times in my life that I can recall feeling competent and confident. But after about a year there, a bigger software company bought out the start-up, and my role was drastically

89

diminished, which made it seem like a good time to have a baby on company benefits.

During my pregnancy with Colin, Jimmie was the kindest and most attentive that he ever was during our marriage. He set up a video camera on a tripod in our bedroom, and standing in the same place every week turning sideways to show off my expanding belly, I'd gush factoids about pounds gained and baby acrobatics to the camera. In nervous anticipation, Jimmie and I attended child birthing classes and bonded together like we never had before.

Collin came into the world at nine pounds, after a long, completely natural labor in which Jimmie participated and emotionally supported me. He even pried himself away from work for the whole month following Collin's birth to stay at home with us. Handling Collin like a fragile egg, attending to his every need, and adoring his every coo and spit-up, we existed in the starry-eyed, sleep-deprived world of first time parents, radiating respect and admiration for each other and the life we'd created.

I was in heaven. Words cannot describe how magnificent it felt to have this little person to love who I'd made in my own body and was completely dependent on me. Collin fulfilled a deep need to be needed that I had had my whole life. The most peace I've ever known was snuggling in the rocking chair in his nursery, breastfeeding and cradling him in my arms until we both fell asleep. I still call upon this scene today when visualizing to evoke feelings of contentment and peace. This euphoric phase ended all too soon as Jimmie resumed his daily grind back at work after a month, and after a six-week maternity leave, I returned to my job part time and hired a nanny to take care of Collin.

Displaying a genuine tenderness and attentiveness to Collin, uncharacteristic of the typical macho male at the time, Jimmie attempted to pitch in and help care for Collin when he was home. He changed smelly diapers without complaint, fed Collin bottles of pumped breast milk, and toted him around in a baby snuggly.

However, if he didn't do something exactly like I would have, it was just plain wrong in my book, and I rarely failed to point it out to him. Picking up on my attitude, before long, Collin would protest loudly when Jimmie tried to do anything for him, which gave me a perfect excuse to exclude Jimmie even further. I then resented Jimmie because he didn't help more, even though I didn't make it easy for him, criticized his every move, and trained Collin to not welcome his participation. I think that I secretly cherished being indispensable to Collin because, even though it was incredibly suffocating, it also felt absolutely wonderful to be so needed at the same time.

When Collin was a year old, we moved from North Carolina to Jacksonville, Florida. I commissioned some freelance public relations work which I did while Collin attended a Montessori preschool a block from the beach three mornings a week. Even working what little I did, I reveled in being a stay-at-home mom. Many days, after picking Collin up from preschool, we'd hit the Dairy Queen drive-through nearby for Banana Split Blizzards and head to the beach. Being thoroughly worn out after an hour of sand and sun, Collin would then go right down for his afternoon nap once we arrived home. This charmed life seems like a sappy, sunny Florida tourism commercial now, but I didn't appreciate it enough at the time.

One reason I didn't enjoy these moments as much as I could have was because this was when my brother, Chris, became sick with AIDS and died. I became a pro at packing Collin, his port-a-crib, walker, pacifiers, bottles, diapers, baby blankets, toys, and the zillions of other things we couldn't do without and hauling them to Atlanta, where I would stay with Chris for weeks at a time to take care of him. My world revolved around extended trips to Atlanta helping Chris, while Jimmie stayed behind and buried himself in his work. We lived in very different worlds with different priorities, which rarely intersected, and we didn't make much effort to bridge the gap. Jimmie was supportive in that he let me go and care for Chris without protest, but we mostly shut each other out during this time, grew apart, and did the best we could individually to survive the storm. After Chris died, I retreated into my own world, frazzled, exhausted, and numb, with nothing left over for Jimmie.

After being in Jacksonville for a year, and still feeling Chris' loss, I became pregnant with Gabe. The new life growing inside of me renewed my hope, strength, and purpose in life. For brief snatches of the day, I could actually think happy-ish thoughts about a new baby boy and dream new dreams for him instead of replaying the horrible scenes of Chris' sickness and death. In my mind, the pregnancy was a divine equalizer, partially filling the hole in my heart. Something taken. Something given.

Being veteran parents, and at a different place in our relationship, Jimmie and I approached this birth in sharp contrast to Collin's. There was no videotape of my expanding belly, no birthing classes, no baby shower, and no bonding together like the first time around. Jimmie continued putting in long hours at the office, and I busied myself with exercising and taking care of the house and Collin.

While I'd planned on natural childbirth again, with no emotional support from Jimmie, I opted for the epidural, and Gabe came into the world at eight pounds, three ounces. The disparity in the pictures snapped immediately after each boy's birth is striking. After Collin arrived, I looked tired in the picture, but an animated, new-mother sparkle lit up my eyes. Cradling a newborn Gabe, I looked into the camera with a relieved, resigned, and flat-eyed stare.

This time, Jimmie only stayed home for a few days. With an infant and an almost three-year-old who still didn't sleep through the night, I became submerged in childcare, sleep deprived and exhausted. Meanwhile, Jimmie focused on his career as usual and had secured a better job in another state. When Gabe was three months old, we moved to Pennsylvania.

In Jacksonville, I'd put my heart and soul into creating a magical nursery for Gabe. Planning and creating it was therapeutic for me because it allowed me to put my energy into moving forward instead of looking back. The brightly colored, jungle-themed border around the middle of Gabe's room had whimsical lions, monkeys, giraffes, and toucans peeking out of tropical foliage. I stenciled black paw prints in a meandering path on the walls and lampshade. A papasan rocking chair sat in the corner under a fabric palm tree on the wall, each leaf a different, cheerful color with a goofy monkey dangling from one. In the dark, quiet morning hours, nursing Gabe in that chair, with it cradling the both of us, I could almost touch the feeling of peace, but it was always just beyond my fingertips.

Jimmie usually relocated first, but because Gabe was only three months old, I didn't want Jimmie to miss out on Gabe's infancy, and I decided to accompany Jimmie with the children to our new state and home.

*

Initially, we drove both cars to Pennsylvania, and I insisted that the kids be fastened in my back seat. Traveling from northern Florida to North Carolina straight through was an 11-hour drive, but we did stop for the night. I listened to Barney tapes until I wanted to strangle his purple neck and peed in a diaper (which I held between my legs, just to clarify) when the kids were asleep, preventing me from stopping. (Rule #1: When traveling alone with a baby and a toddler, never, ever stop if they're asleep!) Cruising by himself in the other car, listening to U2 and Talking Heads, sipping coffee, Jimmie took leisurely bathroom breaks whenever the urge hit. In retrospect, I realize that I chose these circumstances, but I didn't see it that way at the time and was seething mad.

Upon arriving in Pennsylvania, we moved into an older, two-bedroom apartment and put Gabe's crib at the foot of our bed. Having resided in my own house for five years, I was disgusted by the lived-in apartment's stained carpet and the little dirt piles accumulated in the corners of the rooms. I most certainly didn't want my children crawling on it.

Because of this, we moved to a newer apartment in a different complex. Although the third floor accommodations were cleaner, it was considerably smaller, and still not as pristine as my house would have been. Gabe's crib was now crammed into the master bathroom.

"How in the hell am I supposed to get the groceries and the kids up three flights of stairs?" I wondered, as I couldn't leave Collin and Gabe alone in either the car or the apartment with the stairs in between us. I never did figure that one out. So we moved again to a three-bedroom apartment in the same complex on the ground floor. It was a more workable arrangement, but it still wasn't what I'd envisioned for my family. Not even close.

Packing both kids into the car every weekday morning, I hauled Collin to the closest Montessori preschool I could find, which was 30 minutes away. Gabe, who had developed into a car crier, would scream the whole way, which had me wanting to pull my hair out. During the three hours Collin was in preschool, it didn't make sense to drive back to the apartment and repeat the hour round trip to pick him up. Finding a gym near the preschool, I'd put Gabe in the nursery, take an aerobics class, shower, and pick up Collin.

Although it seemed almost ideal, this solution had some major drawbacks. Gabe protested vehemently while in the nursery, which prompted the attendants to come and get me several times in any one exercise class to soothe him. Collin wasn't adjusting well to his new preschool and would cling to me with tears rolling down his little cheeks every morning when I dropped him off. He had loved his preschool in Jacksonville. And being away from the apartment while Collin was in preschool and during Gabe's morning nap didn't allow me to take advantage of this valuable time to get anything done. As any caretaker of small children knows, the time when the kids are at preschool or napping is as precious as gold. The whole situation was nerve-wracking for me.

Contracting one ear infection after another, Gabe was often uncomfortable and unable to sleep day or night, which meant I got no sleep. The pediatrician wanted to put tubes in his ears. I just knew it was the dirty apartment causing his ear infections.

This wasn't what I had had in mind for me or my kids. I recognize now that my attitude only made me unhappier and made a difficult situation worse, but I didn't realize at the time. The children picked up on my sour disposition and stress, which I believe was reflected both in their behavior and sicknesses.

While the circumstances of my life weren't perfect, there was still a lot for which I could have been grateful if I had just noticed it. By holding onto expectations and making constant comparisons to what I thought my life should look like, I contrived my own unhappiness. If I'd just relaxed and looked for it, there was joy to be found in the infectious giggles of two brothers just discovering how to play together, or in our family taking a walk in the beautiful Pennsylvania countryside on a sunny afternoon, or in the excitement in Collin's eyes when he got to ride on a real steam locomotive. Instead, I zeroed in on what was less than great, fueled my anger, and compounded my misery.

After a year of living in three corporate apartments in Pennsylvania, the kids and I returned to our house in Florida, which refused to sell. When it finally did six months later, we joined Jimmie in a different town in Pennsylvania where we'd bought a house which had a Montessori preschool for Collin just ten minutes away.

Life calmed down considerably as we settled into the stately four-bedroom Tudor on a quiet cul-de-sac. Gabe's ear infections even cleared up. (Maybe there was something to my theory after all.) I was delighted to discover a neighbor right across the street with two young boys, and a family beside her with a young son who had a pet duck. Quacking furiously and flapping his wings,

Donald would chase the laughing boys around the yard. Climbing on the playground and testing out the swings of the nearby neighborhood elementary school provided many afternoon outings for us in the chilly Pennsylvania sunshine. I even found a community center nearby with a gym for me, and gymnastics, karate classes, and a swimming pool for the kids. Now this was more like it!

I have rosy memories of bundled up little boys cavorting in the frequent snows and tearing around the neighbor's yard on her son's motorized jeep. When she had one of those expensive play sets constructed in her back yard, it was a happy day for my boys and me as well. Our black asphalt driveway had large dips in it that made little pools when it rained, perfect for stomping and playing in, as the boys discovered. The back of our house had a deck built around a large tree jutting up through the center of it. Instead of grass, the back yard was landscaped with medium sized ornamental rocks that provided the perfect make-believe setting for pirates navigating a deck ship through stormy seas, or for dinosaurs lumbering across the rocks in search of their next meal. Painting, coloring, and gluing decorations to the rocks became favorite rainy day activities.

We had the full basement of our house finished, and when completed, it was big enough to house a plastic Playskool gym, Thomas the Tank Engine train table, air hockey table, bean bag toss 'em game, and lots of other little boy paraphernalia. We could even play a miniature version of plastic baseball down there, and the kids got dizzy riding their bikes in circles around the room. It was like having an arcade in our basement and was our counterpart to the neighbor's jungle gym. When it rained or snowed, we'd corral all the boys in our basement to play.

After a year of apartment hell, my vision of the "perfect life" for my boys had finally materialized. There was only one problem. Jimmie wasn't anywhere in the picture. More and more, his life revolved around work while the kids and I had our own separate existence.

I can't recall many memories with him during that time. Wait a minute. Oh yeah! We toured the nearby Crayola factory several times and indulged Collin's train fascination with day trips to visit historic steam engines.

We stayed in Pennsylvania almost three years until Jimmie landed the next better job in Tampa, Florida. Jimmie went ahead, months before the boys and me this time, but soon enough I once again boxed up our belongings and said my goodbyes. Upon settling in the new location, Collin started second grade at a public school and Gabe went to a Montessori preschool for the first time.

As Jimmie's career progressed, so did his income, and we purchased an impressive home in a sprawling, planned community with a sea of large houses on postage stamp-sized lots, with manicured common areas, a park, a playground, sidewalks, and retention ponds. Being fancier than anything I'd ever dreamed of living in, this four-bedroom house boasted marble tiles, granite countertops, a screened-in swimming pool, and a laundry chute. (I never used it for laundry, but the kids discovered that it made a terrific slide for Pokémon figurines.)

In the two tumultuous years we lived there, things went from bad to worse in our marriage. I felt increasingly more judged and was found inadequate by Jimmie. Nothing I did was right – from the Italian meatloaf I fixed for dinner, to my "mommy khakis", or how I left dirty streaks when cleaning the pool. Because he put in 70 hour weeks at the office, including working most weekends, and traveled frequently, the kids and I rarely saw Jimmie. When he was home, he was tired, stressed, and preoccupied with business matters.

On the rare weekend afternoon when we were all out by the pool, the boys would beg their dad to get in the water with them and play. He might get wet for ten minutes, if at all. I taught the boys how to swim in that pool.

97

Having children polarized and magnified the differences between Jimmie and me that were always there from the beginning. When it was just the two of us, I usually acquiesced to Jimmie putting his needs first; but once the kids arrived, it was a different story. Although I wasn't willing to fight for myself, I was willing to fight for those kids.

So, at this point in our lives, Jimmie and I bickered constantly about whatever the topic was that day. Regardless of the subject of the current argument, there always existed an ongoing struggle for control of the relationship, our lives, and the kids that we weren't aware enough to realize at the time. The tension in our relationship rippled through the kids and manifested as conflict between Jimmie and Collin.

Jimmie and I held very different visions of our family's future. When he came home wanting to relocate yet again, this time across the country, I made the decision to leave him. For myself. For the kids. Ending the marriage felt like a colossal failure that I'd avoided as long as I possibly could, but at this point, it also felt unavoidable. It was the lesser of two evils. We were going to have to move one way or another.

*

In December 2002, Jimmie moved to Boise, Idaho and the kids and I moved back to North Carolina near my parents. I pointed my mommy van north and left our old lives and Florida in the background. I started a newly single life close to my parents near where I had grown up in North Carolina.

A tropical jungle on wheels, the van was crammed full of so many plants the movers wouldn't move, that I couldn't see out of the rear window. Accompanying us on the road trip were eight guinea pigs, two 15-year-old Persian cats, and a two-year-old Jack Russell Terrier. (I did finally figure out how to tell the male guinea pigs from the females and separated them so that they quit multiplying every few months.) Upon stopping to spend the night in a motor lodge, I smuggled the animal menagerie into the room.

The nervous cats never peeked out from under the beds the entire time.

With the kids' and my dad's input, I bought a four-bedroom house in an established neighborhood in the county with large yards and lots of trees. We moved in January, the boys resumed second and fifth grades at the local public school, and I quickly set about making the house into our home.

Because we were used to not having Jimmie around already, the physical actuality wasn't that different; however, this time he wasn't at the office or on a business trip. He wasn't coming home at all. Ever. Mentally and emotionally, this was a monumental distinction. Without him around, stress and anxiety didn't hang thickly in the air, but it was a replaced by a heavy undercurrent of sadness that permeated everything. Things weren't all that different, but they were completely different at the same time.

Both boys were hurting, each in their own way. Gabe resembled his father with strawberry blonde hair that had the slightest bit of curl, wide blue-green eyes, and peachy skin with a sprinkling of freckles across the bridge of his nose and cheeks. He inherited his father's family's athletic build, but had a tender heart that he wore on his sleeve. At seven, he took the split hard. In his baseball coach, uncle, and friends' fathers, he looked for attention and searched for the caring male presence he lacked consistently in his own life.

Gabe, who was bright, adorably mischievous, and usually happy-go-lucky, became the ultimate people pleaser after the separation, trying his best not to set his brother off or elicit a negative reaction from me. When Gabe was eight, he sat in the middle of the upstairs hall outside of his bedroom, with tears running down his cheeks, seriously wanting to know why I couldn't marry his baseball coach, of whom he had become rather fond, so he could have a "real dad". Hiding a slight smirk, I gently explained to him that his baseball coach was already married and that he wasn't really my type.

Collin, the physical opposite of Gabe, looks like me, lanky with olive skin, brown hair, and brown eyes with super smarts, a quick wit, and even quicker temper. After the split, Collin's sadness turned into anger that exploded at everybody and everything. A constant fury smoldered in his eyes, which could look black when he got mad enough, and it didn't take much to send him burning out of control. He was quick to lash out and hurt others verbally and physically, especially Gabe. Screaming "I'm going to kill you!" Collin would chase Gabe around the house with a knife when he felt justified, and he felt justified if he didn't like the way Gabe was breathing.

Dog-eared parenting books with titles like "The Spirited Child" and "How to Parent Boys" filled my bookshelves. As the manuals suggested, I drew charts, taped them to the wall, and handed out stickers for good behavior. Throwing all the book wisdom out the window one afternoon, I rolled around on the floor restraining Collin, who was almost as tall as I was, hugging him tightly with my arms around his chest, and my legs holding his legs still because I didn't know what else to do to calm him down.

Attending regular counseling sessions, weekly "Children of Divorce" classes, and making friends helped the boys gradually acclimate to their new lives and settle down. On weekends, it became the norm for our house to be filled with the sounds of boys bouncing on the trampoline, running around the yard pinging air soft guns, playing video games, and giggling late into the night. After school, our house became a gathering place for friends, and I always made sure that the cabinets were filled with snacks and the fridge stocked with soda.

Gabe played little league baseball. Both boys took karate and fencing classes. Like most boys at that time, they were into collecting Yu-Gi-Oh cards and playing electronic games on every gaming system: PlayStation, Nintendo, X-box, and the computer. Excelling in school, both boys placed into several advanced classes, and I became a familiar face around the halls of their school, volunteering weekly in their classes and eating lunch with each of them often.

For the first time, extended family became an integral part of our lives because we had never lived close to them before. As a single parent, it was important to me to provide the boys with a sense of family, build a support system, and expose them to many different role models, both male and female. We saw my parents often, as they frequently babysat, shared meals with us, and took joint trips to the beach or mountains. The boys and I regularly spent time with my single, male cousin who had a son living with him who was four years older than Collin. We even made several trips to visit Jimmie's aunt and uncle who lived an hour away.

About once a month, Jimmie would fly in from Idaho, and the boys would spend the weekend with him at his hotel while they would take longer trips to visit him in Boise over the summer and for holidays. In between, Jimmie phoned, sent letters, and tried to be part of their lives as best he could.

While life had assumed a comfortable rhythm on the exterior, a current of anxiety and sadness still swelled just below the surface. Like two worthy opponents locked in a deadly battle, the conflict between Jimmie and me remained intense and was still very much a big part of my life. As we had done for the previous two decades in our marriage, we danced round and round in a never-ending power struggle, not making much progress in our new lives and not doing us or the kids any good.

Battles raged over the wheres and whens of the visitation drop off and pick up times. I didn't think it was appropriate that his girlfriend made the boys feel uncomfortable by wearing a night gown in front of them. He didn't like that Steve and his children spent the night at our house. I got pissy because he always returned the kids' clothes dirty after their visits with him. He didn't approve of me letting the kids stay up later and play some of the more violent electronic games. I didn't like that when they were with him all they ate was fast food. You name it, we fought about it just like when we were married.

I, regretfully and unconsciously, encouraged and fueled the boys' anger, pain, and discontent with their dad by informing them of too much of the ongoing conflict, which placed them right in the middle of the battle. By pointing out Jimmie's faults, I could bolster myself, secure them firmly on my side, and confirm what an awful person he was. While I had read enough "Parenting After Divorce" books and knew better than to blatantly bash him out loud, this didn't stop me from emotionally manipulating the kids, without being consciously aware of what I was doing. I needed their love and allegiance desperately to fill my own emotional wounds and deficits, and I truly believed, at that time, that Jimmie was attacking all three of us, not just me. In my mind, my boys weren't separate from me. Blinded by my own hurt and anger, I couldn't see how I was hurting them.

Because I had no identity outside of being their mother, this persona comprised a disproportionately huge part of my sense of self. "The mother" was all there was. I needed the boys to see me as the good guy and their dad as the bad guy to affirm my own self-worth. Because I hadn't grown beyond this point emotionally, for me to do anything otherwise felt like a threat on a primal level. Being so focused on the kids' welfare and the legal entanglements, for years I did almost nothing to meet my own needs, expand my world, or grow my own self-worth.

As was my pattern, I dwelled on what I saw as my shortcomings. Anything less than perfect wasn't good enough for me, and perfect, of course, doesn't exist. Because I felt guilty for the marriage crumbling, for the ensuing conflict between their dad and me, for the boys not having a dad on a daily basis, for the sky being blue, and for just about everything else, I was co-dependent with my boys. I found it difficult to tell them no, and rarely did. Hell, I couldn't even tell the dog no.

Despite these drawbacks, it's not a stretch to say that I was actually a good mother – great even. I could've done better, much better for sure, but I was pretty awesome in many ways. Jimmie's own maternal grandmother used to say what a "good little mother" I was. His aunt bestowed me with the title of "the best mother she had ever seen". Collin's nanny says that I was a fantastic mother. I guess I'm trying to convince you as well as myself. The problem was that I never believed it.

My soul-crushing inner dialogue, partly shaped by Jimmie, and reinforced by Steve and the words of Jimmie's attorney as she viciously portrayed me in court, echoed in my head and ate away at my heart. In my mind, I had a million reasons why I wasn't a good enough mother and had already failed my boys in their young lives, and I couldn't see any way it was going to get much better.

CHAPTER 8

A Mother Is Sculpted

Although the boys only moved 300 miles away, they might as well have gone to a different planet. (Did I really just say "only"?) Two weeks after the judge's ruling, my sons went to Virginia with their father, staying at first in a hotel with his significant other, Sheila, and her son, John. After a month, they all moved into a four-story, five-bedroom house with an elevator, in an affluent suburb of Washington DC, in one of the top school districts in the country. They literally lived five miles from the White House and went to school with diplomats' kids.

When they first left, I operated in full survival mode with the goal being to just try to make it from one day to the next. Even though they hadn't been living with me for the past three months, it felt like they took the oxygen out of the air with them. As with Jimmie's absence when we first separated, the everyday routine wasn't all that different, but the psychological difference was astronomical. Still emotionally shaky and mentally foggy, I desperately wanted to escape from this cruel, childless reality, but there was nowhere to run.

In retrospect, being brain injured was actually beneficial for me because my dulled mental state numbed the impact of their departure – and believe me, it was bad enough as it was.

As if living underwater, I thought, talked, and moved slowly, and my emotions were diluted and diffused too. If I had been clear-headed, the blow of them leaving would have been much too much for me to bear, but because I could only deal with and exist in the present moment most of the time, the happenings didn't pulverize me like they would have before the brain injury.

Don't get me wrong. I did my share of crying and commiserating, and if I could have figured out a sure way to kill myself, I would have. But because my brain was only capable of focusing on one thing at a time, my mind was primarily preoccupied with the task at hand and couldn't endlessly ruminate and drown in self-pity.

Once they left, maintaining contact with the children was challenging and frustrating. Because I could barely talk and because the boys weren't big on speaking on the phone, we mostly communicated through emails. Neither child texted much at the time, which was good, as texting was almost impossible for me. I would often take a picture with my phone and send it to them because that was a fairly simple process requiring that I press only a few buttons.

They left in September and came back for a three-day weekend in October, and for the Thanksgiving holiday in November. Because their visits had to be supervised around the clock, my parents and girlfriend, Julie, alternated staying with us to satisfy the requirement. The supervision was awkward for the kids, the person supervising, and me because we were staying at my house and driving my car, but they were overseeing me. While I found the restrictions humiliating, they did provide powerful motivation for me to improve to get them removed.

Before the kids came in for that first Thanksgiving visit, Julie took me to the DMV office to take the on-the-road and written driving tests. Although I was more nervous than when I was 16, I passed on my first try this time.

Their visits were like a drug fix for me. With the boys in the house, life seemed almost normal. When cleaning up after dinner, looking out the window over the kitchen sink at the trampoline in the back yard, Peter Griffin broadcasting from the TV in the den, and Sonic the Hedgehog running around the playroom upstairs all fed my soul. It could have been any typical night in the past year.

At the end of those early visits, I would openly sob at the airport when saying goodbye as the boys boarded their plane back to Virginia. I didn't want to upset them, but I couldn't help it. Upon their exit, I knew that I was going to fade back into the confusing hell that had become my existence, with no idea who I was, or what I was supposed to be doing. It was hard for me to believe that this was actually my life now.

That first year, the kids flew in on Christmas Day and stayed with me through the following week to celebrate the holidays. I wore myself out going overboard decorating even more than usual. A kids' tree upstairs in the playroom had a sugar-coated plastic candy garland and multi-colored lights, and a more formal tree downstairs was decorated elegantly with all gold ornaments and white lights. Christmas lights sparkled in trees in the front yard, around the porch, and even on the back deck. I wanted the house to ooze "merry and bright" to create the perfect illusion of Christmas, like nothing had changed. But no matter how twinkly I made it, things weren't the same.

Over the following school year, the boys' coming in for a monthly three-day weekend became the norm, and we all adjusted to the rhythm of it and our lives in between. Mine was a solo dance and theirs a hustle with their dad and his new family. I even eventually quit crying at the airport. I waited until I was alone in my car on the drive home.

Continuing to feed the conflict between us, Jimmie would send the boys to visit, no matter how long they were staying, with nothing but the clothes they were wearing and what they had crammed in their backpacks, usually the latest edition of Resident Evil and a wireless controller. Because they were at the ages where they were growing quickly, we'd often have to spend hours of our limited time together shopping for clothes because the underwear I had for them looked like bikinis and jeans were now too short. Jimmie rarely communicated the visitation dates or flight information to me until right before their arrival, making securing supervision difficult.

Occasionally, Jimmie flew the boys into an airport in a bigger city an hour away because fares were cheaper than at the smaller airport five minutes from my house. The same situation existed on the DC end. By the time they arrived at my house, they had been traveling for four hours. When factoring in the return trip, a total of eight hours was required to get from one place to the other, which was a huge chunk out of the three-day weekend for kids who often had homework and school projects to complete.

While these things seem trivial to me now, they irked me then (as I believed they were meant to) because Jimmie and I were still locked in our never-ending power struggle. Over time, these once insulting practices became the norm, and I learned not to expect any different, and was pleasantly surprised if circumstances proved better. Unknowingly, Jimmie provided me with plenty of opportunities to learn to let go of needing control, and to be grateful for and accept what was.

Each of the kids' visits was a marathon rehabilitation session for me, forcing me to venture out of the safe routine I'd established in my life. In my comfort zone, I was competent. With them in town, life wasn't quite so predictable or manageable. Dirty clothes needed to be washed daily, hungry tummies wanted to be fed at regular intervals, and friends had to be picked up and dropped off, which meant polite chit-chat with the parents. When I was by myself, I did a couple of loads of laundry per week, ate whenever I felt like it, and dinner might be a banana with spoonfuls of almond butter. I didn't interact with other people much. While our get-togethers were exhausting for me physically and mentally, they also fed my spirit and furthered my rehabilitation.

Being starved for hugs and the affectionate, day-to-day physical touch that happens between mother and child, I would catch up during their visits. Missing his mother's touch, Gabe would curl up on the couch beside me and cuddle. Collin, who was older and therefore not as touchy-feely, still liked his hugs.

With all of us cozied in the den one night, we watched one of their favorite episodes of *Family Guy*. Still having my brain-injured, child-like mind, I laughed hysterically with tears rolling down my cheeks when the character Chris got pulled behind a refrigerated milk case into a magical Norwegian world where the group, A-ha, serenaded him until he busted back through the milk case. Hitting rewind over and over, the boys delighted in giggling at the clip and their maniacal mother. For a few minutes, it was wonderful to be able to forget everything and just laugh with my boys again.

*

When they came for the summer a year after the suicide attempt, I relaxed the supervision to just telephone contact part of the time, and didn't have a person on-site 24 hours a day. The boys were 11 and 14 years old, I had greatly improved over the previous year, and the court order did not specifically say that the supervision had to be on-site. At a job, a supervisor doesn't stand over a subordinate watching them every minute, I figured.

The first day that the boys arrived, my dad spent nine hours at my house sitting on the sofa, reading the paper, watching TV, and basically wasting his time, fulfilling the court ordered supervision requirement. He didn't spend the night, but did come back the next day for several more hours. On the third day, I took the boys and a friend to the YMCA where they went swimming while I worked out mid-morning. I reasoned that the adult staff at the Y were technically supervising.

After coming home, I was fixing sandwiches for lunch while the boys headed outside to play a game of "wall ball", an old favorite of theirs. My dad was already on his way over to fulfill his supervising duty for the day. Closing the garage door, the boys began to play ball up against it like they had done a million times before over the previous years. Only this time, when Collin reached to grab the ball, his arms crashed through one of the door's glass windows. Hearing the accident, I ran outside to Collin and immediately yelled at Gabe to call 911 and my father on his cell phone. With his arms dripping blood and flaps of skin, muscle, and fat hanging in shreds, I guided Collin around to the back of the house to sit on a deck chair. I'd never seen anything as gross as that, not even in freshman biology when we dissected fetal pigs. Thank goodness he hadn't severed an artery or vein.

While I raced to the laundry room to get towels, Collin remained surprisingly calm and had the wherewithal to raise his arms above his head. Upon returning, I tightly wrapped the towels around his arms.

"Just breathe deep and slow. Everything's going to be fine. You're OK." I kept reassuring him, although I'm not sure I believed it.

Dad arrived seconds before the ambulance and followed it to the hospital while I rode in the back with the EMT and Collin. Once at the hospital, Dad called Jimmie to tell him what had happened and to retrieve insurance information for Collin. Jimmie insisted that a plastic surgeon close the wounds, but because one wasn't available, Collin underwent emergency surgery with the doctor on duty.

Requiring over 90 stitches, Collin looked like Frankenstein with long red cuts sewn together with black thread on the underside of both forearms and the backs of his upper arms. A smaller cut on his chin was glued shut. Collin had to spend the night in the hospital, and while the circumstances were definitely not ideal, I reveled in being able to stay at his bedside and feel like a real mom.

Within two days of the incident, Jimmie filed contempt charges against me for not having the visitation supervised on-site, around the clock, and for my operating a motor vehicle with the boys in it. He cited Collin's accident and other factors, such as the boys staying up late, playing M-rated video and computer games, their diet, and my discussing my "adult relationships" with them as proof that the children were in danger in my unsupervised care.

While initially greatly upsetting, the charges also ushered in a sort of relief. I finished out the visit under the same supervision arrangements. "What's he going to do? File more charges for the same things?" I reasoned.

As was spelled out in the visitation order, the children returned to Virginia for two weeks in the middle of the summer. Before sending them back to me for the month of August, Jimmie demanded that I provide a detailed supervision schedule for the remainder of their summer visit. Because it wasn't legally directed that I had to produce such information, I didn't. In response, Jimmie didn't send the boys back for the second part of their summer visit. I filed contempt charges against him, and he sent them late after I did that. The dance continued.

Still figuring that I couldn't get any guiltier than I already was, I continued to have the visits supervised, with a combination of on-site and telephone support, and drive the boys in the year before we got to court. As the children put down roots, made friends, and invested in their lives in Virginia, I was exploring new therapies, continuing to improve, learning to like my solitude, and carving out a new life for myself. I reached the point where I honestly felt that I had the best of both worlds and was often heard saying, "I love to see 'em come, and I love to see 'em go!"

At the end of the second summer, the boys returned to Virginia a week before school started in late August and came right back down for the Labor Day weekend. Jimmie's significant other, Sheila, had purchased a salon and day spa in the city in which I lived, where she and Jimmie resided before moving to Virginia. Needing to attend to business at the salon, she and Jimmie drove down with the kids, including her son, John. On the way, Sheila phoned me proposing that John spend the holiday weekend with the boys at my house, and I agreed.

When she and Jimmie left the three boys with me with no obvious, on-site supervision, neither of them said a word about it, and Jimmie invited me to bring the crew to his hotel to go swimming the next day. Upon our arrival at the hotel, Jimmie met us in the parking lot, not uttering the slightest concern about my driving the children or the absence of a supervisor.

While the kids splashed around, Jimmie and I sunned ourselves by the pool, exchanged iPod tips, and chatted about meditation and yoga like two civil people. He even invited me to have lunch with him and the boys at the hotel restaurant, although I declined. If I met him on the street, I'd peg him as a pretty cool guy. It was difficult for me to reconcile the man before me, in his "Life is good" T-shirt and Hawaiian flowered swim trunks, with the tyrant who had mercilessly harassed me over the years.

Because of the brain injury and my propensity to live in the present, I tended to remember this sane Jimmie, forgetting the past, and repeatedly underestimated him. And that never ended well for me. As my constitution firmed up, I learned to be wary of him at all times and consider how he could possibly take anything I did and twist it against me – no matter how charming he acted in person.

Behind the safety of our sunglasses, we talked about the past.

"We were so young when we got married. We weren't even who we were gonna be yet," I said. "I know I made a shitload of mistakes during the marriage and in the time since. I want to apologize for anything I've done that you feel I need to apologize for."

"Yeah, the last seven years have been hell," he said, as his phone on the towel beside him chimed a notification. He picked it up, checked it, and began scrolling through a message.

After a long, awkward pause, I said, "This is the part where you say you're sorry."

With his eyes still on the phone, he mumbled, "I'm sorry, too."

When the kids were waterlogged and crisp from the sun, Jimmie walked us to the car and waved goodbye, again showing no concern about me driving or leaving with the children unsupervised.

Because numerous court dates were scheduled and cancelled, we didn't get to court to address the contempt charges from the summer of 2008 until November 2009. Admitting on the stand that he'd willingly left all three boys in my unsupervised care and witnessed me driving them without voicing any protest, Jimmie very sincerely assured the judge that he had erred and wouldn't do it again.

Technically, I won the hearing, but it wasn't quite the slam-dunk I thought it was going to be. Visibly unhappy with the summary rulings, Jimmie stood up and made an emotional plea to the judge.

"In my opinion," he said, "you've made a grave mistake. She isn't a good influence on the boys, and they aren't safe with her." Even though we had been civil, verging on somewhat reconciliatory in our earlier pool-side discussion, this did not surprise me at all. I knew better than to trust Jimmie.

While the judge ordered that the supervision and driving restrictions remain in place, I wasn't sanctioned for contempt of court and neither was Jimmie. Although the court proceedings occurred right before Thanksgiving, the judge didn't make the written details of her ruling known until March of the next year, over two and half years post suicide attempt and brain injury. She instructed that the supervision restrictions were to remain in place for six more months, that I pass a driving test administered by a specific rehabilitation specialist, and that I continue under the care of, and follow the directions of, my neurologist.

Although I wasn't thrilled with her decisions, I was relieved to finally know definite steps I could take to get the restrictions removed and quickly set about meeting the requirements. Certifying someone to operate a motor vehicle was beyond the scope of services provided by the rehabilitation doctor she named. Declining to conduct the assessment, he referred me to a private business that routinely performed such certifications. After a three-hour evaluation including an extensive written quiz, on-the-road driving observation, and vision, reflex, and flexion tests, I passed the driving test and continued under the care of my neurologist, who at that point, I only saw every six months.

*

The judge's order to continue the supervised visitation for six more months presented a challenge because the boys' summer stay for six weeks was included in that period. At the time, my mother, who had been diagnosed with breast cancer months before, had successfully finished chemotherapy, was undergoing radiation, and wouldn't be able to assist much. My father, who was retired, had an active life, busy with volunteering and other commitments. Even though I know that he would have helped me, I wasn't about to ask him to give up his life to come sit on my couch for six weeks. To do so would have been disrespectful to him and his wife.

I'll readily admit that the restrictions were in the best interest of the children immediately after the brain injury, but they were completely unnecessary two and a half years later. I'd substantially improved and the boys were 15 and 12 by then. The requirements were insulting to me, the supervisor, and the boys, and nothing more than a means for Jimmie to continue to harass me and assert control.

Although I detested the ridiculous rules, I'd learned a better way to approach challenging circumstances, and instead of fighting against the situation, I chose to accept and work with it. After asking myself, "How do I make this work for me?" I came up with the idea to hire a supervisor to live with us for the summer. I employed an 18-year-old young man who attended a nearby college, played on the rugby team, and competed in mixed martial arts. Perfect. A natural with the boys, the supervisor gained their respect while also befriending them, like a camp counselor, and even acted as a personal trainer for Gabe.

Like someone who had just discovered religion, I was eager to share the emotional, mental, and behavioral tools that I was finding so successful with the boys. Because I had shown them so many bad examples when they lived with me, I wanted the chance to teach them better. I held daily classes about thought reframing, visualization, and meditation, and assigned reading and practice exercises. Despite their grumbling, I think they kind of liked it, even if they thought their mom was a little weird.

It was an awesome start to the summer, and after three weeks the boys went back to Virginia for two weeks at the end of July, as per the visitation schedule. After they had returned and were in his care, Jimmie filed charges against me causing the Virginia court to enact emergency jurisdiction over custody matters and stop all visitation.

What was the emergency? The boys were already safe with him. To further hassle and insult me, Jimmie's attorney didn't notify my attorney of the filing on the date it was entered, as is standard legal procedure. A courier came to my front door on my birthday, a week after the complaint was filed, and served me notice of the legal action. I then informed my attorney. It's supposed to work the other way around. Having been legally served at my home on my birthday several times before, I much preferred it when Jimmie completely forgot my birthday, as he did during our marriage.

The motion alleged that I hadn't met the driving and supervision requirements. Jimmie and his attorney didn't accept that the driving test I took fulfilled the legal requirement because the doctor that the judge specified hadn't performed it. They also challenged that my hired supervisor didn't satisfy the role even though, within the previous year, Jimmie had employed a "manny" (male nanny), as the kids called him, of the same age with similar qualifications.

Until the matter could be resolved, the court stopped my visitation with the children on an emergency basis. Rightly erring on the side of caution, the legal system acted to shield the kids from danger, not knowing whether the allegations were true or not. The Virginia court held a hearing that next Monday, after I was served notice of the filing on Thursday, which gave me almost no time to find legal representation in another state.

It took six long months to resolve the matter in court, during which I had no visitation rights with the children at all. No Thanksgiving. No Christmas. Regardless of whether the charges were found to be true or not, Jimmie had successfully severed my interaction with the children just by filing the complaint, which I believe was his intent. While the children and I communicated via phone and email, over the six months I only saw the boys for one supervised visit at a hotel and for one meal.

The weekend after Thanksgiving, Jimmie drove them to North Carolina and stayed for a night in a nearby hotel. Although this act may have originated out of the goodness of Jimmie's heart, it may have also come about because a judge shook his finger at Jimmie's attorney, telling her, "Your client needs to make a good faith effort for these kids to see their mother." Because Jimmie allowed the visit, he got to make the rules. He decided that the boys weren't to leave the hotel premises by car with anyone driving. Because the hotel didn't have food service on-site, the kids and I walked to a nearby restaurant for lunch with my father and his wife, who were supervising.

Employing my "How do I make this work for me?" philosophy, I invited family friends to supervise, who came with their children to play in the hotel pool that afternoon. In the evening, three of the boys' friends wolfed down delivered pizza and retreated to their hotel room to play computer games under Jimmie's supervision.

The next morning, my mother visited and supervised me with the kids, and we hiked to a restaurant for breakfast. We had to run across six lanes of speeding traffic to a restaurant that served breakfast. Like that was safer than me or someone else driving the kids in a car?

Three days after Christmas, Jimmie drove the boys to North Carolina again, staying at the same hotel. The trip served a dual purpose as Sheila accompanied him to do business at the spa she owned in town. Because I didn't know that the boys were coming until a day before they showed up, I had mailed them a box filled with candy, snow-in-a-can, gift cards, presents, and other whimsies, for each of the five days before Christmas, and was prepared for that to be our Christmas. Actually getting to see them was beyond fantastic.

Arriving around dinnertime on a Wednesday night, the boys met me with my dad and his wife at the restaurant on the same side of the highway as the hotel. Upon pulling up, I was surprised to see the boys standing outside with two of their local friends. Now, I'm all for them spending time with their pals and maintaining those friendships, but as is true of anyone, their behavior differs depending on the social situation. Around their buddies, they become cool, distracted teenagers, not attentive sons and grandchildren who are interested in interacting with their family. At the end of our meal, I asked how they were getting back to the hotel since we weren't allowed to drive them. No problem. Much to my surprise, Jimmie and Sheila had been sitting in the bar area of the restaurant the whole time.

The boys stayed the night at the hotel with their friends, and spent the next day hanging out with them. That afternoon, they called asking me to run bathing suits over to them, which I did. I was supposed to have dinner with them again that night at the same restaurant with my mother supervising this time, but I cancelled, stating that she didn't feel well because she was undergoing radiation treatment. Although she would have certainly made the meal with the kids possible if I'd requested, I had no interest in doing a replay of the previous night. I'd talked through the situation with my counselor that morning, and she supported my decision.

This was a huge step forward for me emotionally. It was the first time that I made the decision to do what was best for me, over being the do-anything-for-the-kids mom. I made the conscious choice not to see my children if it meant being disrespected and manipulated by Jimmie through them.

*

Over the years, my philosophy had evolved to one of minimizing my legal participation as much as possible, engaging only when it was absolutely necessary to protect my rights. But, in this situation, it was difficult. Damned difficult! In a message to my lawyer, I screamed "DO SOMETHING NOW!" When we finally did get to court in January, six months after the charges were filed, I prevailed on all accounts, and my visitation was reinstated in full without supervision. Three more months passed before this order was written and entered into the legal system. During that time, Jimmie, knowing full well how to work the system, still didn't send the children for visitation. Without being entered, the directives were almost impossible to enforce, and before any contempt motion I filed could be heard in court, the order would most likely be posted. I accepted that once again, the events were beyond my control.

When Jimmie first filed the false charges, I was understandably furious and distressed. As the ordeal dragged on, these feelings receded, and a sense of peace and wholeness emerged as I let the wisdom of the experience shape and teach me. With the boys removed from my life, I was forced to form a more complete self-identity. I began to accept the limits of what I could reasonably affect without overreacting and jeopardizing other priorities in my life. Instead of letting the issue consume most of my financial resources, time, and energy, I focused on my own life and goals, and made solid progress there while I let the other events unfold – impatiently with arms folded and feet tapping, at times.

To cope, I relied heavily on my mental health counselor, the teachings of Pema Chodron, and a daily meditation practice. I discovered that the separation actually allowed my relationship with the kids to evolve and deepen, transcending time and distance. I imagine that it was similar to the process any parent goes through when a child leaves home. I grew to have an unshakable sense of trust in my boys and the universe during our winter of exile.

After resuming the three-day weekend visitation for two months, the boys spent six weeks with me during the summer with no restrictions. It was the reunion I had longed for, but I found myself apprehensive and anxious about their arrival after such a long absence. I was actually nervous about my own children coming to visit!

In the four plus years since they had lived under my roof and during the no-visitation period, I'd gotten comfortable in my solitude and set in my ways. My list of what I called my daily "must-do's", including meditating, working online, writing a blog, exercising, and going to yoga, was long and non-negotiable. With them here, how in the world was I going to get all my stuff done?

While the kids were sequestered in Virginia, I'd moved from the large house in which we lived to a house half the size. The old house afforded space for all of us and more, as they frequently had friends spend the night. We were going to be crawling on top of each other in the new home. My furry family, which had grown to six cats and a dog, most of which I had acquired since the boys left, would freak out at the invasion.

By this time, I knew better than to buy into such feelings and had a grasp on minimizing my anxiety. Every time these kinds of thoughts popped up, I assured myself that everything would be OK and that I could handle it. I chose to use their extended summer stay as a learning experience and stayed open to the lessons it had to teach me. Relaxing the "must do's" to the bare minimum necessary to maintain my mental health, I accepted that the house was going to be wrecked, the cats would be frazzled, and that I'd live if I didn't break a sweat every day.

I cooked and did more laundry in those six weeks for them than I'd done for myself over the entire past year. One timid orange tabby cowered under my bed the whole summer. Sometimes three friends piled in overnight, sleeping on an air mattress and sleeping bags on the floor, and a friend of Collin's from Virginia joined us for a week. And yes, we were on top of each other, but we survived. Thrived even. Packed with lots of laughs and "fun and junk" (the catchphrase for the summer), we had a blast. Within the first few days of their arrival, my worries vanished as I knew they would and, for the remainder of their visit, I fought the urge to tidy up all the time, shushed the nagging voice telling me to eat better or exercise more, and reminded myself to stay in the moment and enjoy the time with my sons. And I did.

*

Having to brave a new school, adjust to a strange home in a different state, with a dad they didn't know well anymore had been tough for the kids. They'd had to fit into a blended family with new rules, and a woman and her son that they barely knew. Collin often described his dad's house as a monarchy and mine as a democracy.

You would think that, when they first left, I would have called them all the time. However, with speech being so difficult for me, I didn't phone them often, or vice versa. I hated talking on the phone, even to them. I did get desperate calls from an unhappy Collin wanting me to do something, somehow, about the conditions and the behaviors that were expected of him in his new household though.

119

"I have to go to bed at 9.00 on school nights," he complained, "They won't let me play M games. They put a limit on my computer time, and I can't have any coke or chips. This really blows!"

Feeling helpless and bad for him, all I could say was, "I'm sorry, honey."

Upon realizing that I couldn't do anything to change his situation, his pleas for help tapered off. Gabe would call just to hear the familiarity of his mother's voice occasionally, even if it was sluggish and stuttered at times. Although Gabe found it very difficult to adjust to living with a younger male, John, and didn't like him at first, he liked the fact that Collin now had someone else to pick on.

Over the years, this unusual arrangement has become our normal. Living 300 miles from my children was certainly never the future I pictured. It isn't how I planned it, but it is what it is. And you know what? It's OK. Good, even. While the adaptation process hasn't been a piece of cake for any of us, we've all grown tremendously and are wiser because of the things that happened. We had to throw out the traditional definition of "mother" and sculpt a meaning that worked for us.

My boys are now fine young men in college, with scruffy beards. At times, I consider myself to be a close, connected mother. At other times, I feel more like a friend, distant relative, or stranger who doesn't know them or anything about them. A girlfriend of mine, who has four young adult sons, assures me that they could live under my roof all of the time, and I'd feel exactly the same way.

Often, I'm not sure what role I'm supposed to, or want to, play in their lives. Although I know that I'm their biological mother – and those heart ties will always be securely fastened – it's confusing to know where I fit in their realities on a day-to-day basis. Rather than keeping in close contact with them, I give them their space, which I believe allows them to enjoy and invest fully in their lives without placing a bunch of expectations or emotional ties on them. They always know that I'm here if they need me.

For this same reason, I don't visit them in Virginia often. For the first three years, I didn't travel there at all because of the restrictions requiring supervised visitation and prohibiting me from driving them. After they were lifted, I wanted to let the boys lead typical, teenage lives on their home turf, uncomplicated by having to make time for their mother every other weekend. Emotional life at that age is turbulent and confusing enough as it is.

Our arrangement may not be perfect, and many would not agree with it, but it feels right to us. The person I am today would definitely make different choices than the ones that led to the tumultuous, life-shattering events for us. In the past, I learned through drama and crisis. Now, I choose a calmer, gentler path whenever possible ... and it's always possible.

I shudder to think how stunted the boys would have been growing up with me as their primary caretaker, continuing on the path that I was on. The turn of events gave them the opportunity to get to know and bond with their father in a way they wouldn't have otherwise. Boys need their dads. The changes brought a little brother and a caring adult female into their world, which are relationships that can last a lifetime and have enriched their lives. As far as I'm concerned, the more people that care about them, the better.

I know, I know. Hold on a sec while I adjust my halo. It sounds cheesy even to me, and believe me, it took years and lots of tears to get to this place. I have to admit, the first time Gabe referred to his dad and Sheila as "the parents", it felt like someone slapped me hard, but I've come to realize that there's room for all of us in their lives and hearts.

Sometimes, I do lament the many things I've missed: school projects, campouts, sleepovers, the first car, 24 hour on-site iPhone and computer support, and even theatrical burps and farts, but I also know that the boys and I appreciate each other and our time together more and have a healthier relationship because of our unique situation.

As I have discovered many times, the best presents in life don't always come in the prettiest wrapping.

CHAPTER 9

Putting On The Ritz

My brother, Chris, was just ten months older than me, and when we were little, Mom used to occasionally dress us in cutesy little matching outfits, like twins. With our similar facial features and his small stature, we could pass for twins, and I always liked to think that we shared that super-special, secret twin-like bond. Because we were born in different years, Chris was a grade ahead of me in school, and I always felt safer just knowing that my big brother was there. My other brother, Ken, is four years older than me, which was a galaxy apart when we were kids. By the time I got to junior high, he was in high school, and by the time I got to high school, he was gone to college. I always felt like the pesky little sister to him, and I'm pretty sure that he thought so too.

When we were young, Chris and I loved to dress up and put on elaborate shows for our parents who endured each one with convincing enthusiasm. When we got a little older, we would pedal our bikes back and forth on the road in front of our house for hours on end, because back in those days (the dark ages with no electronic gadgets), that's what kids did for fun. We never got bored. As far as we were concerned, there weren't enough hours of sunlight in the day to play outside. With the neighborhood gang,

Ken, Chris and I would often stretch a game of kick the can until we were running around the yard in the dimness of the porch light. On many afternoons, we were explorers trekking through the woods behind our house, which used to be farm land and had persimmon, pear, and apple trees, a small lake, and old wooden structures.

As a small boy, Chris was all about dinosaurs. Recognizing them by sight, he could rattle off the eating habits of a Brachiosaurus or tell you matter-of-factly that the T-Rex was the largest carnivore of all time. As a preteen, Chris was obsessed with covering his Boy Scout sash with merit badges. One summer at camp, he earned a coveted badge by swimming the perimeter of the entire lake.

Through the years, Chris played the part of the typical older brother by sitting on my head and farting, and shooting me with a BB gun while I ran as fast as I could in the other direction. (I guess I have him to thank for helping me make the track team in junior high.) As a cheerleader for his little league football team, the Lions, I proudly shook my blue and white pom-poms, yelled, stomped, and clapped with the unbridled zeal that only an eight-year-old cheerleader can have. Because he heard me practice all the cheers at home, Chris knew them well and would often join us screaming cheerleaders while standing on the sideline in his football uniform. Well, maybe he wasn't so typical after all.

In junior high, Chris was on the wrestling team and in me found a convenient partner to practice all his moves, and I could tell you first-hand what a half nelson or a banana split felt like. We swam together on the swim team each summer at the neighborhood pool, and were actually pretty good. Chris went on to swim competitively for several years. When he got to high school, Chris discovered a passion for theatre, joined the drama club, and helped form a mime troupe that performed at pep rallies, football game half-times, and other school functions. At home, Lynyrd Skynyrd, the Charlie Daniels Band, and Blue Oyster Cult bounced off of his bedroom walls.

Like most typical teenagers at the time, Chris experimented with pot and alcohol. One day, he and his buddies skipped school and hung out drinking beer in a shack at the lake in the woods behind our house. When I got home from school that afternoon, his friends came and got me, and I lugged my brother home, passed out in a wheelbarrow, and dumped him in his bed just before Mom and Dad arrived from work. As far as they knew, he was sick.

Another time, he and a friend went to school as usual one morning but never entered the building and instead walked back to our house, which was about a mile from the school. They spent the day joy-riding around town in an orange Volkswagen Beetle our dad had purchased for us both, even though Chris didn't have his license yet. When going around a curve too fast, Chris ran off the road, flipped the car twice, and totaled it. While I was relieved that he wasn't hurt, I was pissed at him for wrecking what was supposed to be my future car, too.

Despite his teenage antics, Chris was always a hard worker, both at restaurants, where he bussed or waited tables, and at school, where he made good grades and even attended an honors program two summers in a row for drama. After high school, he was accepted at the North Carolina School of the Arts for their collegiate theater program and acted in the local Shakespeare Festival.

The summer before Chris left to go to college, before my senior year in high school, our mother rocked our worlds by moving out of the house, and our parents subsequently divorced. Remaining in the house with Dad, I was the only child left at home, but thankfully, Chris' college was only 30 minutes away, which allowed him to come home on the weekends often, and for us to remain close through this tumultuous time. While I managed to maintain a respectable grade point average, cheer on the varsity squad, and hold down my first job at a McDonalds that senior year, I enjoyed my newfound freedom a little too much with no mother around and Dad locked in his own world of despair. After high school, I went to college an hour away, and married Jimmie immediately upon graduating.

In 1984, after switching to a local general college and earning a much more practical degree in communications, Chris settled in Atlanta, Georgia, and began a career in television, doing on-air personality and production work. He eventually ended up behind the cameras in equipment management.

Although the usual distance that just comes with living life crept into our relationship during college and the years immediately after, Jimmie and I moved to Atlanta in 1987. Chris and I delighted in becoming as tight as ever, as young adults loose in the big city. By then, Chris was living an openly gay life which didn't change anything as far as I was concerned. In fact, it made everything even better. "What more could a girl that didn't have a sister want?" I used to tell everyone. His gay life seemed so glamorous and sophisticated compared to my boring, married, high-waisted jeans, yuppie existence. Breaking free of the small town North Carolina mentality, Chris was blazing a new trail and happy to have his little sister tagging along.

In the early and mid-80s, Atlanta was the gay mecca of the South, and Chris was relieved and empowered to be living in a city where homosexuality was so accepted and prevalent. Chris said, although he knew that something was different, it never occurred to him that he might be gay until he went to the School of the Arts and was exposed to the lifestyle.

Because he didn't fit the typical gay stereotype in his everyday life, anyone meeting Chris for the first time wouldn't have immediately pegged him as gay, I don't think. His mannerisms and speech didn't hint at his homosexuality. After years of theatrical training, Chris had a crisp, booming voice, like a radio personality, where he articulated almost too well. Now, when he went out on the town, it was a different story. He enjoyed getting decked out and looking the part of the handsome gay man and would turn heads by wearing leather, chains, butt hugging jeans, and tight T-shirts showing his well-defined pecs and biceps. With a trim, 34 inch waist, muscular body, chiseled jaw line, and prominent cheekbones, Chris was a striking figure.

As an adult, he was shorter than most of his peers at only five feet seven inches tall, and during my teen growth spurt, I grew taller than Chris. I've always felt guilty about that and would have gladly given him the extra half-inch if I could have. His height disadvantage did wear on his self-esteem somewhat, especially when he was younger. You know how cruel boys can be to the short guy at school, especially in gym class. But later, I think his stature actually worked to his benefit; that Napoleon complex helped motivate him. His personality was extra-large and made up for anything he lacked in height.

Having a wicked sense of humor, Chris was known for cutting loose, keeping everyone laughing, and making any occasion feel like a party. Although I suspect that there were deep insecurities behind all the jokes, we didn't consider and weren't concerned with such things in our invincible 20s. We even had a special name for those fits of laughter Chris induced where we'd laugh so hard that we'd cry and gasp for air: the gigglesnorts.

His gay friends were lively, opinionated, and colorful, and even his straight friends were hip and interesting. I felt cooler just being around them. His group went on "tacky Christmas light" tours and threw "tacky Easter bonnet" parties. (Tacky was a popular theme.) They served lasagna made with real Italian sausage on a fashionably set table with a tall vase of white lilies in the center of the table, perfectly finishing the scene. Not a paper plate was in sight.

They threw themed cocktail parties and made martinis in an antique glass shaker and served them in martini glasses that I swear Dean Martin himself could have used. This was a far cry from drinking beer in the bottle that I was accustomed to. His friends lived in grand old houses, sporting large front porches with big white columns and huge oak trees in the yard, that had been divided into tastefully decorated apartments in downtown Atlanta. In the suburbs, my world was full of nondescript apartment buildings with rows and rows of identical little balconies and Pampas grass at every corner, filled with mismatched, hand-me-down furniture that someone didn't want anymore.

Twenty years later, I still cherish and proudly display a few pieces of Chris' antique wooden furniture and his cobalt-blue glass collection in my home.

Intelligent and informed, his crowd had animated conversations and weren't shy about voicing their perspectives on politics, the arts, or the latest fashion faux-pas of the rich and famous. Being welcomed into his social circle was my introduction to a world where young people acted like adults instead of overgrown college kids. I felt worldlier and more sophisticated by association.

Chris delighted in sharing his love of music with me, exposing me to new genres and artists, and stretching my boundaries. His vast CD collection, which back then was a kind of status symbol, included groups like The Beloved, Deep Forest, and Bronski Beat. When dining at a trendy hotspot in the Buckhead area of Atlanta one night, we were thrilled and excited, but played it cool, to discover that our table was right beside Amy and Emily of the Indigo Girls, one of Chris' favorite groups.

Chris loved the charismatic drag queen singer, RuPaul, who favored flamboyant outfits, false eyelashes, and cha-cha heels, and was putting on quite the show long before Lady Gaga. His hit song *Supermodel (You Better Work)* will always make me think of Chris.

When I was with Chris, I gave myself permission to let loose, have fun, and be the person I was never free to be in my real life. One night, I remember feeling especially glamorous and decadent, going clubbing in a skin-tight neon orange tube dress and stiletto heels, wearing a chunky, garish peace sign medallion

Chris had loaned me. It actually looked more like a car emblem than a necklace. When I was with him, anything was OK. The more far out, the better.

While I was completely open to and accepting of his homosexual lifestyle, I have to admit that it did freak me out when other girls hit on me. Normally, this kind of excursion into the big city's downtown district would have scared the shit out of me, but because I was with my big brother, my protector, who knew his way around the city, I could relax and have fun. Chris loved to show me off, and his friends always made me feel like the belle of the ball.

Gay bars undoubtedly have the best dance music, and boy oh boy, Chris could dance! Blending the latest moves he saw on the dance floors with his formal training at the School of the Arts, Chris concocted a funky, fun, hypnotic, flawless style that was all his own. At a club one night, with our mother no less, everyone on the dance floor stopped their gyrating and formed a circle around Chris and cheered him on as he freestyled to *Putting on the Ritz*.

While Chris was social almost every night of the week, I only accompanied him occasionally. Jimmie and I lived in one of those nondescript apartment complexes on the outskirts of Atlanta with our two Persian cats. Although Jimmie seemed to genuinely like and care for Chris, he didn't join Chris and me on our escapades around town dancing, but he would occasionally join us for dinner or brunch. I have to give Jimmie credit here. Because he was so damn good looking, Jimmie fitted right into the gay scene, and when he hung out with Chris and me, he could have easily been mistaken for Chris' companion instead of mine. Jimmie let me run around with Chris as much as I wanted without protest, and was accepting of his lifestyle and friends.

A friend of Chris', Mike Mason, who is now an accomplished journalist and writer, perfectly captured Chris' spirit and energy in this eulogy:

Chris Hampton was a man with a genius for living. He knew what clubs to go to, what CDs to buy, which thrift stores were cool, which gym everyone was at, where to get a custom 50's swimsuit, who to call, who to insult, when to arrive, when to leave, how to go all weekend without sleep, how to keep the boss from suspecting on Monday morning.

Over the years, I saw him on a hundred dance floors, a small whirlwind pulling friends into a joyous orbit, and today I cannot bring myself to understand that the center of so much has collapsed.

Here's the first thing I learned about Chris: he was not a guy to shrink from battle. Ten years ago, he worked as a waiter at a restaurant on Peachtree Street called Cafe Society. It went bankrupt suddenly, and one of the first conversations I had with Chris concerned his determination to sue the owners for back wages. This was not to be an exceptional conversation.

For as long as I knew him, there were disputes – dramatic, almost Shakespearean – involving car accidents and rent deposits and break-ups and jobs. Chris was quick to draw his sword, sing a war whoop, and charge the enemy. I loved that about him.

He was restless. I suspect that he hated silence and emptiness, that he cherished noise and furor, and friends, and a full Filofax. For the last few years, he insisted to me that he'd become a homebody. I never believed it. This was the guy who dragged me to a Christmas party where a leather-clad woman with a bloody nose let her Doberman eat his way through the buffet. This was the man who showed up at a Halloween party looking like a cross between Peter Fonda in Easy Rider and Liza Minelli in Cabaret, with just a dash of Pee-wee Herman.

To this day, there is a ball of crumpled metal underneath the front bumper of my car because Chris said something, I can't recall what, that made me laugh so hard I drove over a parking curb at 4.00am at the Cove.

I remember Chris rising out of the Chattahoochee River, a laughing tangle of love beads and algae, yelling as our raft sailed past:

"love ya, mean it, miss ya already!" Somehow he was waiting for us at the end of the race. That much was typical: I often felt he was waiting patiently for the rest of his friends to catch up.

Here is what AIDS wants: it wants us to stop living as fully as Chris lived. AIDS is a dark angel passing overhead, and it reaches for the brightest of us, like Chris, because it hopes that by extinguishing their stars, it may also snuff the spirit of an entire community. It hopes that those who are left behind will lead compromised lives, perhaps lives not even worth living, because of the losses we have suffered.

Today, I think the dark angel has lost a battle and Chris has won. The sicker he got, the more we learned from him about living fully, and drawing our swords, and refusing to compromise. Imagine the mortification above. The dark angel of AIDS looks down upon us now and instead of seeing a light extinguished it sees scores more burning brighter.

Occasionally, I have a dream about the day a cure is found. On that day, the dark angel comes crashing to Earth and I am there when it lands, miraculously, in Piedmont Park, among rows of gay men lying on the grassy hillside. We are not pleased. I find I am holding the love beads Chris Hampton used to wear. So, I walk over and wrap the necklaces tight around the monster's greasy neck. Before long, the fallen angel is flapping angrily along the ground, toward the sewer, unable to fly again because the crowd has ensnared it in love beads.

Goodbye Chris. Love ya. Mean it. Miss ya already.[1]

*

In 1987, at the age of 25, Chris tested HIV positive. One morning at my desk at work in midtown Atlanta, tears rushed to my eyes as I sat clutching the phone when Chris called to tell me the terrible news. Choking back sobs, I tried to remain calm and talk coherently to him, but I know the quiver in my voice must have revealed the terror I felt. When I hung up the phone, I sprinted to the nearest bathroom.

On a night soon thereafter, Chris and I hugged each other and cried, because we didn't know a lot about AIDS for sure, but we knew that, barring a miracle, being HIV positive was a death sentence. I took Chris' hands in mine, looked into his eyes, and promised, "I want you to know that, no matter where I am or what's going on in my life, I'll be there for you. Whatever that means. Whatever you need."

At the beginning of the 1980s, reports began to emerge in California and New York about a small number of men who had been diagnosed with rare forms of cancer and pneumonia. The cancer, Kaposi's sarcoma (KS), normally only affected elderly men of Mediterranean or Jewish heritage. The pneumonia, Pneumocystis Carinii Pneumonia (PCP), was usually only found in individuals with seriously compromised immune systems. But the young men contracting these diseases had previously been in good health. The only common characteristic was that they were gay. Over the next decade, what came to be known as AIDS, grew to become the equivalent of a global disaster, killing millions.

In 1994, Tom Hanks won an Oscar for portraying a gay man with AIDS in the movie *Philadelphia*. I remember cowering in the dark theater, bawling my eyes out as I watched the movie in horror, knowing that I was glimpsing Chris' fate.

*

Chris maintained good health for several years after testing HIV positive. He went about his life as usual, burning the candle at both ends, working hard and playing harder. Nothing really changed, but at the same time, everything had changed. A black cloud followed him around now, and no matter how furiously he danced, how many trips he took, or how much festivity he crammed into his life, he couldn't shake it.

The ominousness of his HIV status impolitely oozed into the pauses of our conversations and rudely sat down with us at meals. We didn't talk about his plans for the future anymore.

On one hand, I wanted to tell him to slow down a little. Take it easy. On the other hand, I wanted to encourage him to have fun and live life to the fullest while he still could. He chose the latter. Even as the protective sister in me cringed, I always admired that about him. Chris didn't do anything if he didn't do it 100 percent, and AIDS didn't change that.

During the height of his sickness, I once asked him, "Is it just not worth it to you if you can't go full force?"

"No." he replied without hesitation.

Chris lived this philosophy right up until the end. When he felt especially bad, he'd soak in the tub, finding comfort in the warm water just like I did when recovering from my brain injury. He had a large Jacuzzi tub in the house where he lived during his illness, and because he spent so much time in the bath, he accumulated an array of tub toys. His collection of squirty frogs perches on the ledge of my bathtub today.

Three weeks before he died, Chris visited a friend in New York City. Chris wasn't feeling well the night that his friend had a small gathering in his tiny urban apartment, which only had one bathroom. Chris, the guest of honor, stayed in the bathtub the entire evening, greeting everyone who came into the bathroom from his watery perch and chatting while they took care of their business.

In 1992, Chris' T-cell count, a marker of the strength of a person's immune system, steadily nosedived, he started getting sick frequently, and his lifestyle and health condition became hard to keep secret. Years earlier, he'd come out to our mother who despite, or because of, her strict Catholic upbringing, was liberal, progressive in her thinking, and supportive of Chris. She knew about his HIV positive status shortly after he found out.

Our father, however, was more of the traditional Southern mindset, and while not judgmental, was more conservative in his thinking. Because our dad was remarried with a teenage stepson at home, Chris worried that Dad and his wife would feel as if they had to protect the stepson from being influenced in some way. Chris didn't tell Dad about his homosexuality or illness until it was absolutely necessary.

After attending a business symposium in South Carolina in January 1995, Dad drove the rest of the way down to spend the weekend with Chris in Atlanta. Chris' partner, whom he lived with, was conveniently "out of town" for the weekend. After a packed Saturday during which they stopped by a gay book store owned by Chris' close friend, saw *Pulp Fiction*, and dined at a trendy restaurant, Chris turned to Dad on the drive home and said, "I guess you've noticed that something's different down here with me and my friends. I'm gay."

"Well, Chris," Dad said, "I never really thought about it. It never even occurred to me."

"I realized it when I went to the School of the Arts, but I've known something was different for a long time. I just didn't know exactly what." Chris explained.

Looking at the road ahead, Dad paused and said, "Chris, it doesn't matter to me. You're my son. I love you. Nothing will ever change that."

Relaxing his jaw and exhaling, Chris replied, "That sure is nice to hear."

After finally coming out to Dad, Chris felt like he could finally breathe freely after having to sip air through a straw for years. Conversely, Dad now couldn't catch his breath. Although he loved his son dearly, this shocking information was tough for him to digest, and upon returning home, he was quiet and sullen for days before sharing the news with his wife.

Chris disclosed his homosexuality to Dad, but he didn't reveal that he was HIV positive, and as his eyes sank deeper into his head and his pants got baggier, hiding his sickness became increasingly difficult. While Chris' condition was painfully obvious to some, Dad saw Chris so infrequently and AIDS was so far off of his radar, he didn't realize that his son was sick.

In the spring of 1995, for the first part of a visit with Dad in North Carolina, Chris concealed the vial taped to his forearm delivering medicine intravenously under long sleeves. Eventually, he stripped down to short sleeves, revealing the apparatus. Sitting in the afternoon sunshine on the white wicker settee on the front porch, Chris told Dad that he was sick.

Pointing to the vial in his arm, Chris explained, "I have an infection. It's called AIDS, Acquired Immune Deficiency Syndrome. This thing is giving me medicine for it around the clock."

"Chris, I don't know anything about that. What'd you call it? Do you have a doctor?"

"Yes, I have a doctor who specializes in AIDS, and we're doing everything we can to fight this thing and get it taken care of."

While Dad thought the vial was awfully strange, Chris didn't act overly concerned about the situation, so he wasn't either.

Because I had had way too many almost slip-ups, Chris coming clean with Dad was a major relief to me. If I felt frustrated and stifled trying to keep the secret, I can only imagine how hiding his health status from his employers, colleagues, and others must have weighed heavily on Chris. Because Dad and his wife now knew, they also could shoulder some of the emotional burden and assist with Chris' care.

Ken lived in California, which prohibited him from helping Chris much, and although our mother was closer in North Carolina, she was single with a demanding job and busy life that limited her availability. Thankfully, Chris had built a strong network of friends in Atlanta and was able to remain independent for as long as possible. Just four months before he died, Chris stopped working and only required intensive help for the last three months of his life.

To my father's credit, Chris' fears were completely unfounded. Our father and his wife were both loving and supportive of Chris, and honest about his lifestyle and disease. They even attended weekly classes at a local AIDS organization to educate themselves. It was there that Dad learned the crushing truth that his son was going to die. Dad's wife, who had worked for the Social Security Administration her whole career, took care of filing for Chris to get disability benefits. His first check came the week after he died.

While Chris watched too many of his friends become sick and die, he also began to get the opportunistic infections that came with the onset of AIDS: shingles, KS, thrush on his tongue, and the sweats. Chris underwent radiation treatments for the KS lesions, the purplish/reddish cancerous splotches on the skin that became an AIDS-defining illness. I wince when I remember his thigh, raw and blistered from radiation, looking as if someone had pressed a hot iron on it. While these health annoyances were enough to slow Chris down, he didn't hit the brakes too hard just yet.

For most of 1994, Chris and his partner, Tom, shared a home on the outskirts of Atlanta. In the spring of 1995, Tom moved out of the house but stayed in the area and in Chris' life until he died. Having already lost one partner to AIDS, Tom said that he just couldn't bear going through the ordeal again. There wasn't any path that wasn't going to be extremely painful with a tragic ending for both of them. Tom moved to California immediately after Chris' death.

All too quickly, Chris progressed to the nastier invaders that came with AIDS: cytomegalovirus (CMV), pneumonia, and wasting syndrome. These wretched illnesses would land Chris in the hospital, and then he would rally, and bravely but more haggardly go on with his life until the next round of sickness. He had no choice but to slow way down by this time and became a homebody. Chris' decline over this period makes me think of my boys' electronic games where a zombie gets mercilessly riddled with bullets. With each shot, another gaping wound appears and a chunk of the zombie gets blown off but, with parts grotesquely hanging on, the zombie always manages to resurrect and stumble forward.

One way doctors monitor the progression of AIDS is by a person's T-cell count. The HIV virus attacks the T-cells and uses them to make more copies of HIV, which weakens the immune system as more T-cells become damaged, leaving it unable to protect the body from illness and infection. We became all too familiar with Chris' plummeting T-cell number. Calling Mom one day, he joked, "Well, I'm down to the Seven Dwarfs," when his count dropped to seven. A normal count would be between 600 and 1,000.

*

Jimmie and I only lived in Atlanta for about year and left in 1988. During Chris' initial sickness in the early 1990s, we lived in Raleigh, North Carolina and while there, I completed a course on being an AIDS buddy to prepare myself to be Chris' caregiver. In July 1995, when Collin was a year old, Jimmie and I moved to Jacksonville, Florida. Jimmie's growing income allowed me to quit work, stay home with Collin, and keep the promise I'd made to Chris. I would pack up Collin and travel to Atlanta frequently, staying for weeks at a time to help and console Chris as best I could. Months passed in a blur of trips back and forth, with family members and friends also visiting to say silent goodbyes.

By this time, Chris had a permanent port implanted in his chest to deliver daily IV medications, and to keep him independent and at home, because he and I could administer his meds, which took hours daily. I learned that it was imperative to get all air out of the syringe of medicine before pushing it into the port to prevent air from entering the blood stream, which could be deadly. I was absolutely terrified that I was going to hurt Chris instead of helping him and that someone was going to find out that I didn't really have any idea what I was doing. But I was damn determined that I was going to help my brother, despite my fears.

There were always plenty of things to do about which I felt more competent, such as cleaning Chris' fashionable but dirty house, or cooking fattening foods that I could only hope he might be able to keep down, or tackling his and Collin's laundry. I would try to keep Collin quiet so as not to disturb Chris, and stressed to Chris how important it was to not play the TV or music too loudly so as not to wake Collin. I needed the valuable time while Collin was sleeping to do other things, but felt incredibly guilty about silencing Chris. It was his house. He was the one who was dying. He should have been able to play his music as loud as he wanted.

At the time, I felt like Chris had a love-hate relationship with Collin and got annoyed having to accommodate him. I believed that Chris resented Collin for demanding my time and attention, and for being a responsibility that prohibited me from being free to take care of him. In hindsight, I realize that this was what I was feeling. I felt like a green Gumby doll stretched to the max, with Chris pulling on one arm and Collin tugging on the other in opposite directions. I was never as good as I wanted to be for either one of them.

Still breastfeeding Collin, I had the bright idea to pump breast milk for Chris to drink to transfer the antibodies from me to him to boost his immune system the same way it does for a newborn. In theory, I was correct; however, Chris wouldn't do it.

Over the year, Chris and I rode the AIDS rollercoaster, holding on with white knuckles, never knowing whether an exhilarating high, or heart-in-your-throat drop was around the curve. We might end up sobbing, cussing mad, and laughing hysterically all in the same day. One night when we should have been resting, we reminisced about childhood antics and got the gigglesnorts for the last time. The night he spiked a fever of 104 degrees with alternating periods of violently shaking chills and profuse sweating, we stayed awake out of frustration and desperation. After trying ibuprofen, acetaminophen, an alcohol bath, and a cool bath, with no success at bringing the temperature down, I paged the doctor at 2.00am thinking that she could help.

"There's nothing else to try," she said, "Just keep doing what you're doing."

Not knowing what else to do and following my instincts, I crawled in the bed with Chris during one of his shivering sessions and spooned him, pulling him close to give him my body heat and love.

For Chris' 33rd birthday, September 30, 1995, we went all-out with a party at a swanky Atlanta restaurant. Ken flew in from California. Our father and his wife came in from North Carolina as well as our mother, who brought her mother, our 82-year-old grandmother. En route to the restaurant, Grandmom revealed with a girlish giggle that it was the first time she had ever ridden in a limousine.

With 30 of his friends, we celebrated Chris' birthday, his life, and his special Chris-ness. His friends, who had helped care for him, were just as much a part of Chris' family as the blood relatives, and we were all connected by our love for this man. Despite everyone sharing the unspoken understanding that this would be Chris' last birthday, the poignant gathering was filled with genuine smiles and merriment. In his usual fashion, Chris kept us laughing as he dispensed his humor from the head of the table like a king ruling over his court.

Grandmom, who didn't know Chris was gay, stole the show when she quipped, "There are so many handsome young men here. Why didn't you invite any girls?" The whole place cracked up.

After the meal, we raised our glasses and made tearful toasts to Chris. I'm grateful to have had this opportunity to let him know how much he meant to so many people. Wouldn't it be great if it were customary to celebrate people's lives *before* they died instead of after?

Jimmie was in Atlanta the night of Chris' birthday party, but didn't attend the celebration, opting instead to stay at Chris' house with Collin. I'm forever grateful to Jimmie for making the evening possible financially, and for supporting Chris and me in this way.

As Chris got sicker, I informally set about trying to fulfill his last requests. The Dairy Queen Blizzard, Godiva truffles, and pimento cheese and pickle sandwiches were easy enough to manage. But I couldn't get my hands on any fresh blackberries, as they weren't available year-round then like they are now. Every time that I add blackberries to my Greek yogurt, I think of that fact regretfully.

Chris would have extended hospital stays, then enjoy a few weeks at home until another sickness debilitated him and put him in the hospital again. In the hospital, I would pop up Collin's portable crib in one corner of his already cramped room. Although I didn't like Collin being that close to the deadly disease and could tell that the nurses frowned on it too, I was going to take care of my brother no matter what. Not having any well-defined spiritual beliefs at the time, I told myself, "If there is a God, surely, he won't let my baby get AIDS."

Chris' hospital stints were dotted with awkward moments, such as when the nurse wheeled a portable potty into his room, and I helped this grown man take a crap in front of his sister. Tender moments were sprinkled in, like when I used my expensive moisturizer to massage his feet. One night, Chris had an epiphany and realized that his Lexus meant nothing to him, and that his friends and family were his real valuables. An otherworldly spiritual moment unfolded when we were alone in his room one evening, and Chris started talking to someone at the foot of his bed that I couldn't see. He said it was our paternal grandfather, Pawpaw, who had been dead for more than 20 years.

*

For Christmas in 1995, Ken flew into Atlanta from California with his daughter shortly after Chris got back from his bathtub party weekend in New York. Upon taking one look at Chris,

Ken convinced him to go to the hospital. Having driven up from Florida for the holidays, I was already in North Carolina with Collin, and Ken and Chris were supposed to join us in a few days. The information coming from the hospital was not good and indicated that this was serious. So, Dad and I left that night at 11.00 with Collin strapped in his car seat in the back for the five-hour drive to Atlanta. Not too far down the highway, I was pulled over for speeding. After explaining to the officer why a woman, her baby, and her father were racing down the highway late at night, he told me to slow down and sent me on my way.

By Christmas Day, which was on a Monday that year, Ken, my mother, my father, and his wife were all in Atlanta. In a wheelchair, Chris came to a waiting area of the hospital with his oxygen tank and IV pole in tow, and we exchanged Christmas gifts.

Enjoying the hustle and bustle of the season, Chris had always been a last minute shopper, buying gifts right up until Christmas Eve most years, and hadn't gotten any gifts before entering the hospital. He and I made a list, and I'd gone to the Lenox mall across from the hospital the day before and bought his gifts for everyone. There was only one problem. I couldn't buy my own gift now could I? Chris gave me a diamond and ruby tennis bracelet that he had gotten for me earlier that year.

By this time, Chris had been in the hospital for a week, and although he wasn't getting worse, he wasn't getting better either. I realized that more formal arrangements had to be made to take care of him for when he returned home. Being worn out emotionally and physically, I knew that I wouldn't be able to provide the level of care that he would need.

As I was so good at doing back then, I realize now that I had constructed a self-imposed hell for myself. With Chris and Collin being my priority, and Jimmie's wants and needs coming next in line, taking care of myself was nowhere on the list, and I didn't know how to ask for help. While caregiver burnout is common, I'd had the tendency to ignore my own needs my whole life, and this was nothing new for me. Mom said that I made it difficult for others to assist Chris and made it very clear that I was the one taking care of him. Although I can certainly see how I did this, I also think that if someone had wanted to help out in a big way, they could have made it happen.

Over time, I have no doubt that I would have found more balance. Organizing a "share the care" team based on a book I read, I put the word out to Chris' friends that we were organizing a caregiver family for him and held the first meeting in the hospital auditorium. I was pleasantly surprised at the good turnout, and told myself confidently, "This could actually work." Chris never came home from the hospital that time.

Each family member took shifts staying with Chris around the clock at the hospital while his two-bedroom house served as home base for everyone, using the beds, couch, and an air mattress on the den floor for sleeping. I marvel at, and am proud of, how a group of people not prone to getting along – I mean at all – otherwise pulled together and made peace under these stressful circumstances.

With a miniature Christmas tree sporting wacky ornaments, like one saying "Wake up Barbie. Ken is gay," framed photos of family and friends, artwork from his house on the walls, cards taped to or sitting on every surface, a throw from home at the foot of the bed, and his beloved CD player, Chris' room was as comfy and warm as a hospital room could be. One night, Chris and I listened to music, reminisced, laughed, cried, and grieved for each other all in a few hours, swimming in a warmth and intimacy that has had to last me decades. We could have been at home on his couch. With a shaky voice, watery eyes, and Everything But The Girl's *Acoustic* CD playing in the background, Chris told me, "Above all else, I just want to be remembered and know that my life meant something."

On New Year's Eve, the medical staff told us that it was time to put Chris on a respirator if we were going to. Chris had always stated that he didn't want extraordinary measures taken to prolong his life. Before the morphine drip began, while he was still coherent, I sat by Chris' bed in the ugly mauve, fake leather chair, took his bony hand in mine, and with tears running down my cheeks, told him, "Chris, your blood oxygen levels have dropped to the point that the docs say you need a respirator. I know that this isn't your wish. Is that still true?"

"Right."

"So, we're not going to do that. We'll just see how it goes from here without it," I choked out in between sobs, "I want you to know that it's been an honor and privilege to be your sister. You've been the best brother and friend that a girl could ever want. I love you dearly. You've waged an admirable battle against AIDS, but now it's time to rest."

Chris just stared up at me with a vacant glaze in his big, brown eyes. I'm not sure if he understood what I was saying fully, but it was what we'd agreed to when he wasn't facing death, when there was still life behind those eyes.

Once again, acting instinctively from my heart and sniffling a now runny nose, I crawled over the metal bed rail and eased myself down gently next to Chris on top of the tangle of IV tubes. Making sure I wasn't causing him pain, I spooned my brother one last time, memorizing his scent, sharing his pain, and saying goodbye.

Having the medical power of attorney, I ultimately had the responsibility to decide to put him on the respirator or not. Although not using life support was in accordance with Chris' directives, to let him go went against every fiber of my being.

From then on, Chris slipped into unconsciousness more and more frequently. Relatives rushed down from North Carolina for a final visit. That afternoon, when a lucid Chris was sitting up in bed, socializing, and watching football, everyone breathed a communal sigh of relief.

Around 7.00pm, Dad and I headed to the hospital cafeteria for dinner. When we returned, Chris had taken a turn for the worse, was unconscious, and in the process of dying. His vitals sank lower and lower while his labored breathing became slower and shallower.

Death didn't happen quickly, like in the movies, and for years, I didn't remember his passing as being peaceful because the memory was infused with my own pain and horror. I realize that this was my frame of mind at the time of his passing, and can now look back on the scene and feel the grace and love that was present. Ken described Chris' transition as "beautiful and holy with a powerful, palpable love and light energy in the room," with his daughter's birth being the only experience with which he could compare it.

A compassionate nurse set the tone and gently guided us through the ordeal. Mom, Dad, Ken, and I spread out so that one of us held each of Chris' hands and his feet, with a person at his head. Time passed in slow motion. We watched for more than an hour as Chris' breathing abated, with the pauses in between his raspy, strained breaths becoming longer and longer. I fervently sent him love and light, and wished him peace as I watched the scene through my tears in disbelief.

Chris' lips were chapped and cracked due to breathing oxygen through a mask for weeks. A piece of skin on his upper lip fluttered with each breath he took, but in the prolonged pauses between breaths, it lay still. Each time the skin was inert, I thought, "This is it." But Chris would take another shallow breath one more time until the flap was frozen and his chest motionless forever.

Putting her stethoscope over his heart, the nurse said, "It's awfully quiet in there."

Mom stayed with his body while Dad and I went to a pay phone, looked through the yellow pages, and called a funeral home to arrange for pick-up of Chris' body. I then phoned Jimmie and told him simply, "It's over." After a long pause, he cried. Ken wandered off by himself.

*

We returned to Chris' house hours later, and because it was New Year's Eve, there was a bottle of champagne sitting on the kitchen counter. At Mom's suggestion, we opened the bottle and toasted to Chris. Having just witnessed such an intense scene, we were all in very different places emotionally. At the time, clinking glasses didn't strike me as appropriate at all; however, I now love the idea of paying respect to him in this way. Chris was disappointed that his illness forced him to miss a New Year's Eve party that he wanted to attend. Mom has always said that his soul left his body so that he could go to the party after all.

In one of our heart-to-heart talks during his months of sickness, Chris and I made a pact that, when he died, if possible, he'd come back and visit me to let me know that he was OK. That night as I lay in his bed, in shock, with scenes of the day replaying in my mind, I felt his presence at the foot of the bed. While I didn't see an apparition, I had a sense of knowing that he was there and felt his energy. The presence moved into my body through the soles of my feet and traveled up my legs and torso. At that point, I raised my right hand off of the bed and looked at the back of it. Upon seeing his hand, not mine, I got freaked out and the experience stopped instantly.

Two days later, Dad and I retrieved Chris' ashes from the crematorium, and even though I know that such a business isn't really supposed to be warm and inviting, I don't think I've ever been to a creepier place. Distraught and ashamed that we had let his body go there, I felt like I owed Chris a big apology.

His ashes were put in a handcrafted piece of pottery that we took from Chris' house. Positioning my hands on each side of the vase, I hoped to detect a hum, a current, or something that felt like Chris. Nothing. All I felt beneath my fingers was the cold vase. It was completely incomprehensible to me that all that remained of a person that I knew as Chris, the brother I loved so much, was now in this vase.

CHAPTER 10

Like The Deserts Miss The Rain

A celebration of Chris' life was held in North Carolina two weeks after his death. Family members and friends got up on stage to share memories and heartfelt words. For the first time that I can remember, we were publicly honest about Chris' homosexuality and cause of death.

Regrettably, our grandmother discovered that Chris died of AIDS from the obituary in the newspaper. We'd never explained it all to her, and she had never pressed for gory details and told everyone that he had cancer.

Chris' friends in Atlanta held a memorial service one afternoon in early February before the gay circuit party, Masquerade, later that night. The gathering felt more like a fashionable cocktail party, with food and drinks, a slide show, and people telling stories about Chris. It was anything but solemn, and I think Chris would have liked that. Craig, our cousin from North Carolina, and I met at Chris' house before the engagements and went together.

That night we got decked out, met up with Chris' friends, and attended Masquerade, which as the name suggests, was a costumed event. At a vintage clothing store, I purchased a groovy retro two-piece outfit from the 70s which looked like something Julie from *The Mod Squad* would have worn. The scoop necked, bandeau top's sleeves fanned out at the elbows into giant lace wings, and the spandex skin-tight hip huggers flared into ridiculously huge bell-bottoms. I finished the outfit with chunky platforms, of course. Ken wore a jester costume that he'd made himself, complete with sparkly painted-on designs, a floppy cone hat, and jingling bells. Our cousin sported a Phantom of the Opera look with a black suit, knee-length cape lined in red satin, top hat, and cane. At 11.30pm on the fourth floor, friends of Chris and members of his krewe, like at Mardi Gras, gathered and toasted him with champagne. Enjoying ourselves Chris-style, we danced until we were dripping wet with sweat and partied until the sun came up.

At one point, a friend, Randy, that I had worked with in North Carolina years earlier and hadn't seen since, emerged from the colorful haze of bodies and lights, came dancing over to me, and hung love beads around my neck. At first, I thought I was hallucinating. It was an epic night, and Chris would have been proud of us.

But the party ended, and we all reported back to our real lives. Returning to Jimmie and Collin in Florida, I numbly went through the motions of my everyday life. As the old saying goes, "Life goes on," right? But, it doesn't say how in the hell you're supposed to do that exactly. Life did go on, but nothing was the same anymore. I wasn't the same.

*

Immediately after Chris' death, I was relieved and happy, yes happy, that Chris was no longer suffering. I had wanted the ordeal to be over for a while. Throughout his sickness though, I had never allowed myself to think about what life would be like without Chris. Probably out of self-protection.

147

Every morning, I got up and tried to remember how to live: for Chris, Collin, and myself. Collin deserved a mother who laughed, played, and sang even if it was forced and fake. I attempted to pick up the pieces of a neglected marriage and reconnect with Jimmie, who had been understanding through this difficult time, but had nonetheless grown more distant. We had become like polite roommates, not sharing ourselves any more than necessary, and not bothering to fight either.

Life in the sunshine state wasn't very sunny. I cried a lot. I sat a lot. I didn't eat a lot. My sorrow morphed into a rage. Throughout Chris' decline, I didn't feel one flicker of anger, which was good because he was mad enough for the both of us. Like a master restraining his dog on a leash, Chris kept his fury in check, but it could be heard in his acrimonious comments and acerbic wit. At the end, Chris showed a flat, resigned acceptance of the inevitable, I think because he was simply too weak to be mad anymore.

Now I was the angry one. I was livid that Chris had been taken from me and that we had been forced to grope our way through that heinous illness. I just couldn't make sense of it. Above all, the thought that nagged at me mercilessly was, "Where the hell is he?"

Although I knew that he was dead physically and that I believed in some kind of afterlife, I hadn't decided what that meant precisely. He'd already tried to visit me once, but from where? Was he accessible to me? How did I reach him? Was he OK? These questions gnawed at me constantly as I went through the motions of my daily life.

I started devouring every title I came across about life after death, and contacting the spirit world. Reading these books, I uncovered an overwhelming amount of common sense, confirmation, and comfort.

In *The Séance* by Suzane Northrop, I found do-it-yourself instructions for contacting a spirit. Even though I felt a little silly, as directed in the book I notified Chris' spirit of our designated meeting time and sent him reminders as the date approached. By the glow of a candle one July night, after Jimmie and Collin were asleep, I envisioned myself surrounded by a protective white light and followed the guided visualization spelled out in the book. The journey began with deep breathing and relaxation exercises followed by imagining myself ascending as in an elevator. After going up, up, up, the doors of the elevator opened to:

... [a] golden field of flowers, tall grass surrounded by trees, sunlight filtering through. Feel that you are warm, protected, and loved. Looking across the field, you notice a bench. Be aware of what the bench looks like and concentrate on who is sitting there waiting.[1]

The elevator doors opened to an English garden with a majestic old tree, ivy covering its thick trunk and blanketing the ground underneath, in the center of the scene. The air was hazy, but not in a gloomy or spooky way. The setting had the feel of a spring morning when the sun is just behind the fog, illuminating the mist, ready to burst through. Twenty feet in front of me, Chris sat on a concrete bench under the canopy of the giant tree.

Intense warmth, love, and joy flooded my body upon seeing him, but these sensations were more than just physical. I was the feelings. While I visualized a body for myself and Chris, I was also very aware of us as energetic masses, alive and buzzing with light. Chris looked like he had in his late 20s with a healthy color to his filled out face, full head of hair, and robust frame. After a long hug, I nestled beside him on the bench and glanced at my questions I had for him on the paper in my hand, which I'd written out before in real life. Without reading the list to him, his answers were instantaneously transferred to me.

As is common after a death, controversy swirled around the directive in Chris' will, which left all of the insurance money to my mother while Ken, Dad, and I received tokens of remembrance. He left me his CD collection. That was it. While I most certainly didn't take care of him expecting something material in return, this gesture felt like a punch in the gut that knocked the wind out of me every time I thought about it. Although my higher self assured me that this shouldn't matter, it did. Even knowing that Chris told our stepmother, "You and Dad are set. Debbie has Jimmie. Mom is all alone," didn't make me feel better about the whole thing.

Because my family had never talked about the specifics of his will, this turn of events took us by surprise. I guess I had wanted to think that I was a bigger person and whatever his wishes were wouldn't matter to me. About this controversy, his spirit told me simply, "It's her [Mom's] lesson to learn." His words didn't bring immediate acceptance, but his message did allow me to feel that the action was intended for a deeper reason.

Although foregoing life support at the end was Chris' wish, I had tremendous guilt for having been the one to make the final decision to not put him on the respirator. I know this doesn't make intellectual sense, but I felt as if I'd just let my brother die, which was in direct conflict with what I'd been busting my ass to do over the last year of his life.

Two months before Chris passed, research discovered that a combination of the existing drugs used to treat AIDS, dubbed a drug cocktail, was proving effective at slowing the progression of the disease and prolonging life. During the month of Chris' death, the FDA approved the use of protease inhibitors, a potent new family of anti-AIDS drugs. Six months later, the FDA sanctioned the first of a new class of drugs known as non-nucleoside reverse transcriptase inhibitors. Other significant treatment advances also happened soon after Chris' death, and the health of many AIDS patients improved radically with people literally coming back from the brink of death. The reversal was so dramatic that the phenomenon became known as the "Lazarus Syndrome".

This scenario was perfect for me to second guess myself and conjure up a million "what ifs?" What if I'd put Chris on the respirator? What if he'd stayed alive for just a little longer? Would he have made it? Would he be alive today?

"You did the right thing. I'm fine. I'm happy. I'm not in pain or cold anymore, and I'm always close." Chris' spirit reassured me. He was always freezing in the last year of his life.

Although visiting with Chris' spirit brought a sense of peace and helped to fill the gaping hole in my heart a little, the respite was short-lived because I wanted more. "Oh, I get it." I thought, "It'll be like it always was, only he's in spirit now." After the first visit, I expected Chris to be on-call and show up whenever I requested his presence. I scheduled a few more visits with him during which I felt as if he came through vaguely, like the grainy picture of a TV with bad reception, but never as strongly as the initial meeting. If I had had my way, Chris would have been my shadow.

The information and love that I received in his visits helped me to begin processing his death and believe the concepts presented in the books I'd been reading. At the time, I thought these communications allowed me to heal. However, I now know that I closed the wounds just enough to carry on with life while stuffing the unresolved pain even deeper.

In April following Chris' death, my father, his wife and her son, and my cousin, drove down to Jacksonville, Florida with Chris' ashes. We convoyed to the Gulf side of the state, chartered a boat, and spread his remains in the water. His house was sold shortly after his death and all the affairs of his estate were settled and closed. That was it. Nothing left. Chris was gone. All the physical evidence I possessed that he ever existed was his CD collection and my "box of Chris" containing pictures, cards he'd sent me, his glasses, a few articles of clothing, a one-eyed "Poochie" dog, a stuffed animal from his childhood, a match book collection, and other odds and ends. Because the clothes carried his scent for years, I used to bury my nose in them to get a whiff of Chris. Now, they just smell old. I couldn't understand how in the hell this could be all that's left of a person.

At first, I missed Chris every single day, in a million ways. Like the brown crinkly leaves on a dead limb of a tree, part of me had shriveled up and died during his illness. The night he left, the world became a meaner, scarier place, and I became smaller and "less" – less capable, less hopeful, less trusting, less me, less everything good, because Chris had been a big part of that good. He was my safety net, the one person in the world that I knew had my back no matter what.

You know that one person you call when you feel like a complete idiot, like you've totally fucked it up this time, like you took a romantic trip to San Francisco and ended up getting plastered and peeing on the carpet, and they make you laugh and feel like everything is going to be OK, when you originally felt like bawling your eyes out? Well, he was my "that person."

Holidays and family gatherings weren't nearly as merry and bright anymore, but they came and went anyway. So did I. So did everyone else.

*

A year and a half after his death, my second son Gabe was born. As the years marched on, I busied myself taking care of the kids, the house, and the husband. I went on with my life, or rather my life went on without me. Chris' love became a distant memory, like a book I knew I had read, but couldn't quite recall. I knew how the story ended, but the details, the colors of the whos and whats, were blurry. I couldn't feel anything even remotely close to the energy of who Chris was anymore and sometimes questioned whether he was ever really here or if I'd imagined it all.

Scenes of Chris' sickness and death ate away at my soul, bit by bit, every day. Because I dwelt on the painful memories, they grew stronger and more predominant until I couldn't even feel the good ones anymore. It was as if the laugh track for the happy memory movie in my mind was erased. While the pleasant recollections were still there and I could see them, I couldn't feel the joy that went with the happy occasions. The pain of the past became an integral part of who I was. The agony of Chris' death was a medal I wore proudly and never took off. I'd earned it, hadn't I? By holding onto the ache, it proved how much I loved him and how special he was to me, and the sadness and anguish became my connection to him.

There have been a few times over the years during which I felt Chris' presence clearly again. The CD collection he left me includes the one we listened to in his hospital room just before he died. Another CD by the same band, Everything But The Girl, has seven different mixes of one song, *Missing*. The main chorus of the song has the verse, "And I miss you like the deserts miss the rain."[2] I've always known in my bones that this song was a message, a "hello" from Chris to me. While it was common to hear the song on the radio around the time of his death, I stop dead in my tracks and feel a jolt of electricity every time I hear it now.

Seven years after Chris died, I'd just moved to North Carolina with the boys after leaving Jimmie. Sad and alone at the grocery store one night, hearing that song over the intercom had me sobbing uncontrollably in the middle of the canned goods on aisle five.

Although I couldn't discern a solid connection to Chris anymore, I hoped that I had some special pull in the spirit world with him there and that he could manipulate things here on Earth to go in my favor. After my divorce, I was actually mad at Chris because he had "let" that happen to me, and later, because he didn't brainwash Steve into wanting to spend the rest of his life with me.

A desire to be with Chris was a pivotal factor in my suicide attempt. I believed that the deep bond we shared was unique and that I'd never experience anything like it again. I now know that a large part of why we love somebody is how we feel about ourselves when we are with that person, and with Chris, I felt valued, respected, and adored. He loved and accepted me and all of my imperfections, and I could be completely myself with him. Years after my suicide attempt, I had an epiphany and realized that what Chris gave me was authentic love and that it wasn't something unique to him. I'd just never experienced it with anyone else, but that didn't mean that I couldn't. I thought the feelings of love and acceptance died with Chris, but they didn't.

Along that same line of thinking, I came to understand that to be estranged from my own heart was to be disconnected from Chris. By the time I tried to kill myself, I was out of touch with the essence of Chris, which really means that I had no self-love or acceptance. The Chris-ness that I missed so much was the same caring and kindness that I needed to extend to myself.

I have no doubt that he helped me to survive the suicide attempt and guided me throughout my recovery. There really is no medical reason that can explain why I survived the initial insult to my body or recovered fully. The resulting brain injury forced me to be still, quieted the chaos in my head, and caused me to turn inward. During recovery, I reconnected with my own heart and learned to love myself, which linked me to Chris once again.

On several occasions, especially early in my recovery, I could feel his almost constant presence and love. Many times, in meditation, I perceived his energy as a palpable, tingly warmth, much like being wrapped in a protective blanket of love. I know it sounds sappy, but the sensation was so strong and pure that it often made me cry. There were many days that I don't know that I could've kept going without this boost.

In fact, on March 10, 2009, at 8.22am, the phone rang. When I saw the caller ID, I did a "What the what?!" double take. The caller ID digital screen read "Hampton, Chris W," but the phone number was my father's, and he was on the other end of the line. At that time, Chris had been dead for 14 years and the phone had never been in his name. How in the heck? I took a picture of the phone just to prove to myself and others that it really did happen. For several days, when Dad dialed anyone, Chris' name would show up as the originating caller. When Dad called the phone company to ask about a possible explanation, they couldn't explain this strange, wonderful occurrence, but had heard of similar happenings before.

When I tried to commit suicide, I had one middle aged cat and dog. After the attempt, having lost custody of my kids, alone and desperately in need of companionship, I adopted a spunky gray and white kitten from the animal shelter and named him Smoky. Smoky had the loudest purr of any cat that I've ever heard. The thunder coming out of this little kitty could rattle the windows. Every night during the first year of my recovery, Smoky would position himself on my pillow, curl up around my head, and purr us both to sleep. I later read that the vibrations of a cat's purr have been proven to have healing qualities for cats and humans.

These days, I don't feel that Chris is around helping me anymore because he knows that I've got this now, but I can always find him whenever I want to, because connecting with him really means tapping into my own heart energy. I took care of him when he needed it, and he was here for me when I needed it. Now, I honestly don't fear the future because I know that, whatever happens, he's there for me, which really means I'm there for me.

Now don't get me wrong, this doesn't mean that I think everything is going to be rainbows and unicorns. Far from it. It means that I know that, no matter what comes my way, I can handle it. I by no means have a death wish. But I do believe we'll be together again one day, someway, somehow, in whatever form. And I look forward to it.

CHAPTER 11

The Best Teacher of The Worst Kind

I don't know which caused my 13-year-old heart to race faster, the flash of Jimmie's golden hair or his dazzling smile. He moved to my small town in North Carolina the summer before my eighth and his ninth grade, but it would be years before he even knew I existed, although I was aware of his entrance on the scene immediately. Everybody was. With his tanned, athletic body, mane of blond hair, and dreamy blue eyes, Jimmie was the stuff of schoolgirl fantasies. Voted best looking and most popular the first year he attended our junior high, Jimmie was the guy all of the other boys wanted to be like and secretly hated at the same time.

In contrast, I was a painfully skinny, awkward preteen, all arms and legs, with long brown hair, and nicknamed "monkey" among my friends. I don't even think I wore a training bra, but I did wear braces and that attractive metal headgear with the wire encircling my head looking like some kind of alien antennae. I was enrolled in all the nerdy classes, and I wasn't voted best anything.

Jimmie didn't notice me until yearbook camp at the end of the summer before my junior year, his senior year. By then the monkey had ditched the braces, filled out, and grown into her body and looks. Now on the varsity cheerleading squad, I had upped my coolness factor considerably.

My best friend, Laura, who was also on the yearbook staff, was at camp as well. We were giggly teenagers with surging hormones looking to add some excitement to the fascinating subjects of picture cropping and copywriting. So, we started passing notes with Jimmie and his friend, and hanging out with them whenever we had some free time. I was astonished to find that Jimmie's flirtations were aimed at me. Holy shit!

While I'd kissed a few boys and let Gary Sharpe finger me in a hot and heavy make-out session that summer, I'd never even been on a date and here was Mr Best Looking zeroing in on me. Me?! His attention scared me to death but had me walking on air at the same time.

The story almost ended there because I kept nervously thwarting Jimmie's advances once we returned home, out of girlish anxiety. Finally, one rainy, September afternoon at a junior varsity football game with friends, I found some gumption and we had our first official get together. You couldn't even call it a date, but I was surprised and disappointed that he didn't try to kiss me when dropping me off at my house after. Because Jimmie had a reputation for being a "ladies' man", at first I'd only agree to go on group outings; however, before too long, we were flying solo. And not long after that, I lost my virginity in the back seat of his Chevrolet Chevette hatchback one night at a popular parking spot in the woods of my neighborhood. Somehow, he even made a metallic green Chevette seem cool.

Like most high school romances, we had exhilarating highs, dramatic arguments, and histrionic break-ups. Never having been in a relationship before and now being coupled with "Mr It", I was neurotically immature and insecure. As I'd rocketed from a nerdy nobody to dating the most to-die-for guy in the school, my emerging self-worth and identity became inextricably all tangled up in having Jimmie by my side. He wrote in my yearbook, "I thought I was a jealous person until I met you."

After graduating that year, Jimmie went off to college an hour away and wanting his freedom, broke off our relationship. My young heart was crushed in the way that can only happen with a first love: I was completely devastated and thought it was the end of the world.

During his freshman year at college, which was my senior year in high school, even though we weren't a couple, Jimmie and I always made it our business to know what the other one was doing. Friends, enemies, and mutual acquaintances made sure that neither of us missed the tiniest move the other made, even if we would have rather not known at times. When he was home for the weekend from college, we often ended up at the same parties and clubs, and hooked up several times during the year. I don't know about him, but I made sure that we "just happened" to be at the same places. Not being nearly as subtle, he'd often show up at my front door out of the blue late at night for a booty call. Even though I pretended to pay no attention to him, Jimmie was always on my radar screen.

With my father newly divorced and in a relationship, and both of my brothers away at college, I was a high school senior with a driver's license, a car, and unprecedented freedom. While I maintained respectable grades and held down a job serving burgers, I went a little wild and had a senior year to remember, partying and fooling around, but didn't date anyone seriously. I was beginning to understand the magical spell my looks and body, both in full bloom by now, could cast over the male half of the population, and was getting a kick out of learning how to use them. I reveled in my bewitching powers while enjoying attention, free drinks, admission into clubs at no charge, and receiving flowers for no reason. Although I now know that all of this didn't really mean anything, to my budding teenage ego, it meant everything.

Looking back, I can see how the drastic change of my external appearance, coinciding with dating Jimmie, only made me more insecure and stunted the development of my inner self. As my self-worth became firmly rooted in my appearance, my internal feelings of inadequacy and low self-esteem were only magnified. The outside didn't match the inside anymore. In my heart and head, I was still the awkward monkey with braces and headgear.

I went off to the same college that Jimmie attended the next fall. The very first week I was at school, he showed up at my door, and we were together from that day forward, with a few break-ups along the way. Officially, I always maintained my own room on campus or an apartment off campus, but we were inseparable and spent almost every night together. For his last three years at college, he lived in a mobile home, purchased by his father, just a couple of miles from campus. With a washer, dryer and spare bedroom, the trailer was the height of luxury compared to the living arrangements of most of our friends and perfect for us to play house.

The summer before our final year in school, I actually broke up with Jimmie for a few months and dated someone else. That was a first. I wrote in my diary:

He does not love in bed or anywhere else. Still, I feel drawn to him and sympathetic and caring towards him. I could never hate or dislike him. I don't like the way he treats me, but I like him. I guess all these years, I just kept thinking it would get better – and it did sometimes, but it also got worse.

Because Jimmie took five years to get out of college and I took four, we graduated at the same time. With a computer science degree, he quickly found a solid first job in Kansas City, Missouri. While I'd earned a versatile business degree, I hadn't really given much thought to what I was going to do with it after graduation. In a hastily thrown-together ceremony, Jimmie and I were married and set out for Kansas City the day after the wedding with all our belongings packed into an 18 foot U-Haul.

I did love Jimmie for what I knew love to be at that time. However, I think a major reason I got married was because I was too scared to venture out into the world on my own. At our wedding reception, I broke into an ugly cry for a good ten minutes. While everyone probably attributed the waterworks to my leaving and moving halfway across the country the next day, part of me knew that I had sold myself out.

From the start of the marriage, we fell into the pattern of me following Jimmie's jobs all over the country for higher positions, more money, and I think sometimes just for the heck of it. After Kansas City, we lived in Dallas, Atlanta, Orlando, Durham and Raleigh, North Carolina, Jacksonville, Florida, Lansdale, Pennsylvania, and Tampa. He was always in search of a better job, a better city, a better life, a better whatever. I'm not even sure. I suspect that his quest, like that of many young adults, was really about proving something to the world, to his father, and to himself.

Jimmie, ambitious, hardworking, and perfectly looking the part of the handsome young executive, climbed the corporate ladder quickly. His ascent, while financially rewarding for our lifestyle, turned out to be bad news for our relationship because I allowed his career to dominate, while not insisting that my wants even be considered in our lives. Early in our marriage, I was more than happy to depend on Jimmie and let him take the lead while I peeked timidly over his shoulder from my comfort zone. That way, I didn't have to bear the brunt of the financial responsibility or put myself too far out into the big, scary world. Over the years, as Jimmie became more powerful, I became more powerless and unhappy. In between packing and unpacking, I found low-paying, administrative jobs wherever we landed. Always starting over and never getting anywhere in a career. Always compliant and submissive. Always feeling isolated, resentful, and lost in my own life.

In August 2000, after 11 moves, Chris' death, two miscarriages, and the birth of two sons, I found myself in Tampa, Florida, in an expensive, elegant home. Jimmie and I had been married for 15 years at that point. The most recent move to Florida was the third to the state during the marriage, and the third move to a different state in the previous five years. By now, I was a stay-at-home mom with three-year-old and six-year-old boys who were both precious and challenging. I was a corporate widow, a professional mover, and an angry, bitchy woman. I was tired. Tired of moving. Tired of being a single parent. Tired of being lonely.

When we relocated, Jimmie usually preceded the family to the new state and job for months. When the whole family was settled in one place, he was absent from home a lot of the time, putting in long hours at the office during the week, working most weekends, and frequently traveling for business. We crossed paths very little, and when we did, we argued.

In December, three months after the kids and I joined him in Florida, Jimmie announced that he wanted a divorce.

"I'm not happy. You're not happy. I don't think we're doing ourselves or the kids any favors by dragging this thing out. It's only getting worse. I think we should separate."

"No," I told him, "We've been through phases like this before. Let's go to counseling. We made it bad. We can make it good again."

Half-heartedly, he agreed.

We attended weekly marriage counseling sessions for months and implemented changes that did perk things up for a little while. With regularity, I'd hire a babysitter, wear unfamiliar high heels, short skirts, and thongs, and we dined at restaurants that didn't have chicken fingers on the menu. Tenuously, almost shyly, we started to discover each other as two adults instead of the all too familiar personas of the frazzled mom and the gotta-go-to-work dad.

Our future was beginning to brighten until I divulged in a counseling session that I'd had a brief, extramarital affair nine years earlier. Until that point, I would say that we were your average married couple with different priorities, facing the typical stressors of a young family and being pulled apart by life. We didn't communicate well, try to understand, or have much compassion for each other. After hearing the news of my indiscretion, something in Jimmie snapped and went crazy. Deeply wounded and hurt, he was furious, but I got the impression that he was incensed that someone had tarnished his possession more than anything else. He immediately withheld my mail, got a private post office box, cancelled my credit cards, reported my debit card lost, removed half of the money from the joint checking account, and opened an individual account for himself.

With cold eyes, he told me that he wanted a divorce as soon as possible.

"You're on your own from now on, you lying bitch. You've sponged off of me long enough. You're not going to get shit from me. I'll make sure of that."

One afternoon when I returned home from taking the children to a neighborhood picnic, he went off on me.

"Did you pick up any men and get some action in the parking lot? When the kids get older, I'm going to tell them what a whore their mother is. I'm going to take them away from you. The worst thing that ever happened to them was having you for a mother. I'm going to have their DNA tested. They're probably not even mine."

I didn't have a name anymore as Jimmie called me "whore" more often than not, even in front of the children. He shoved me around so much that I called domestic abuse shelters for information and lived in fear for my safety in my own home.

"Don't fuck with me or I'll kill you. If you tell anyone I said this, I'll deny it and still kill you," he said as he slugged me in the back of the head with his fist.

I couldn't believe this was the Jimmie that I knew and that this was actually my life. We had argued in the past, but nothing like this.

Jimmie threw me out of the master bedroom, put a new lock on the door, and relocated the family computer into the bedroom, denying me access to it. By that time, email was my main means of communication with friends and family, my support network, in other states. I moved into the guest room at the end of the hall upstairs, past the boys' rooms.

Behind the locked master bedroom doors, Jimmie rifled through the boxes of personal stuff in my closet, reading the diaries that I'd written in high school and college. Those diaries were the intimate musings of a young girl coming into adulthood who was confused, enjoying her newfound womanly powers, questioning herself and her decisions at times, and madly in love at other times. Those thoughts were never meant to be seen by anyone else's eyes, much less his.

The ramblings on the pages of the diaries only fueled his anger even more, and the already volatile situation turned into a bomb ready to detonate at any minute. Daily, Jimmie delighted in telling me, "Today's the day," meaning that I was going to be served divorce papers, and watching me squirm like a worm on a fish hook.

"Ooh, Debbie, what ya' going to do? Kill yourself? Go ahead. We won't miss you. Make it easy on everyone," he taunted me.

Feeling like a spring coiled too tight and living in constant fear, I couldn't sleep or eat and dropped ten pounds in a matter of weeks. I was functioning enough to accomplish what I absolutely had to for the kids, but beyond that, all I could do was chain smoke and drink coffee.

On May 14, 2001, Jimmie called me from work three times during the day, which was unusual, but because he was being at least cordial and communicative, I took it as a good sign.

During the last call, around 5.00pm, he was unusually nice and indicated that we'd talk when he got home. After nonchalantly walking in the door an hour and a half later, Jimmie called for me to come to the front door. Through the window beside the door, I could see a courier standing there to deliver the divorce papers he had threatened me with every damn day. That's when I escaped in my mini-van, attempted suicide in the Wal-Mart parking lot, and ended up in the hospital psych ward.

My mother flew in from North Carolina upon getting the news that I'd tried to kill myself, and showed up at the hospital an hour after Jimmie the next morning. When she arrived, he became extremely agitated, ordered me to tell the nurse to ask her to leave, and became so confrontational that the nurse called security.

"As long as she's in the state, I won't be back to visit you or bring the kids up here," he commanded. "It's either her or me. You choose," he spit out as he stormed out of the hospital room.

My neighbor later relayed to me that he'd told her that he was afraid my mother was going to file domestic violence charges against him.

I was transferred to the hospital's psychiatric ward, stayed there the required two days, and was released. Genuinely happy to be alive, I was anxious to get home to my kids.

Jimmie, however, had very different plans for me. Calling my dad, Jimmie told him that he'd "better come get his daughter", because he'd filed a restraining order against me restricting me from going near our house, the children, their schools, or their activities. He was thorough. Driving down from North Carolina with his wife, my father checked me out of the hospital's mental ward and took me to a nearby hotel where I nervously contacted a lawyer to find out what my next step was and my rights at that point. Because I couldn't go home, I was going to travel back to North Carolina with Dad. To get the necessities needed for the trip, lawyers had to arrange for me to visit the house, accompanied by police. I couldn't believe that I had to get permission to go to my house where I lived with my children, and be escorted by police.

With me sitting in the back seat, the police officers pulled their marked car right up in the circular driveway in front of our million dollar house at around dusk the next day. For reasons that I still cannot fathom, a police helicopter hovered overhead shining its searchlight down on the house and yard for the entire duration of my visit, like I was some dangerous criminal on the loose. I'd like to know how Jimmie managed to arrange that one. The officers informed me that I had 15 minutes to get my belongings.

Accompanied by a policewoman, I entered the house through the same door in the kitchen that I'd slipped out of the night that I had avoided being served the divorce papers. I wasn't feeling so triumphant now.

The in-laws, who'd driven from out-of-state to help take care of the boys in my absence, quickly ushered the children into the playroom and closed the door. The playroom was adjacent to the den which was open to the kitchen, through which I had to walk to retrieve my things from the guest room upstairs. As I passed by, I could hear my sons screaming and crying for me in the other room. Because I was visibly upset and sobbing, with my hands shaking so badly that I could hardly open drawers and shove clothes into a paper bag, the policewoman felt sorry for me and helped me gather my things. I could still hear the children protesting loudly as I made my way back out of the house.

While in North Carolina, I attended a daily outpatient counseling program at a local hospital, saw a private mental health counselor, and had long, emotionally charged talks with Jimmie on the phone. Feeling like a fish out of water and desperately wanting to get home to my boys, I did whatever I thought would help reunite us. After having experienced the full extent of the callousness Jimmie was capable of, with the verbal and emotional torment before the suicide attempt, and the restraining order after, something inside of me shifted towards him. Sadly, but long overdue, I realized that I couldn't trust him, and that I had to protect myself from him, my own husband. It wasn't supposed to be this way.

There had been many signs pointing in this direction over the years that I'd conveniently ignored. I didn't want to see them and managed to explain them away to myself convincingly enough, although there was always a part of me that never really quite bought it. I preferred to live in my illusion, telling myself whatever I needed to, in order to keep the life that I knew intact. Ignorance is bliss, until it's not anymore.

While I was in North Carolina, I recorded telephone conversations between Jimmie and me in which I said whatever I thought I needed to say to get back to my children. That was my only priority. Being out of the house put me at a significant legal disadvantage in the event of a divorce, both with the kids and materially.

I wouldn't say that I completely deceived Jimmie. Part of me did want to erase all traces of the recent ugly events, glue the pieces of our lives back together, and somehow, some way, be a family again. I moved forward in discussions with him, cautiously aware that I had to regain my position, first as mother and wife, before I could make any decisions about anything else. Although my heart wanted to reconcile and I was emotionally open to it, my head knew better. After my childhood home, life with Jimmie was the only existence I'd ever known. Being with him was my comfort zone even if it was uncomfortable as hell, and on some level, I wanted to return to it.

After five weeks in North Carolina, I flew back to Florida, stayed in a hotel, and after what seemed like an eternity, finally got to hug my sons' necks. Jimmie and I had intense meetings to discuss the possibility of my returning home. For one talk, we rendezvoused in the lobby of a hotel and went behind the building and sat on a picnic table, overlooking a lake, to have privacy for our heart-to-heart. We hugged desperately as if grasping each other tight enough would allow us to hold onto the life that we had known together. After agreeing to a legal document outlining many specific conditions for my going home, and another week in the hotel, I moved back into the house. Jimmie and I stayed together for two more years.

During this time, I was genuinely open to whatever unfolded in our marriage and wasn't masquerading under entirely false pretenses. If things improved, great. If they didn't, a powerful self-preservation instinct had kicked in that would help me get through whatever was ahead. Being careful not to rock the boat, I played "the good wife" while I stashed money in a secret bank account and bided my time. I didn't know exactly what I was waiting for, but I knew that I would recognize it when it came around.

In the spring of 2003, Jimmie started actively looking for another job and eventually accepted a new position with the same company in Boise, Idaho. Our family visited the area to check it out as a potential new home base, and nothing about the place or the relocation felt right to me. To go halfway across the country with someone I didn't trust anymore would isolate me further, commit me to several more years with him, and make unraveling our lives even messier.

"I don't want to go to Boise. I just can't see it being a good thing for me or the kids," I told him.

He proposed the idea of a "commuter marriage", in which he migrated wherever his career took him while the boys and I permanently stationed ourselves in one location, with him flying in to visit regularly. He could have an instant family whenever he felt like it and have his freedom too, and this arrangement would be much cheaper than a divorce. How convenient!

I knew immediately that this was the opportunity I'd been waiting for. The scenario would work perfectly for me to make my escape. I couldn't have masterminded a more ingenious plan, and Jimmie had concocted this one and handed it to me. The boys and I would move to North Carolina, making it our permanent home while he went to Idaho, but we would stay married. In August of 2003, Jimmie started the job in Idaho living in corporate housing. The boys and I remained in Florida for five months with him visiting occasionally. During this time, I traveled to North Carolina and found a house for the boys and me, on which Jimmie put down a large down payment and signed the loan. At the end of December, Jimmie returned to Florida to supervise the move, we split up all of our belongings, and everything was loaded onto two trucks headed to different sides of the country. We spent that night in a hotel and planned to take off the next day, driving to our respective new homes.

In the morning, with the kids at school, Jimmie and I went to the empty house to perform the final clean up. On the floor in the den, we had sex for the first time in a year and a half and the last time ever. I think, intuitively, we both knew that we were saying goodbye even if we didn't utter the words out loud. Unbeknownst to him, I had already filed for divorce in the state of Florida and after the moving truck had unloaded, and the kids and I were safe in North Carolina, I informed him over the phone that I was divorcing him.

For a while after the brain injury, I had that visual memory of us having sex on the floor in the vacant house, but I didn't recall the surrounding circumstances. I couldn't figure out why in the hell I would have done that. As my memory came back in color, others filled in the details, and I read notes that I'd kept for legal purposes, the mystery was solved. I was intimate with Jimmie so I didn't clue him in as to my real intentions. But also because I'd been with this man for over two decades, and on some level I still loved him.

When my lawyer and I started digging around in preparation for the alimony trial, I discovered that Jimmie and a woman that had worked for him for the previous five years, Sheila, were formally investigated at their place of employment in Tampa for having had a romantic relationship the year before he and I split. I didn't know anything about this when it was happening.

Sheila started working for Jimmie in Jacksonville, Florida, followed him to Pennsylvania, back to Florida, and then to Idaho. While Jimmie and I were married, Sheila was also married, we were friends, and had family cookouts together with the kids. Upon joining Jimmie in Idaho, Sheila left her husband in Florida.

With this new bit of information, the last years of my marriage began to make a lot more sense. I no longer wondered why a year of weekly couples counseling never seemed to really improve anything for us. I no longer wondered why Jimmie would actually propose the idea of a commuter marriage and think that that was OK. I no longer wondered why he was so stressed and in such a bad mood the last year we were together, while he was under investigation at work and had to keep it all a secret

Jimmie had miraculously kept everything hidden from me. I believe that he was positioning himself for a divorce, but I agreed to an option that would cost him much less money, allow him to continue to control me and the kids, and give him his independence too. Looking back, I have sympathy for the young Debbie who often took her sons to have lunch with him in the cafeteria at his work. Although I didn't know any of this was happening then, his co-workers did. What's the female word for cuckold?

Honestly, I did have an idea that something was going on over the years, but I didn't acknowledge the signs because I didn't want to face the reality, instead preferring to remain in my protective bubble of ignorance. What you don't know can't hurt you, right? Wrong. It sneaks up and bites you in the ass. When we lived in Pennsylvania, I found a receipt for a bed and breakfast located in a nearby picturesque township. The hotel stay was for a weekend when the boys and I had been visiting family in North Carolina.

Jimmie explained the hotel trip as him and some friends hanging out for the weekend. Chilling with the guys at a B&B? Right. I knew that this didn't add up, but being a stay-at-home mom with a three-year-old and an infant, I wasn't prepared to deal with what I might find if I dug deeper. So, I didn't. I wanted to believe him, and to acknowledge anything different would have shattered my reality.

That same year, I gave Sheila all of the baby gear from my boys when she became pregnant with her son. While I have grown tremendously since then and have done much healing around this whole situation, I'm not so evolved that I don't want to kick myself in the ass every time I think about that.

Today, she and Jimmie are married. After I tried to commit suicide, and Collin and Gabe moved to Virginia with their dad, she and her son accompanied them, although they weren't yet married. Although it took many years and tears to get to where I could say this, I genuinely appreciate her presence in my sons' lives. She has been nurturing and kind to them, and they care about her, although I can't say that I appreciate the way she got there.

*

At 39 years old, after 18 years of marriage, I began life as a single woman. I'd never been "unattached" for long since the age of 16, so this was terrifying new territory for me. Although there had been brief intervals during the six years in high school and college that Jimmie and I dated during which we had separated, this was very different. I was all grown up now with kids, pets, a leaf blower, a set of matching dishes, and a mortgage. I had spent my entire adult life being Jimmie's other half. I didn't have the slightest idea how to do single.

Even though I had initiated the divorce, I was still in a total state of shock. My heart hurt as I grieved the end of the life I'd known and the death of hopes and dreams I had held for our family.

There would be no growing old together and watching the boys turn into fine young men. No romantic stories to tell the grandkids about how Grandma and Grandpa were high school sweethearts. My mind was dizzy with the thought of a future crammed full of so many question marks. I felt like a major failure, because after going through my parents' divorce as a teenage girl, I'd always smugly promised myself, "I'm never doing that to my kids!"

At first I functioned on autopilot, keeping busy settling into the new house and situating the kids, to allow myself to feel much of anything. However, soon enough all of the boxes were unpacked, the pictures were on the walls, and the kids were enrolled in karate. I fell into the routine of numbly going through the motions of looking after the house and the kids, doing what had to be done, and holding it together. After the kids went to bed or when they were away with their father, I found myself with way too much time to mope and alternated between licking my wounds and pouring salt in them. Jimmie usually came in to see the kids one weekend a month and flew them to Idaho for longer holidays. When they were gone, nothing could keep me busy enough to prevent the sadness and loneliness from settling into my bones.

Even though I never questioned my decision to leave the marriage, I didn't feel very confident venturing forward into the world alone, yet I knew that it was exactly what I needed to do. Jimmie and I were locked in an ugly financially and emotionally exhausting legal battle. The sadness permeating my world after the divorce was different than the suffocating wall of blackness I experienced when Chris died. This was a 1,000-pound rock that I had to drag around behind me every day while still taking care of the kids, the house, and life's little details, and pretending that I was OK.

I understood that it was expected to have wildly fluctuating moods with the drastic changes occurring in my life, but knowing this didn't make them any easier or less unpleasant to navigate.

While I was too scared and sad to be excited about my newfound freedom and the possibilities ahead most of the time, I would catch a whiff of the scent every once in a while. Sometimes, I strapped myself in, rode the emotional roller coaster, and actually managed to see the humor and wisdom in the shitty feelings and situations. At other times, I sank deep into a well of despair and felt as if I was drowning.

Being without a man for the first time ever, a single mother of two young boys, and a female homeowner determined to do-it-herself led me to make some rather poignant observations that I wrote down, planning to compile them into one of those bathroom books, entitled *One Hundred Things I Have Learned Since My Divorce*. Some jewels from the collection are:

- *I have learned that you can be married to someone for 18 years and look at them sitting across the table from you in some fancy lawyer's office and realize that they're just as much a stranger to you as the nice girl who led you to the room and gave you a bottle of water because your mouth was dry.*

- *I have learned that taking well-timed naps is a viable self-defense mechanism. When you're asleep, you don't have to think, feel, worry, or even exist.*

- *I have learned that little boys don't value sleep in quite the same way, and if you zonk out on the couch one Friday night, they might just stay up until 4.00am playing video games.*

- *I have learned that you shouldn't attend a wedding too soon after you get divorced or you'll end up crying so hard that snot runs out of your nose, and it'll have nothing to do with the blessed union you're witnessing before you.*

- *I have learned that little boys don't like to see their mother cry.*

- *I have learned that if you read too many self-help books right in a row, it isn't all that helpful.*

- *I have learned that getting a coffee maker on Valentine's Day is actually better than getting nothing at all.*

- *I have learned that certain appliances given as wedding presents may be stained and crusted, but they will still be working long after the marriage isn't.*

- *I have learned that corn dogs, macaroni and cheese, and a few grapes for dinner can pass for cooking with your kids, especially if you give them some ice cream for dessert.*

- *I have learned that making wholewheat, banana and raisin pancakes on Sunday morning for your kids is a complete waste of time, although you might enjoy them.*

- *I have learned that it's better to buy two 50 foot extension cords instead of one 100 foot cord when trimming the bushes in the yard with the electric trimmers. That way, if you cut through one cord, you still have one left – until you cut through that one too.*

- *I have learned that when you cut through the extension cord with the electric trimmers that it can blow a safety fuse and that all you have to do is hit the reset button on the outlet on the garage wall. You don't have go without power in that part of the house for a day and a half until the electrician gets there, and you don't have to pay him 100 dollars to push the button.*

- *I have learned that if your entire downstairs is rapidly flooding with raw sewage gurgling up from the toilet, turning off the water valve at the base of the toilet does absolutely nothing to stop the deluge nor does screaming hysterically at your children and the neighbor who came over to help.*

Just keeping the house, the kids, and myself functioning in our new life was a drama, a tearjerker, and a comedy, sometimes, all in the same day. I kept busy, kept to myself, and vacillated between wallowing in self-pity and tasting morsels of optimism. Slowly I began to have a couple of good days in a row, felt like I could breathe again, and thought I could glimpse a light flickering at the end of the tunnel. I just hoped like hell that it wasn't a train about to flatten me.

CHAPTER 12

My Shaman Lover

When my ring finger had been naked for ten months, I decided it was time to dive into the dating world. Because my life had always revolved around a man, filling this void seemed like the next logical step to me. After the divorce, I found myself in uncertain territory everywhere I turned. Besides the obvious biggie, being a single parent, there were all kinds of things I now had to learn to tackle on my own about which I felt less than qualified. Like having the oil changed in the car before it's gone 10,000 miles or replacing the HVAC air filters before they're caked with an inch of crud. Being able to attract a man was one area in which I felt pretty competent.

Because I'd just moved to the area and didn't work outside the home, meeting men could potentially be challenging. Match.com to the rescue. The internet was just starting to explode, and online dating sites, which were perfect for me, were skyrocketing in popularity. Everybody was using them and they were way better than a singles bar. I could sit at home in my bathrobe with zit cream on my face, flirt outrageously, and let my fingers and uploaded pics do all the work.

I don't care how fascinating your hobbies are, a person is judged primarily by their pictures on a dating site, and I felt good about my chances here. I posted a flattering profile picture, attractive and sexy – but not the trying-too-hard-to-look-sexy pose which ends up not being sexy at all – wrote a witty, flirtatious profile, and was deluged with winks and responses, giving a much-welcomed boost to my bruised ego.

As I sifted through the replies, I quickly picked up some computer dating savvy. A few observations I wrote for my bathroom book reflect my snarky mindset at the time:

- *I have learned that when men describe themselves as "athletic and toned" on an internet dating site, it means that they have a small beer gut and can probably climb a flight of stairs without hyperventilating.*

- *I have learned that when men describe themselves as "about average" on an internet dating site, it means they have a fully developed set of man boobs and look like they're about to give birth to twins.*

I took much pleasure in and spent way too much time engaging in online conversations, which felt like seductive dances and eventually led to first meetings. Because all this dating stuff was new to me, like an awkward teenager, I wasn't good at any of it. I was especially bad at being honest about my interest in a man and didn't know how to say a polite, "Thanks, but no thanks."

Rendezvousing with an online date for the first time the smart way, I met the gentleman at the restaurant for dinner. While knowing that it was a no-go for me 15 minutes into the meal, rather than being up front I agreed to follow the poor guy somewhere after the meal to continue our evening. Instead, when he turned right, I turned left and sped home. Like that was nicer than just telling him the truth? That stunt was preferable to having what would have been an uncomfortable conversation.

Another time, I registered with one of those hoity toity matchmaking agencies where rich men turn to find companions. The service arranged a blind date that turned out to not be a good pairing on any level. The guy showed up looking like he was straight out of *The Sopranos* with gold chains around his neck and his shiny shirt unbuttoned too far down his gorilla-ish furry chest. All evening, I couldn't stop staring at the hair plugs going halfway down his forehead even though I kept commanding myself not to. In the middle of the dinner, I excused myself to go the bathroom and called a girlfriend on my cell. Between giggles, I begged her, "You have *got* to help me figure out a way to get out of this!" Because we couldn't devise a feasible plan, and because he had driven an hour and a half to meet me, I was polite and finished the date.

*

Meanwhile, back online, I started chatting with a charming, handsome man who was two years older than me and only lived three miles away. His messages were smart, intelligently humorous, and grammatically correct. It was Steve.

For our first, in-person meeting I showed up at his house with a six-pack of Coronas which I sipped, while he nursed a gin and tonic with a twist of lime. We sat on his side porch steps and talked for hours. Over the years, I've probably watched him make hundreds of drinks, and from that very first night, I've always thought there was something incredibly sexy about the way he poured the alcohol and mixer onto the sparkling ice cubes, then sliced the lime and squeezed the wedge into his glass. Hell, he could have scraped gum off of the bottom of his shoe, and I would have thought it was sexy. Conversation was easy, effortless, and titillating. I felt that spark, that zing, that elusive "it" with him. When we kissed at the end of the night, a delicious electrical charge surged through my body all the way down to my toes.

The animalistic attraction between us was so powerful and undeniable that it was damned difficult to make it to the respectable third date before having sex. Every cell of my body buzzed with the rush of the new romance and lust for this man.

It was the same physical pull that I'd felt with Jimmie in high school, but I also found myself strongly attracted to Steve's mind this time. He was smart and charming with a dry, cynical sense of humor with the slightest edge of hard-won wisdom. Interacting with him was like an invigorating mental tennis match. He would drive a remark over the net, and I'd return with a clever comment to which he'd hit a witty comeback. His words were charged with innuendo, which I was challenged to decipher and reply with equally enticing retorts. Or maybe they weren't. It's entirely possible (and most likely) that I was playing mental tennis by myself, but because I thought that's what we were doing, that's what was happening for me, and I liked it. It felt like oh-so-satisfying mind sex.

Steve had his story, lots of stories actually, which he'd told so many times to so many women, that he could recite them backwards, forwards, and sideways. His anecdotes portrayed a childhood of poverty, emotional abuse, and neglect by his birth mother, and I have no doubt that there was some truth in all of them.

When he was a boy, Steve lived in a mobile home with his half-sister and half-brother who each had a different father from his own, whom he never knew. At a young age, too young, the children were left at home by themselves while relatives did the bare minimum to help out. He told of one instance in which an aunt and uncle brought over some burgers and fries for him and his siblings, because they were too little to fix anything for themselves. Instead of coming inside, talking to the kids, and serving them the meal, the couple tossed the bags of food into the trailer through a cracked front door, as if throwing scraps of food to wild animals. Right then and there, Steve told himself that he was better than that and promised to make a very different life for himself.

As a teenager, while playing hooky from school one day, Steve picked up a game of tennis with a man he thought was a random stranger at the local public tennis court. That man, Larry, turned out to be the county truancy officer searching for him, and rather than turning him in and getting Steve in trouble, Larry struck a deal with him that would change his life. Larry agreed to play tennis with Steve regularly if he'd commit to going to school. Over time and tennis, Larry befriended Steve, often inviting him home to have dinner with him and his wife. At 16, Steve petitioned the court and had himself legally emancipated, and Larry and his wife, who were childless, adopted him. Steve moved in with them and finished high school.

Steve worked hard and put himself through college, going to different schools over many years, and after trying out several careers, ranging from photographer to various sales positions, he found success as a financial analyst. When visiting one of his clients, he met an attractive receptionist, turned on the charm, and asked her out to dinner that weekend. They dated for a brief time, nothing serious, and lost touch. Steve was surprised to discover that she'd given birth to twins some nine months later. After doing the math and suspecting that the children were his, he contacted the mother and went to visit the children for the first time.

I wonder how many women have heard him say, "I went into that house praying like hell the kids weren't mine. And after seeing them sleeping in their little cribs, I was praying like hell they were."

Their mother confirmed that he was the father.

Like a skillful artist painting a picture with his words, Steve told his stories much better than I can, punctuating them with sentimental details in just the right places so they tugged at your heart and made you want to respond with a big sympathetic, "Aaaww." He was revealing enough to make a woman feel as though there was a real openness and connection there. While his tales were intimately personal, they weren't at the same time, because he was reciting rehearsed lines like an actor, as he had numerous times before. More often than not, his touching testimony had the intended effect and activated the "save the lost puppy" instinct in a woman.

With masterful skill, Steve spun his web, and women like me walked willingly into the tangle of silky threads, although I can honestly say that I don't think he acted consciously with ill intent. The Pied Piper of women was just who Steve had come to be and how he had learned to successfully cope given his emotional wounds. These bits and pieces of Steve's life story, his baggage as he called it, were the disjointed fragments of himself that he hadn't figured out how to put together to heal and become a whole, healthy adult. As many before me, I wanted to adopt the puppy, take him home, and make it all better.

I don't mean to criticize or mock Steve because I actually have a great deal of respect and admiration for him. He had a good heart and was doing the best he knew how to do with who he was at the time. To survive his childhood, Steve learned to gauge and manipulate every opportunity and person that came along to his advantage.

To protect his younger self, he had to shut down emotionally and not allow himself to trust, rely on, or be vulnerable with anyone, because doing so meant getting hurt. As a child, a person needs to form secure and positive attachments to caregivers. When this goes awry and the very things that should make a person feel safe and secure, and allow them to go on to live a fulfilling life, are in fact threatening, a person's brain learns that relationships and intimacy are dangerous and to be avoided.

Steve adapted and not only survived a cruel childhood, but the skills he developed allowed him to later thrive in some areas, like sales. Although he could read people like a psychic to close a deal, his adaptations weren't very helpful when it came to having lasting relationships.

As if every childhood wound added a stone, Steve built an impenetrable wall around his heart for his protection. While this barrier served him well when he was younger, it became a barricade that kept him isolated from happiness and love as an adult. Like two adjacent pieces of a puzzle, the imprint of his wounds matched up perfectly with my own jagged edges.

Looking back, what was going on is all so obvious to me now, but I played right into the destructive patterns unconsciously at the time. I spent huge amounts of energy focused on Steve's behavior and problems while remaining oblivious to my own faults and not taking responsibility for my part in the toxic relationship. Instead of always pointing my finger at him, I should've turned it back around to myself and started making changes there. Goodness knows, I had more than enough emotional work that I needed to do, but I wasn't ready to go there yet and was suffering from the "let me fix him, and we'll live happily ever after" syndrome. The attraction between us was so strong because the relationship was so unhealthy, but it felt like love to me.

Steve always drove an impressive set of wheels, usually a luxury sedan or sports car, wore expensive Italian shoes, and owned several homes throughout the state, from the mountains to the beach. Even though he had a successful career in the conservative banking industry, Steve never adapted himself to fit the mold and refused to wear the standard khakis and pastel button down uniform. He rejected the popular "good life" formula comprising doing the nine-to-five commute with the masses to eventually retire in front of the TV or putter around a golf course. He had a curiosity and thirst for life that I suspect originated from an uneasiness with himself. If he was always on the move and distracting himself, his feelings and memories couldn't catch up with him.

Although Steve changed his car about as often as he changed the woman in his life, he maintained several interests, which kept him in perpetual motion, but were also the constants in his world. He bought and sold baseball cards, and I'm not talking about the baseball cards that little boys collect. I mean rare cards that are auctioned on eBay for hundreds and even thousands of dollars. My guess is that the rush of the hunt and acquisition fueled this hobby, and like women or cars, he could get rid of a card when its newness and shine wore off.

Steve's most consuming interest was music. Late into the night, he would spend hours scouring the internet looking for obscure talent, purchasing music, and making CDs. (This was before the iPod.) Tracking artists he liked, Steve would plan dates for us to local shows and weekend trips to out-of-town performances. I found this hobby of his exciting compared to most of the 40-somethings I knew whose interests included the kids and yard work.

Steve shared his love of music with me, introducing me to new artists that have become important parts of my life, especially as I healed from the brain injury in isolation. The shows, artists, and songs that he and I shared became the threads woven throughout our relationship, stringing together snapshot moments over the years.

Annie Lennox brings to mind an outdoor concert at the beginning of our romance when Steve and I were head over heels in love, and everything was still all hearts and rainbows. Darden Smith makes me think of a weekend trip to attend an intimate, acoustic show after which we had Mexican food and beers with the singer at a little eatery next to the venue. Eddie Money reminds me of a local performance during which Steve and I argued so much – something about a female client giving him the tickets to the event at dinner a couple of nights before – that we hardly even saw the show.

Every time I hear Patty Griffin I can picture us sitting on a blanket spread out on a grassy hill before the outdoor spring concert, where Steve turned to me with a big smile on his face and warm eyes and said, "I love you." The thumping, gotta-move-your-booty bass in Prince's tune, *Right Back Here In My Arms*, takes me right back to the night I did a shaky striptease for Steve, because I was nervous, tipsy, and wearing three inch heels.

Music was as essential to Steve as air, because in the world of melody and lyrics, it was safe for him to feel. Music allowed him to come into the land of the living and experience the emotions he dared not expose himself to otherwise. When we had sex, Steve always had to have music playing in the background, to set the mood and get the juices flowing, but also to get his emotions and feelings going, I think.

He would often burn compilation CDs for me (the old equivalent of making me a playlist) and in my mind every heartfelt sentiment, every term of endearment, and every expression of longing uttered by the singers were his words to me. I later learned that making and giving CDs to a woman was one of his signature moves that, like his collection of stories, felt intimate and special when you think it's just for you.

Having been married to Jimmie for 18 years and having dated him for six before that, even with my wild senior year, my sexual experience paled in comparison to Steve's. At the time of our relationship, Steve, who'd been married one time for 13 months to the twins' mother, was in his early 40s. With no shortage of women over all those single years, he picked up a few tricks in the bedroom, which really opened my eyes … and legs.

The physical attraction between Steve and me felt like an undeniable force of nature, which was so strong that even others sensed it. While we were sitting at a bar one night having drinks, a man came up to the two of us out of the blue and said, "I want to see you two kiss." After Steve and I enjoyed an especially long and slow one, just for extra effect, the man shook his head and exclaimed, "Mmm-mmm! That one had molasses in it." One night, after dinner and drinks with another couple, we all went back to Steve's house to shoot some pool in his basement. Without the slightest provocation or warning, the woman stripped off her top and attempted to initiate a foursome. Awkward! Steve and I were very surprised, to say the least, and politely declined.

Sometimes, other people didn't have to pick up on it for themselves. After a dinner and a few drinks, Steve and I returned home to relieve my mother, who had been babysitting. While chatting with her in the den, I leaned over and not-so-quietly whispered in Steve's ear, "I can't wait till she leaves so I can take you upstairs and fuck your brains out."

Steve was a drug I craved physically, emotionally, and mentally, and I had to have a regular fix to satisfy my habit. Nothing and no one else would do. I found the natural scent of him intoxicating. I loved the way he tasted. I melted at his skillful touch and adored the way my body came alive in response. I don't know if I craved sex with him so much because it was a means to see him or because I actually liked the sex that much. Probably a little of both. In our relationship, I confused sex with love, and every steamy tryst fed my heart. Over the three years we were in each other's lives, whether we were officially dating each other or he was seeing someone else, we rarely went very long without being physically intimate.

Knowing what time my kids caught the school bus in the mornings, Steve would ring me up right after they went out of the door. And because he lived so close, I could be at his house in just minutes for a roll in the hay, without even making him late for work. For these morning quickies, I often would wear sexy lingerie or nothing at all under a trench coat. (Good thing I never got stopped by a traffic cop. Although, I probably could have easily gotten out of a ticket!) Steve used to say, "Why go to the store for ice cream when it's in the freezer?" Or, in this case, delivered.

Under Steve's tutelage, I blossomed, explored new sexual boundaries, and embraced a liberation and sensuousness that I didn't know I possessed. He initiated me into womanhood and encouraged my progress, while I played the enthusiastic student.

When I got a home equity loan through his company, Steve set everything up so that all I had to do was show up and sign the paperwork. One afternoon at his office, he and I followed a woman with a stack of papers requiring my signature into a conference room to finalize the loan. Wearing a mid-thigh skirt with a garter belt and no underwear, I made sure to position myself so that Steve had a good view. I'd never seen this normally smooth and collected man as flustered as he was that day.

I've decided that Steve was what Elizabeth Lesser refers to as a "Shaman Lover" in her book *Broken Open*. A shaman is a person in a tribal society who acts as an intermediary between the natural visible world and the supernatural invisible world. Shamans are on speaking terms with the spirits, both the good and not so good ones. A shaman can serve as a person's guide into the darkness, through it, and back into the light.

Lesser writes:

The Shaman Lover is a man or woman whose destiny is to heal the heartsick with the sweetness of love, and to give the gift of fire to those whose passion is frozen. Some call the Shaman Lover a temptress or cad, a siren or a snake; sometimes the Shaman Lover has bad medicine to offer. Sometimes the smartest response to the allure is to run away. But sometimes the Shaman Lover has been sent to us by fate to blast us open, to awaken the dead parts of our body, to deliver the kiss of life. And, if we succumb, we are changed forever.[1]

Some additions to my bathroom book from my escapades with Steve are:

- *I have learned that a 45-year-old man who has been married one time in his life for 13 months can accumulate the world's most impressive collection of coffee cups and Tupperware and will add many of your prize specimens to his collection.*
- *I have learned that it's as much fun as I thought it would be to grab the two front tails of a man's dress shirt and rip it off of him, sending all of the buttons flying to the floor.*
- *I have learned that I have enough guts to tell a man who gets pissed about me tearing his favorite shirt off of him that: "If a woman thinks you are sexy enough to rip your shirt off, you should feel damn lucky about it!"*

- *I have learned that a vibrator does get the job done quickly and efficiently, but leaves you wanting so much more.*
- *I have learned that if you need to replace the batteries in your vibrator more often than you need to charge your cell phone, you probably need a new hobby.*
- *I have learned that if you have noisy sex while a dog is in the bedroom, he'll jump up and down popping his head over the edge of the bed repeatedly with a look that says "What ya' doin?" Boing. "What ya' doin?" Boing.*
- *I have learned that if you do have noisy sex while a dog is in the bedroom and you do manage to ignore him, he might get so upset that he takes a nervous poop on the floor, which finally does get your attention with its foul stench.*

*

After the divorce, I was searching for some way or someone in which to find my value and identity, and I latched onto Steve like a drowning person clutching a life preserver. I criticized myself brutally for being so needy because I didn't want to be that way and knew better, but I still was. However, I put on a strong front, not wanting him or anyone else to see how desperate I really felt. There's a world of difference between looking brave and being brave.

Often, when my boys were away with their dad, Steve would stay over on a Saturday night. Relaxed Sunday mornings spent sipping coffee as we chatted at the kitchen table were some of my most cherished times with him. It was usually here that we had our most intimate discussions, and I felt the closest to him. Inevitably, he would refuse my invitation to let me fix him breakfast and make his exit all too soon, and I'd be left standing in the kitchen feeling like my guts were hanging out. Over and over, I'd stuff them back inside, slap on my game face, and go on with my life.

Steve and I were always doing the on-again-off-again thing, with him initiating the break-ups every time. The longest we were ever officially in a committed relationship was only a few months, and I highly doubt that these were exclusive periods for him. Each time he walked away, I promised myself that I was done. That was it. I wanted it to be over because I knew that our relationship wasn't healthy for me, but like a drug addict, I kept relapsing.

Sometimes when the kids were with their dad and Steve and I weren't dating, I'd park outside the front of his house on an adjacent side street where I knew he couldn't see my car. As two silhouettes crossed in front of the window beside the door, I would watch one switch off the frog-shaped lamp with the tortoiseshell shade on the foyer table as they headed to his bedroom. I knew the landscape well. From the street behind his house at night in the winter, with no leaves on the trees, I had a clear view in the sliding glass doors of his basement, where he was often on his computer playing with music.

Occasionally, I'd sit in my car in the parking lot outside of his office around lunchtime, watching for him to leave to see where he went and with whom. Knowing where he kept a house key hidden outside in a drain pipe to the left of the side porch, I would let myself inside periodically to thoroughly snoop around and check out his answering machine, caller ID, and computer.

A handsome male friend told me that he once had a woman crawl through his doggie door at two in the morning. I can smugly think, "At least I didn't do that!" (Steve didn't have a dog door or I'm sure I would have.)

It's hard for me to believe that I was actually one of those creepy stalker chicks. Even as I was committing my covert operations, I felt terribly ashamed and disgusted, but I couldn't stop myself, which only made me feel worse. Looking back, I feel bad for the woman who was so caught up in this man and so desperately looking outside of herself for love and validation. I'm sorry that instead of extending compassion and understanding to her, I was so harsh and judgmental of her. I was my own worst enemy. Steve was merely a reflection of my own beliefs about myself and played his part perfectly to allow me to act out my drama. With my father nicknaming him "the user" and my cousin calling him "Jimmie-lite", he was more than qualified for the role.

I now know that there was a physical basis for my obsessive behavior because of the chemical changes taking place in my brain. Studies have shown that romance happens primarily in our heads. Our brain sizes up someone as a potential mate in a game of "hot or not" almost instantly by unconsciously taking into account traits of the other person, such as symmetry of features, voice, and scent. If our gray matter likes what it encounters, a cascade of chemical changes occurs in the brain. Dopamine and norepinephrine are released to spark that euphoric in-love feeling. As the romance progresses, the stress hormone, cortisol, decreases and the love-bonding hormone, oxytocin, increases. Physical contact keeps oxytocin levels riding high.

In the brain, romance is identical to addiction. Studies using functional magnetic resonance imaging (fMRI) scans show that love lights up the brain's reward pathways in the same pattern as cocaine or nicotine. Being in love is a goal-oriented motivational state, and upon rejection, the "in love" neurons are still compelled to seek their reward, a fix of the lost love. Research shows that the brains of people who have been rejected, even weeks later, were still addicted to the love interest and go through withdrawals, just like with a drug. Heartbreak and physical pain are rooted in the same regions of the brain and intricately connected. Love really does hurt. Over time, the rejected person's brain adapts to their love's absence with neural circuits rewiring and neurochemical levels normalizing.

I never got off the dizzying merry-go-round of the romance long enough to give my brain time to stabilize. The capricious nature of my relationship with Steve, with sporadic but ongoing physical contact, joined with my emotional neediness and low self-esteem to forge a strong obsession.

In his book, *The Heart of The Soul*, Gary Zukav explains that this type of addictive sexual attraction is never really about sex, and the cravings signal a person's feelings of emptiness and desire for meaning, purpose, and value in life.[2] Weakness is drawn to similar weakness. The sex provides momentary relief from the physical urge, but doesn't satisfy the underlying emotional need. The addictive attraction is never really to the other person, but to the illusory image of that person and the promise of them fulfilling an underlying emptiness. According to Zukav, while such sexual interactions may seem intimate, they actually act as barriers to intimacy, because both individuals are exploiting the other seeking to fulfill their own need. Each person is both the predator and the prey.

After two and a half years of riding the crazy chemical love rollercoaster, Steve and I dated for four consecutive months in the beginning of 2007. My brain calmed down and didn't feel the need to spy on him anymore. During this time, Steve purchased a house 55 minutes away from the town in which we both lived because it was centrally located within his job territory, and his children lived another hour past the house. That's when I bought the vacant lot beside him, and with his encouragement and participation, began interviewing contractors to build a home on it.

Shortly after buying the lot, Steve broke up with me. Our joint plans had given me a false sense of security about our future together, and I'd fooled myself into thinking it was going to be different this time because we were taking steps towards a life together. I'd let my guard down and begun to live in my fantasy world again. As in my marriage, there were signals, like nights when he was inexplicably absent and unreachable on his phone or a woman's number repeatedly showing up in his recents, that should have jerked my ass right out of the fairy tale and plopped it squarely back into reality with a thud. But as I was so good at doing, I ignored them.

In the weeks following Steve's departure, we spoke regularly, and, like always, he strung me along, leaving the door open just a crack for the possibility of reconciliation. On his cell, I left a desperate message.

"We need to talk. I think there's a chance of salvaging us. I think we can work things out. But we both have to want it and really put some effort in. I'm willing to try. I hope you are. I need to hear from you by Tuesday. Please call me."

I left this voicemail before showing up at his house unexpectedly, feuding with him in his garage, and forcing three adults to hide in a closet. Since that incident, he'd gone silent, not returning my calls. On Wednesday, with no response from him, I attempted suicide.

*

I didn't hear from Steve for more than a year after I tried to kill myself. My father handled tidying up any loose ends, such as Steve buying the lot back from me and returning my personal items. He left me alone, thank goodness, as I wasn't a viable mind-tennis partner anymore, and in the condition I was in mentally, emotionally, and physically, I didn't dare contact him, no matter how much I thought about it and wanted to. Being as I was nothing close to the Debbie he'd known, the last thing I wanted was for him to see me like that.

My hunger for him was like my cravings for the cigarettes and wine. Although a very real urge existed on a physical level, I knew that there was no way it could be satisfied because the old Debbie simply didn't exist anymore.

When Steve reached out to me in the spring of 2009 through an email, I could tell he was carefully choosing his words, as if tiptoeing through a minefield. But before long, he was making me CDs and telling me his stories. Because of the brain injury, I didn't remember his history in detail and asked him to remind me. When the same phrases and jokes that I'd heard before hit my brain, I recognized the well-worn script.

While we never really dated per se, we were friends with benefits. We continued to see each other randomly over the coming years, probably when he was in between girlfriends. Or maybe not. I didn't inquire. Every interaction with him furthered my emotional healing, and amazingly to me, noticeable physical healing always accompanied emotional gains. Because our contact had ended so abruptly and painfully, I have no doubt the suicide attempt left unclosed wounds in both of us, and our reconciliation allowed us to heal.

Once again, Steve acted as my Shaman Lover, leading me out of the darkness. I guess because I still really craved him on an emotional level, he was one of the few people I let into my small post brain injury world. The limited interactions between us provided me with the opportunity to re-learn how to be a human being, who knew how to be around other human beings, at a time when I wasn't brave enough to associate with anybody other than close family members. With Steve, I got to practice the dynamics of being an adult again just doing the things normal adults do: chatting on the phone, dining at a restaurant, spending time with another person, and being interested in their day, their life, and what they have to say.

When browsing at the bookstore on a Saturday afternoon, I told Steve that I couldn't resist the aroma any longer and was going to get a latte at the in-store coffee shop. When I returned with my steaming drink, he said "That's OK. I didn't want anything. Thanks anyway." In his own way, he was teaching me that it would have been polite to consider the other person in this situation.

Steve was surprisingly non-judgmental and understanding during this period in my life when I was very vulnerable. Or maybe he had always been that way, and I just never noticed because I was too busy criticizing him. The fact that Steve wasn't ashamed to be seen with me in public, when I believed myself to be so inadequate, meant the world to me.

Albeit brain injured, I'd turned into his dream woman because I wasn't demanding, didn't latch on, and had no children in my daily life to have to work around. Steve's typical pattern of getting close and retreating, which I used to find infuriating and anxiety producing, was now just right. At a time when I felt completely undesirable and unlovable, I appreciated his sporadic but nurturing attention and was grateful that he didn't place a bunch of expectations on me or my time. Now that I had nothing, what had been too little before became more than enough.

I also got to practice making myself a priority and establishing boundaries with him, as all of my rehabilitation "must-do's" came before him. Not used to this kind of treatment from me, he asked, "Is there someone else?"

"Yes, there is," I told him, "me."

"You're not a giver anymore. We're both like the female end of an electrical plug now and just don't fit together anymore," he continued.

Although I know he didn't mean this as a compliment, it was an indication of how much healthier I was becoming.

He even taught me how to have sex again. While I did remember the basics, the rest came back like riding a bike, only with different motions, and I read books named *Blow Him Away* and *Penis Genius*. Steve was in his element in the role of sex ed teacher, and once again, I enjoyed being his willing student. There was an honest, vulnerable, and intimate quality to our relations that hadn't existed before.

"I think that was the best sex I've ever had," he said after one of our lessons.

Maybe we were finally authentically expressing instead of performing.

During the period of our involvement, I was reading self-help books (other than sex manuals) and consciously trying to apply what I was learning. The familiar pangs of attraction and wanting to hook onto Steve did show up, just as they had in the past. At one lunch date, I remember my physical response to him being like a dog salivating over a bone. The juices were flowing and I think I may have even foamed at the mouth a little. My body really, really, really wanted to act on the strong urges it felt, but I was damned determined not to behave in the ways I had that had landed me in the helluva mess. For the first time in my life, I started to observe my thoughts, wants, and bodily reactions without acting on them. I wanted to be like an oak tree standing tall and firm, instead of a leaf being blown around haphazardly by the wind.

One Saturday afternoon, Steve phoned giving me the, "Neither of us is dating anyone. I don't see why we can't just spend time together," spiel that had actually worked many times before. He'd fix his signature chicken and pasta dish with the homemade tomato sauce while I sipped a glass of red wine and chopped salad fixings. Then we'd cuddle on the couch, drink more wine while watching a movie, and end up in the bedroom. Oooh! My body wanted to say "yes", but my head vetoed the idea.

"I refuse to let lust rule my life anymore," I told him.

More and more in my dealings with Steve, I learned to intentionally choose my behavior and broke free from my knee-jerk patterns that had proven so destructive. When I'd find myself stuck in the old obsessive loops and urges, I'd literally argue with my thoughts, reframe my thinking, and consciously choose my actions in accordance with who I wanted to be.

When Steve called and told me "this just isn't going to work for me", I felt the familiar hurt initially, but instead of reacting, I reasoned with myself that nothing had actually changed. All that was different were the expectations and thoughts in my head that I had held about the relationship.

At Steve's encouragement I bought an iPod, which he loaded with music and taught me how to use. Once again, music built a bridge between us. The songs on that iPod were my closest companions over the isolated years of my recovery, like an ever-present friend who just always happened to be in whatever mood I was in.

*

Jimmie and I continued our legal entanglements for nine long years after we divorced, six of which were post brain injury. The lawsuit alleging that Steve and I had cohabitated was finally dropped as part of a financial settlement in 2012.

For both of these men, I have nothing but the highest appreciation and gratitude ¬– uh, now, that is – but believe me, I didn't when they were the leading men in my life. Without each of them playing their part of teacher so well, I wouldn't be who I am today. Pema Chodron tells us that if we learn to open our hearts, anyone, including the people who drive us crazy, can be our teacher.

I'm a much better person because of their influences and am able to make a more fulfilling and happier life going forward because of the lessons I learned during my relationships with them. Steve's always said, "If you like where you are, you can't complain about how you got there."

Some philosophies believe that on a soul level, before incarnating in the physical world, we enter into contracts with other souls to engage and interact with each other for karmic evolution and growth. All I can say is that, boy, these guys did a good job of upholding their end of the agreements!

I'm thankful to Jimmie for forcing me to step into my own power and become independent. Even after we divorced, he pushed me to become a self-sufficient, whole person. I'm glad to have finally graduated from his school. Picking up where Jimmie left off, Steve prodded me to be emotionally mature, come into my own power, and begin to love myself and others authentically.

These romantic relationships were all about physical attraction, ownership, and control. My understanding of love was the stuff of fairy tales because I believed that happiness, fulfillment, and completion could be found in the arms of another. This myth of love that I'd been fed since I was a little girl turned out to be dead wrong.

In Buddhism, love has nothing to do with desire or attraction; both are believed to be forms of attachment. Another Buddhist philosophy, that everything in life is impermanent, makes the notion of "happily ever after" false to begin with. Unhappiness and pain stem from trying to cling to a relationship in an attempt to make it permanent. When two people meet, it's already the beginning of an ending, and accepting that concept of impermanence is essential to unconditional love. A person must first love themselves before they can give or receive authentic love and find peace and happiness with themselves or anybody else.

Some final observations from my bathroom book are:

- *I have learned that a cat rolling around on her back in a sunny spot on the driveway can almost always make you smile even if you feel like you have nothing to smile about.*

- *I have learned that I should be more like my cat. She's independently aloof, entertains herself easily, and only allows those who have earned the privilege to touch her.*

- *I have learned that I tend to be more like my dog. If you show me some affection, I just might hump your leg, lick your face, and follow you around until you tell me to "go home!"*

- *I have learned that goodbyes are just as much a part of life as hellos and that you better get used to both.*

CHAPTER 13

So Much Healing, So Little Time

After ten weeks of outpatient therapy, it was scary as hell to hear the neurologist say, "Well, all we can do at this point is wait and see." His only advice to me was to sing out loud.

He might as well have told me to go home and twiddle my thumbs. At the time, I wasn't cognizant enough to have an opinion or ask questions, but knowing what I know now, his direction lacked a basic understanding of how neuroplasticity can be directed to repair the brain. All I knew then was that it felt pretty darn shitty to not be told of anything I could be doing to improve. I thought, "I actually have to do something to get better, don't I?" Unbeknownst to me, rest, lots of it, and time, were essential to let my brain heal as much as it could on its own.

However, I did like that without therapy appointments, I could sleep as much as I wanted and that everybody, for the most part, left me alone, which meant that I could make it through most days without having to perform even once. For the next year, I slept an inordinate amount, lived one day at a time, and even though I didn't know it, rewired my brain with the mundane tasks of everyday life acting as my therapy. Although I improved considerably naturally, I plateaued at around a year post-injury with impaired mental processing, unreliable short-term memory, and disjointed thoughts and speech. But I'd recovered enough to find my hard-headedness and get downright pissed off.

"There HAS got to be something else I can do. I'm NOT staying this way. If I'm going to live, it sure as hell isn't going to be like this!"

For the first time, my inner child stomped her foot, dug in her heels, and got bullheaded about investing in herself instead of somebody else and pledged, "I will get better, dammit!" Like a hound dog with its nose to the ground, I sniffed out every scrap of information that might lead to something to help me, and began doing all I could independently to improve. As the mental fog dissipated, the more determined I became, because I saw that what I was doing was actually working. The more I did, the better I got, and the better I got, the more I did.

Following every glimmer of hope I could uncover, working towards recovery became my singular pursuit from the minute I opened my eyes until my head hit the pillow again. For the first time in my life, I had no one else to focus on. My kids were gone. There was no man in the picture. All my friends had vanished. My parents had their own lives, and my brother lived all the way across the country. There was only me, and healing became my reason for being alive.

*

In February 2008, eight months after the suicide attempt, my friend Julie, whose pills I'd swiped, told me, "I've got a surprise for you, and I know you're gonna love it."

Although she wouldn't tell me where we were going, she did tell me, "Wear exercise clothes, and bring a towel and water."

"What in the world?" I thought.

She took me to a Bikram yoga class, which was unlike anything I'd ever experienced. She was right. I loved it.

A Bikram yoga class is 90 minutes of Hatha yoga in a room heated to 105 degrees with 40 percent humidity. Developed by Indian yogi Bikram Choudhury, a class consists of 26 postures with long, tongue-twister Sanskrit names. The heat increases flexibility and decreases the risk of injury, allowing a person to rework their body. Think of a metal sword. When cold, it's rigid and inflexible, but when heated, it becomes pliable. My first classes were excruciatingly long and difficult, but strangely satisfying at the same time. At the end of a class, I always felt like I'd accomplished something, but I wasn't sure what.

When I first started Bikram yoga, I was still in the mindset of the old Debbie, with the ego in full force: yoga was all about looking good and being better than everyone else in the room. Although this thinking got me through my first hard-as-hell hot yoga classes, it contradicts the basic philosophy of yoga. Over time, my attitude evolved, along with my practice, until yoga became about concentrating on the postures and being aware of my body and breath. On a good day, instead of trying to figure out what that tattoo on that girl's arm was, or if that guy was wearing a wedding ring, yoga was an experience between me and the mirror.

The heat and humidity in hot yoga led to profuse, almost comical, sweating, which is beneficial detoxification through the largest organ of the body, the skin. But it isn't pretty. After 90 minutes in the hot room, I literally looked like I'd been swimming but, ironically, I left the yoga room cleaner than when I went in. I can't say I smelled better.

Because of all of the pills I swallowed in the suicide attempt, detoxing was important to my recovery, and I would feel more clear-headed after every class. Three months after beginning yoga, I sweated through a challenge sponsored by the studio in which I completed 60 classes in 60 days. This sweat-a-thon cleansing was probably the best thing I could've done to rid my body of residual drugs. This happenstance was just one of many uncanny, perfect coincidences on my recovery journey.

Hot yoga greatly improved my balance and coordination, and helped relax muscles that were clenched as a result of the brain injury. Because breath is the most important element stressed in yoga, doing the breathing exercises helped me learn to breathe while talking again.

Any style of yoga has brain benefits, which isn't surprising considering that it started 5,000 years ago in India as a meditative–spiritual practice. It's actually a form of biofeedback in which you're retraining the brain's reaction to stress in the body. As you calm your breath and relax facial muscles while holding challenging postures, your brain learns to not automatically invoke a stress response. So, your brain figures out that it's OK to chill out even though your body is experiencing stress. Eventually, this pattern spills over into your life outside of the yoga room, and you find that you don't get so worked up when stuck in traffic, when the kids won't stop squabbling, or when rushing around frantically to meet a deadline at the office.

Studies have found yoga to be associated with increased gamma-aminobutyric acid (GABA), a neurotransmitter that tends to be low in people with depression and anxiety, and oxytocin, a hormone that helps the brain tune in to social cues and promotes bonding, and decreased cortisol, the stress hormone. Learning to consciously control the breath and focus the mind, both fundamental elements of mindfulness, are also pillars of yoga.

Practicing yoga helped my brain reconnect with my body and improved my balance, coordination, and spatial awareness. As I repeated a posture over and over, more neural connections were formed in my brain's body maps, and nerve fibers were created through my nervous system to that part of the body.

Yoga helped transform my life and facilitated my recovery physically, mentally, and emotionally. It encouraged me to adopt a healthier, gentler perspective towards life and myself. What I have learned in the yoga room has transferred to life off the mat. I went on to own a hot yoga studio with some other yogis, which I sold after a couple of years, but I'm still a hot yogaholic. My body and mind don't feel right without it.

*

When I heard about neurofeedback, it sounded like it might help me. So, I jumped on the computer and located the closest available services. Although the practice was much less common back in 2009, I was fortunate enough to find an experienced provider, Dr Durbin, just ten miles from my house.

Biofeedback, which is widely used and accepted, teaches a person to improve their health and physical performance using signals generated by their own body, such as heart rate and breathing. Neurofeedback is a specialized form of biofeedback for the brain in which a person's body learns to actually alter their brainwaves. The learning occurs at a subconscious level and results in permanent, physical changes in the brain.

Neurofeedback has been around since the 1960s but is still considered alternative therapy. However, the information I read indicated that neurofeedback had been successful in improving many conditions where the brain doesn't function optimally, including chronic anxiety, autism, ADHD, depression, brain injury, stroke damage, addiction, seizures, learning disabilities, and more. The therapy had also been used to perfect and heighten focus, concentration, and overall performance in the healthy brains of athletes or musicians. So, I was willing to give it a try. While I'm convinced by the wealth of research on neurofeedback and my highly successful personal experience with it, it's not covered by insurance or part of the standard medical system.

In neurofeedback, EEG sensors are placed on a person's head and ears to pick up their brainwaves at the sensor sites. Computer software monitors the activity and interprets the EEG data to provide visual and/or auditory feedback to the person training.

Training can occur in the context of a video game, like a rocket ship going faster or a Pac Man gobbling up dots quicker, when brainwaves meet the set criteria. When the brain doesn't perform to the desired level, the rocket ship stalls or Pac Man stops chomping.

When I first started, I would concentrate intensely, commanding my brain to perform, which was the equivalent of trying really hard to be psychic. This didn't work. Eventually, I found out that I didn't have to actually try to do anything because my brain learned automatically.

As we moved around training different sites on my head, I got to the point that I actually liked to initially get low scores because this meant that we'd discovered a part of my brain that could do some major improving. Better brainwaves meant a better me. I came to think of all my impairments from the brain injury in this way. Anything that was difficult for me was an arrow pointing exactly where I needed to focus my efforts to get the most gains.

I had just finished reading Lynn McTaggart's book, *The Intention Experiment: Using Your Thoughts to Change Your Life and The World*[1], in which McTaggart explains how our thoughts, intentions, and consciousness affect our lives and the world around us. Citing empirical data, McTaggart makes a strong case for the power of the individual mind and collective consciousness. I got the bright idea to have my brother Ken, one of the best brains I knew, contribute remotely to a neurofeedback session and sent him an email asking him to lend me some brain power at the time of my appointment the next day.

The next morning, my scores were consistently around 20 points higher than normal on every site we trained. It worked! I found out later from Ken that he didn't even read the email until after I'd completed the session. Something worked. I'd upped the scores with the power of my own mind.

Because neurofeedback is a learning process, the results occur gradually over time, as a brain makes permanent physiological changes allowing it to perform differently and self regulate even when not training. After my first ten sessions, my speech and thoughts came together. My sleep became deeper and more restful, which I believe allowed my brain to start doing some serious healing. Once I saw that the neurofeedback was working miracles, I did it as much as I could, up to four times a week. Dr Durbin didn't work on Fridays, or I would have done it five.

With my frontal lobe functioning optimally, maybe for the first time ever, my emotions stabilized, and I became calmer and more positive, with a stronger constitution than before the suicide attempt. Like the wind makes temporary ripples on the surface of a lake that then returns to stillness, the tumultuous emotions that I'd known all my life shifted to fleeting disturbances on the outskirts of my being, rather than earthquakes shaking me to my core.

As my memory and mental processing speed improved, time magically stretched out. "Time expanded again," I would excitedly inform Dr Durbin regularly.

With a faster brain, I had greater mental stamina, could accomplish more, and life became much easier. Before long, a good day included not just emptying the dishwasher, but also sweeping the floor, exercising, doing laundry, and maybe even running a few errands. My capacity continued to increase with the neurofeedback until I was what anyone would consider normal. I still took daily naps, but I didn't zonk out and have to sleep every few hours anymore.

Dr Durbin would train a specific site on my brain's motor strip, and I could feel the corresponding area of my body waking up, with a pins and needles sensation I named "the tinglies". My gait and body movements became more fluid and natural, while my balance and coordination were greatly enhanced. As the muscles of my hands and jaw relaxed, my manual dexterity and speech improved.

In addition to providing neurofeedback, Dr Durbin was a valuable resource for information and support. She suggested books, supplements, computer programs, and websites to better my brain, as well as social and educational activities to facilitate emotional, social, and mental healing. At her encouragement, I enrolled in a local self-improvement course and found a supportive community of self-help junkies.

Dr Durbin taught me how to breathe more effectively with a device called a capnometer and suggested that I do respiratory therapy on my own with a tool I bought online. Proper breathing is so important to ensuring that the brain receives adequate oxygen, and I needed to breathe right for my brain to work right. Who would have thought that I'd ever have to learn how to breathe?

Like a developing Polaroid picture with colors emerging and figures taking shape, I came back into being almost completely under Dr Durbin's care. Life became manageable, promising, and joyful even. After participating in neurofeedback therapy for a year and a half, I stopped seeing results and began searching for my next healing option.

*

In the dressing room after a yoga class, a woman was handing out business cards for her Body Talk practice. Encouraged by the results I was getting with the alternative therapies I had tried so far, I was interested in anything that might prove helpful. Summoning my courage, I spoke with her and took a card.

Body Talk is like acupuncture without the needles. It's based on the belief that the body innately knows how to heal itself, but like a computer, can get overloaded and malfunction. A Body Talk practitioner doesn't offer a diagnosis, just a "rewiring" session using muscle testing and light tapping on the head and sternum to re-establish channels of communication within the energy circuits of the body.

Not knowing anything about Body Talk, I went in for my first appointment expecting some kind of massage, and was surprised and disappointed when all the practitioner did was tap on my head and chest, and wiggle my arms around. But afterward, I was surprised that I felt emotionally lighter and more clear-headed. So, I went back. At one session, I was amazed to feel the traumatic 25-year-old memory of being raped in college exit my body from an area right above my heart.

Some believe that the trauma of our past experiences is stored in the musculature and connective tissue of our bodies, contributing to depression, creating tension, and blocking circulation, which can lead to pain and disease. Count me as a believer.

*

Also in the dressing room after yoga one day, a woman told me about the success she experienced treating her neuropathy with acupuncture. While she was initially skeptical, she had been astonished to find that acupuncture didn't just mask her symptoms and ease the pain; it resolved and prevented the condition.

By this time, I viewed my recovery as a scavenger hunt. Clues about where the next prize might be located could show up anywhere in my life at any time – especially in the yoga studio dressing room. It was my job to spot a clue, gather more information, and follow the lead.

After my first acupuncture appointment, the change in my perception was so profound that the drive home was scary. Buildings had sharper edges and the yellow lines on the road jumped off of the pavement. It was as if the lens through which I was looking at life had been focused. Strangely enough, I didn't even know that I'd been out of focus. My thinking was also faster, clearer, and more capable. As if I had taken a smart pill, my brain became more efficient and able to concentrate while I felt revitalized with increased life energy and strength. Even though my new way of seeing the world was improved, I found the unfamiliar view a bit unnerving.

For the first few years, I did cranial acupuncture, in which needles were stuck all over my head and attached via clips and wires to a machine that sent electrical impulses into them to provide stimulation. (Amazingly, I never did glow in the dark.) Evidence suggests, and I believe, that our brain is like a battery that, thank goodness in my case, can be recharged.

I've had acupuncture needles stuck almost every place imaginable: in my ears, fingertips, wrists, in between toes, and behind my knees. While they didn't really hurt, I can't say that the needles felt great going in. Once in place, however, I couldn't feel them at all – unless I moved. If I fidgeted during treatment, which could last 30 minutes or more, I experienced what was like small electrical shocks where the needles were inserted. So, I tried to do my best impersonation of a corpse.

When the inevitable itch happened, I learned to experience the sensation literally for what it was: my brain's interpretation of some electrical impulses, labeling it an itch, or my butt falling asleep, or whatever. The "whatever" was up to me. It's interesting to experience an itch without automatically and mindlessly scratching it. If my brain doesn't define it as something that needs to be scratched, it becomes just a sensation. In this way, acupuncture was not only a remarkable healing tool but also an exercise in mindfulness.

Acupuncture has been practiced for over 2,000 years and is based on the belief that there are energy channels called meridians running throughout the body. These meridians carry Qi or chi, life energy. Illness or pain occur when energy becomes imbalanced or blocked along these meridians, and acupuncture restores the natural flow. Medically proven to speed healing, improve circulation, and increase nerve growth, acupuncture is backed by science. Studies have shown that painkilling endorphins and important mood regulating transmitters are released throughout the body when acupuncture points are stimulated.

I continued acupuncture long after I recovered from the brain injury for wellness support, computer elbow, and other aches and pains that popped up. An acupuncturist's goal is to support the body to maintain wellness, rather than treat the symptoms of sickness.

*

Although I rarely watched television, I had an undeniable sense one afternoon that I just had to watch *Oprah* because I had a strong feeling there would be information on the show that I needed. When Dr Oz came on talking about the healing properties of hyperbaric oxygen therapy (HBOT), I knew immediately that that was the message for me.

I found a private HBOT practice located 15 miles from my house. Like neurofeedback, I was very fortunate in this situation as well because HBOT facilities were few and far between, then and now, and an independent service not affiliated with a medical center and not requiring a doctor's prescription was even rarer.

Like neurofeedback, HBOT isn't new and isn't part of the established medical system in the United States. However, it is more readily used in European countries and Canada. Upon researching it, I found a wealth of scientific evidence confirming its substantial health benefits. The American medical community, however, has failed to accept it as of yet, and few insurance companies will cover it, under any circumstances. HBOT was in the press for a while because Michael Jackson slept in a HBOT chamber, proclaiming it to be his fountain of youth. Often used by athletes to optimize performance and heal injuries, HBOT is also gaining popularity as an effective cancer treatment.

In HBOT therapy, a person is exposed to increased atmospheric pressure in a room or inflatable chamber, permitting them to breathe pure oxygen at a higher level than found naturally in the atmosphere. The extra pressure allows a person's blood to dissolve up to ten times more oxygen, which not only increases the oxygen in the blood but also permits it to pass into tissue, cells, and the brain more easily. After continued HBOT treatments, the tissues of the body are permanently changed.

Initially with HBOT, I experienced substantial healing on all fronts, but the most dramatic benefit was mental. Like the sun bursting from behind clouds, my brain fog cleared and the invisible veil of the brain injury that separated me from the rest of the world evaporated as I returned to full consciousness. I've continued HBOT over the years, as maintenance, and still feel it working its magic. If I go too long in between sessions my speech suffers, but then improves immediately after time in the chamber.

Over decades of offering HBOT services, my practitioner has witnessed many "little miracles" as she calls them. One client post-stroke came in using a walker, couldn't speak, and had little sensation in her hands. After a year of HBOT, she was walking with no aid, spoke normally, and was happy to be able to feel it when she burned her hand on the stove. My HBOT provider has also seen several autistic or brain damaged children begin to speak and people with paralyzed limbs regain movement.

In my opinion, HBOT can aid the body with just about anything, and has been proven to be beneficial for a wide variety of conditions. HBOT is the most effective treatment for the type of brain injury I had, encephalopathy, which, sadly, no medical professional ever told me. It's also the first-line treatment for anoxic brain injuries, where the brain is deprived of oxygen, which may have also been a factor in my case. HBOT is proving to be so helpful with traumatic brain injury and post-traumatic stress disorder cases in war veterans that the Federal Government is actually starting to endorse and offer treatment.

*

Norman Doidge's book, *The Brain That Changes Itself* [2], became my bible during my recovery. I even gave a copy to my neurologist and told him that he needed to read it. (This was not an isolated incident. I'm sure he loved me!) If I had to single out one spark that ignited and fueled my recovery, it would be the information within the covers of this book, with the subtitle, *Stories of Personal Triumph from the Frontiers of Brain Science.*

Backed by scientific research, Doidge tells of the astonishing adaptability of the brain, and in doing so, turns many "truths" touted for decades about the brain, upside down. Researchers and doctors used to believe that after childhood, the brain was hardwired and not capable of significant change. Like a machine or computer, the brain could accomplish many impressive things, but also like a machine, it was believed that it couldn't rewire itself or grow new parts. Wrong.

In the 1990s, it became widely, scientifically accepted that the brain is malleable or "plastic" and continually changes according to stimuli received. This phenomenon, known as neuroplasticity, means that the brain and nervous system change structurally and functionally as a result of input, including experiences, behaviors, and thoughts.

Learning about neuroplasticity and recognizing how I could utilize it infused me with so much hope, because here in black and white was evidence that my brain could repair itself. I'd discovered a magic wand. While my injury was unique, the principles in the book weren't, and on its pages were detailed instructions for how to fix my brain. All I had to do was adapt the information, get determined, and get busy. This knowledge was in part responsible for my obsessive drive, because I understood that whether I recovered or not depended on how hard I was willing to work for it. Repairing my brain was up to me.

Your brain is like Play-doh, minus the funky smell, because it's malleable and constantly changing. The gray matter between your ears physically adapts every day in response to everything: actions and behaviors, senses and perceptions, thoughts and imagination, and whatever else happens in your world.

This "plastic paradox", as Doidge calls it, can work both for and against you, because an incredibly resilient brain is also a very vulnerable brain.

The same neuroplasticity that allows a person to alter their brain in positive ways also carves not-so-good habits into their brain. Over time, neuronal connections strengthen because of repetitive action or thought: binging on Netflix, indulging your sweet tooth, having a cocktail to unwind, smoking cigarettes, biting your fingernails, or worrying. These activities become wired into the brain and can become addictions. People have cravings because their plastic brain becomes sensitized to a substance or experience.

When the craving is satisfied, their brain gets a shot of dopamine, the feel-good neurotransmitter that's an essential component of neuroplasticity. The same squirt of dopamine that makes someone happy when a craving is fulfilled also assists in making the neuronal connections that lead to addiction. When a person quits a habit, neuronal circuits become weaker and less active over time without reinforcement.

There's a catch to neuroplasticity. It only occurs when a person is paying attention to and focusing on the stimuli, whether intentionally or not. With deliberate intent and action, you have the ability to change your brain and life for the better. Neuroplasticity has the potential to improve brains in many situations, ranging from mental illness to addiction to injury. Neuroplasticity also has significant implications for every aspect of human nature and culture, including medicine, psychiatry, psychology, relationships, politics, business, and education. Doidge writes, "Any change in how we understand the brain ultimately affects how we understand human nature."[3]

I leveraged the power of neuroplasticity to heal my brain. Like Dorothy in *The Wizard of Oz* discovering that the ruby slippers already on her feet possessed the ability to transport her home, I had the magic wand in my hand, or head, all along. Something as drastic as a brain injury had to happen before I actually bothered to read my brain's owner's manual to figure it out.

The science of neuroplasticity is relatively new, with unknown limits. Neuroplasticity doesn't mean that our brains are infinitely malleable, but it does mean that we've grossly underestimated what our brains are capable of. Neuroplasticity unleashes a world of possibilities. On a personal level, each of us has the power to change our life. On a broader scale, the same brains that practice prejudice, hatred, and warfare have the potential to be kinder, more compassionate, and less aggressive.

*

After discovering my brain's incredible morphing ability, my life became all about sculpting my brain. I determined that the best way to encourage neuroplasticity and neurogenesis, the birth of new brain cells, was through aerobic exercise. Scientific evidence shows that physical exercise is MiracleGro for any brain at any age. Research has documented that exercise increases the production of new brain cells, various neurotransmitters, a group of chemicals called nerve growth factors (BDNF), angiogenesis, the formation of new blood vessels, and blood and oxygen to the brain.

To experience the most brain benefits, you ideally want an exercise that gets your heart pumping while keeping your head working, like ballroom dancing for example. However, studies show that even walking at a comfortable pace for 40 minutes three times a week can enhance the connectivity of brain circuits, combat age-related decline, and increase performance on cognitive tasks.

Spurred by vanity, I'd already been going to the Y and working out regularly. Little did I know how well my ego had been serving me. To encourage neuroplasticity, I began exercising no less than 30 minutes daily, usually longer. Every day. No excuses. Again, my obsessive tendencies worked to my advantage here. With no job, no kids around, no friends, and no relationship, I didn't have much else to do. What seemed like awfully pathetic circumstances were actually perfect for me to work at my recovery full time.

I started jogging with my senior Jack Russell Terrier, whose short legs and need to sniff and leave what I called "pee mails" every few feet had me running in one place a lot, but that was OK. My goal was just to keep moving. A small lake with a one-mile paved trail was a block from my house, and two times around was a perfect workout. Releasing my old pal from his leash, I would pass him on my first lap and pick him back up on my second.

At first, the coordination of my arms and legs wasn't smooth when jogging, but over time, running became more natural, as my brain made the necessary connections. Because of neuroplasticity, I knew that physical actions performed repeatedly would rewire the corresponding parts of my brain. Hence, if I found a motion awkward or challenging, I understood that this was precisely where I needed to work to rebuild pathways in my brain.

After running every day, I'd complete various activities to direct neuroplastic growth in specific parts of my brain. I did jumping jacks, or tried to, rather. At first, my hands and feet wouldn't cooperate despite my chanting, "Hands up, feet open. Hands down, feet closed."

With each hand, I bounced and threw a tennis ball and caught it, not allowing myself to quit until I had ten successful catches in a row, gradually raising the bar to 50. My son's idle basketball saw action again as I practiced dribbling and took shots at the hoop on the garage. Once I mastered dribbling the ball, I added movement while dribbling and thinking up animals' names starting with each letter of the alphabet, like in rehab.

While I can't say that I ever got good at it, I tried to juggle. In this case, becoming proficient wasn't as important as just performing the movements repetitively. I wouldn't let myself be finished until I'd tossed the beanbags up ten, 20, then 30 consecutive times without dropping one, even if it meant standing there until my arms ached. Of course, almost every time, a beanbag would inevitably hit the ground on the very last rotation. Dang it!

After attending a "jump and pump" aerobics class at the Y, I added jumping rope to my post run activities. At the class, I ended up having to hold the rope and jump in place because I couldn't skip rope to save my life. Soon after, I bought a rope and vowed, "I WILL jump rope again like a third grader, dammit!" When I could hop over the thing 20 times without getting tripped up, I beamed with pride.

In other classes, like kickboxing or tai chi, I had to watch, learn, and try to execute movements in time with the rest of the group. Again, I used difficulty as an indication of where I needed to concentrate my efforts to make neuroplastic improvements. Because the movements were challenging, they were good for my brain, but not my ego. By this time, I did realize that other people's attention wasn't focused on me, and even if it was a little bit, I didn't care that I looked goofy, because I was on a mission.

After months of running every day, I began to mix up my daily exercise. Initially when swimming laps, I gulped mouthfuls of water because I couldn't coordinate the arm strokes and breathing. After hours in the pool, my brain figured it out. To work on my lung strength and capacity, I forced myself to breathe only a few times while crossing the pool. Eventually I could swim laps regularly with only one breath and pushed myself to swim a few every workout without taking a breath.

Often, I cranked up the tunes and danced around my bedroom for exercise. Before the brain injury, I used to love to dance. After, I could manage a convincing robot, but didn't move well enough to be comfortable dancing in public. I still enjoyed getting my groove on with no one watching though. When dancing, I incorporated cross-lateral movements that involved crossing the midline of the body with the arms and legs, for instance, touching a knee or shoulder with the opposite hand. Cross-lateral movement forces the two sides of the brain to work together, speeding up communication and strengthening pathways.

Crawling is a cross-lateral movement that fundamentally wires the brain. Babies crawl before walking for good reason. Every day, for months, I got on all fours and crawled around the house, which was surprisingly hard work for me, but lots of fun for the dog. Getting all excited, he'd weave in and out of my legs and arms thinking that I was down on the floor to play with him. So, I'd make a game of it, throw his squeaky toy, and we'd race to it. He always won.

I discovered rebounding – bouncing on a mini-trampoline – to be great fun and an awesome workout. Rebounding provides detoxification benefits through the lymph system, which is the metabolic garbage service of the body. Lymph fluid bathes your cells, delivering good stuff and taking away the bad, and it relies on the movement of your body to work. Several times throughout the day for months, I would hop on the mini-tramp for a two-minute health bounce. Rebounding has been shown to improve everything from sleep, depression, digestion, lymph edema, and more.

I still rebound today for a convenient workout. Collin keeps me supplied with techno music that's just right for energetic bouncing with its fast thump, thump, thump.

*

During the second year after my brain injury, in my "try anything and everything phase", I incorporated weekly massage. I specifically sought out a massage therapist who specialized in craniosacral therapy, which combines massage with chiropractic care. The craniosacral system includes your brain, spinal cord, its surrounding membranes, and cerebrospinal fluid. The therapy gently works with the bones of the head, spinal column, sacrum, and the pulse of the cerebrospinal fluid, and isn't what you typically think of as massage.

Like Body Talk, the technique employs a very light touch with holds to release restriction and compression along the craniosacral system. The practice feels like energy work and has been scientifically proven to yield valid medical benefits for many conditions. Craniosacral massage aided me in relaxing tense muscles and helped my body to become more balanced.

Physical touch signals the brain to release oxytocin, the feel-good neurotransmitter most closely associated with orgasm and breastfeeding. Oxytocin has been shown to buffer the effects of stress, ease pain, and aid the neuroplastic process. Human contact, bonding, and touch are as essential to a person's well-being as sunlight, food, and water. Since I wasn't getting hugs from my boys or anyone else, the massages provided me with nurturing human touch.

My massage therapist was trained to work with temporomandibular joint (TMJ) disorders, would put on plastic gloves, and work inside my mouth on my jaw joints. Massaging here proved helpful in easing muscle tension, resulting in clearer speech.

At three years after the suicide attempt, I'd made significant progress in my recovery, and probably appeared normal to the casual observer. Although I wasn't quite all of the way there yet, life was leaps and bounds better than it had been three years earlier. I'd adjusted to my solitary existence and had even grown to like it. Being alone was now my comfort zone, and although I was becoming more at ease in the company of others, it was still a taxing, nerve-wracking effort. Whenever I knew that I was going to be around people, or even when my kids came to visit, I would feel anxious.

Even though I spent almost all of my time alone, I was far from bored. I kept a packed schedule with my must do's: exercise, yoga, brain training, meditation, and my therapies, and had become active on Facebook, where I'd joined brain injury, stroke, and other brain related communities. Reading the postings of the other people online, I often had the "me too!" feeling and took comfort in knowing that I wasn't alone. While communicating with a brain buddy, I learned about Brainwave Optimization® (BWO).

Based on the same principles as neurofeedback, BWO utilizes computer technology to identify brainwave imbalances and make adjustments in real time during therapy sessions. Similar to neurofeedback, BWO is a non-invasive method that guides the brain to a balanced state of functioning by placing sensors measuring the electromagnetic energy of brainwaves at specific sites on the head. A computer translates the brainwaves into sounds that represent and train optimal patterns for the brain, which are fed back to the trainee via earphones. All the person receiving the treatment does is sit in a comfy chair, listening to strange bing, bing, bong, bong music while colorful waveforms chart their brain's activity on a computer screen.

Like many of the therapies that were proving successful for me, BWO wasn't backed by scientific research yet, and wasn't widely available, but that didn't concern me. What mattered was if I saw favorable results. Fortunately, I located a provider an hour from me who had just opened for business, and I was her first client in April 2010. Another uncanny coincidence?

The first step in BWO is for the practitioner to assess the current functioning of the brain to determine treatment. During the assessment, I watched the computer screen charting my brain activity like I had during my neurofeedback sessions. When at rest, a calm, balanced brain should have low activity that is fairly stable and consistent. The screens depicting my brain activity at rest looked as if someone had angrily and erratically scribbled all over them with black marker. The practitioner administering the test managed to hide her shock at the time, but later told me that my brain maps were the worst she'd ever seen and knew right away that I was in for a long training regimen.

One BWO treatment consists of ten sessions. I did 80. I'd drive the hour up there, complete a session in the morning, break for lunch, do another in the afternoon, and drive back home. With BWO, I crossed the finish line to fully become myself again. While it didn't happen overnight, returning to full mental capacity finally happened. Technology in the area of neurofeedback has quickly evolved and improved. Today, there are many therapies offered, similar to BWO, which train the whole head at once and are much faster. I have done multiple sessions over the years with other systems, as maintenance, and always feel that I benefit.

*

I took all of my rehabilitation "must-do's" very seriously for years, because I knew that if it was to be, it was up to me, and as far as I was concerned, it was going to be. I saw every minute of every day as time to work on myself and heal my brain, which meant I didn't socialize, date, watch television, or talk on the phone. If I was awake, I was working on improving my brain.

Gathering miscellaneous supplies, I did my own manual dexterity rehabilitation exercises daily. I shuffled and dealt cards, stacked cups and coins, picked up rice and beans with tweezers and chopsticks, learned to knit (or tried to), colored with crayons and markers, wrote longhand, and twirled a pencil between my fingers. For years, I sat at the computer completing brain training for an hour or more every day.

Motivated by the knowledge that if I took a break, the formation of new pathways in my brain would also take a break, I was as militant about my cerebral workouts as I was about my physical workouts. Neuroplasticity must have consistent repetition and focus to happen. I discovered free online sites with puzzles, word games, and memory challenges, and bought brain training software. As I write this, the scientific community is still testing and debating the effectiveness of computer brain training, but I can tell you without a doubt that it helped me dramatically and was crucial to my recovery.

In the third year after my brain injury, I sought out and

worked with a speech pathologist at a local university. This was after visiting the speech therapist covered by my insurance and being told that there wasn't anything they could do to help me. The speech pathologist determined that I had a voice, not speech, impairment. For six months, I shouted, sang, and made funny faces as we worked on volume regulation, voice strength, air control, and not bursting into sentences or trailing off at the end. I had to re-learn the speaking mannerisms that had come naturally to me before the injury and unlearn the bad habits that I had adopted since to compensate.

I left every session with more exercises to practice at home. Turning the radio off during my hour's commute to and from BWO, I'd pass the time and miles with my vocal homework, singing songs, or reciting nursery rhymes. I also got reacquainted with Dr Seuss and other childhood favorites while reading out loud daily.

In my fourth year post injury, I gradually phased out many of my daily must do's, deciding that I could live with writing and talking a little funny, and could accept it if I never improved any further. At some point, I decided that I had to stop getting myself prepared to live and actually start living. Although the thought scared the shit out of me, I longed to break out of my protective shell and become part of the real world again.

CHAPTER 14

Healing From The Inside Out

For most of my life, my mind hasn't been my friend. My brain has bullied, ridiculed, criticized, doubted, abused, and limited me. And that was on a good day.

For sure, all of the ugly shit really happened; there's no denying that. But I was the one who poured salt on my wounds by dwelling on the trauma, and replaying the painful scenes over and over in my head. By bringing the past into the present, I kept hurts alive that should have been long dead and buried. The realization that I was torturing myself was a colossal "aha!" moment for me, and I figured that if I was doing it, I could stop it. With this radical departure from the victim philosophy that I'd subscribed to my entire life, I found the motivation to heal my mind, body, and spirit.

It's been irrefutably proven that the mind and body are intricately linked in ways not fully understood. I know this to be true first-hand, as I witnessed the relationship time and again during my healing journey. Carolyn Myss, a medical intuitive and author, writes in her book *Why People Don't Heal and How They Can*: "An awareness of the innate connection between our body-mind and our spirit can catalyze a healing."[1] She asserts that healing and change are actually one and the same, and that a strong, focused willpower is essential for repairing physical tissue. In the first year after the brain injury, her book became one of my guides for spiritual and physical recovery.

Myss proposes that people don't heal for a number of subconscious reasons; one being that a person becomes defined by their injury. Participating in a brain injury support group at a local hospital, I saw this in action. Although I did find it comforting to be in the company of others whom I felt weren't judging my deficits, I got irritated that these meetings often turned into "woe is me" gripe sessions. I didn't want to sit around, eat Cheetos and cupcakes, and commiserate about all that was wrong. I wanted to talk about what we could do to make our brains and lives better.

After flooding the group with too much "helpful" information in emails and meetings, I stopped attending after a year. Although I was still impaired and frustrated by my challenges, I simply refused to allow my brain injury to define me and my life. I was more, and wanted more for myself.

According to Myss, another reason people don't heal is that their illnesses give them permission to live reduced lives, with minimal expectations and responsibilities. Sickness allows a person to rely heavily on others and holds a certain amount of power. Often, being healthy is equated with being alone. Already by myself, I didn't have anyone around to lean on or manipulate, or I guarantee you that I would have tried.

As any situation in life, health challenges and healing can be approached from the perspective of either a victim or a learner. The attitude we choose either increases our fear and struggle, or healing and wisdom. For the first time in my life, instead of feeling like I'd been sucker punched without a damn thing I could do about it, I was damned determined that I was going to decide how this story played out.

*

Like a good girl, I went to the requisite mental health professionals immediately after the suicide attempt. Nobody quite felt like the right fit, but I played the game, said what they wanted to hear, and appeared to make progress. Although it didn't do much for me, my seeing a shrink made everyone else feel better. In the past, I hadn't found therapy to be all that helpful, and I didn't then either, even as messed up as I was. I'd always thought I was smarter than the therapist, not in an arrogant way, but in an "I know more about me than you do" way. Although I was never dishonest, I made sure that this was true because I wasn't completely forthcoming and never gave anybody a chance to be of any real help.

Unconsciously, I concocted an image of myself for the counselor, like I did for the rest of the world, and because I was the creator, I worked their professional wisdom right into my picture, assigning whatever meaning I wanted to it. In other words, I may have received wonderful advice, but my skewed perspective colored it so that the teacher couldn't teach because the student wasn't ready to learn. The picture I painted of myself wasn't angelic by any means, but I wasn't finished being the victim and blaming everyone else yet.

Going to counseling had proved to be an expensive, nonproductive practice for me in the past. Treatment after my suicide debacle was no different, and I quit seeing a mental health counselor after six months. Besides not finding the therapy beneficial, it was impossibly difficult for me to talk for an hour. Around this same time, I also stopped taking my antidepressant cold turkey. During the six years I'd been on a happy pill, I attempted suicide twice – not too successful in my book. Although ending the drug abruptly worked fine for me, I understand it's recommended that a person wean themselves off an antidepressant gradually with the support of their doctor.

Immediately following the suicide attempt, my family considered sending me to one of those expensive, inpatient mental health facilities for an extended stay. I envisioned a spa that you read about the rich and famous going to after they shave off all their hair and rip up a picture of the Pope on live TV, or whip out their willy and urinate in public at 9.00 in the morning wearing a woman's evening dress. It would be equipped with a well-stocked workout room, couches with overstuffed cushions, and seafoam green walls.

But my family couldn't find one appropriate for me because I couldn't talk or write, which excluded programs including discussion groups or journal keeping. Despite my inviting vision of a rehab facility, I decided that if I was going to get better emotionally and mentally, it had to happen inside of me and didn't matter if I was at home or some fancy facility in Arizona. I have no idea where that brave person had been all of my life, but it was about time she showed up!

A girlfriend mentioned that her sister had seen good results with a local, energetic healer. Always having had an interest in spiritual, new agey stuff, I was intrigued. Five months after the suicide attempt, I contacted the healer and began bi-weekly visits.

Lakota, a tall, thin, wise-looking man, had adopted the Native American name, and it suited him. Instead of a framed degree and professional certificates, pictures of enlightened beings and thank-you cards from people he'd helped dotted Lakota's walls. Although his only training was 60 plus years in the school of life, Lakota helped me more than any of the mental health professionals I'd been to up until then, who had impressive initials behind their names.

At the beginning of a session, we'd talk for 30 minutes during which he'd counsel me and guide me through Emotion Freedom Technique tapping, a form of psychological acupressure. Then I'd lie on a massage table for 20 minutes while he hummed and waved his hands over my body, working with my energy, while the CD of his Indian guru chanted in the background.

In our talks, Lakota shared his colorful, hard-won wisdom with me and after a few weeks, I started to hear the same anecdotes over and over. Either Lakota had memory issues or he believed in learning through repetition. He told me his story about the Charles Manson documentary at least ten times, but I do remember it and the point. So, job well done, Lakota ...

Charles Manson, a convicted serial killer, who became an icon of evil in the late 1960s, headed a hippie cult, "The Family", whom he manipulated into brutally killing others. The documentary portrayed Manson's hard childhood, filled with emotional and physical abuse. To his surprise, Lakota found himself actually feeling compassion for this brutal killer. In the same way, he guided me to find compassion for the "evil" people in my life. He taught me to consider their possible perspectives, reasons, and wounds that may have caused them to behave as they did, rather than assuming ill intent. Lakota helped me realize that others' behavior towards me has very little to do with me.

By showing me that all of us are "doing the best we can with who we are at the time", Lakota encouraged me to extend compassion to others and myself. As I adopted this philosophy, I slowly began to unclench my fists and release the fear, anger, and pain that I'd held onto for years. Just by shifting my perception in this way, the world became a kinder place with less suffering for me, and the past was forever changed because I could now view it with compassion.

Lakota also suggested books for me to read, supplements to take, and continued to tell me the same stories as well as some new ones over the next year. Lakota died of pancreatic cancer four years after I met him. On the day after Christmas in 2011, my brother, Ken, and I sweated through a Bikram yoga class. After class, I told him that I'd had the strong sensation that Lakota had visited me in spirit to tell me goodbye during the class. I later found out that he'd transitioned during that time.

*

While under Lakota's tutelage, I was reading voraciously, trying to heal and grow on my own emotionally. If anyone had seen me during this time, they would have surely thought that I was still suicidal, or crazy, or both. I would have long crying spells, and I don't mean that I shed a few dainty tears. I mean whole-body, shoulders-heaving, snot-pouring, can't-catch-your-breath, wailing sobs. A dam had burst in me and all the pent up tears that I never cried in the years past came rushing forth. During these crying jags, I'd sometimes pummel the bed, throw pillows, and scream at the top of my lungs. Because my injured brain didn't have a stranglehold on my emotions anymore, I was finally free to express myself fully.

All of the feelings that it absolutely wasn't OK to show during my marriage came gushing out of me. The grief and fear that I hadn't allowed myself to express in the aftermath of the divorce spewed forth. The pain of Chris' sickness and death bubbled up and oozed out. I couldn't have stopped the purging if I'd wanted to; and I didn't want to, because even though it wasn't fun, I knew that it was exactly what I needed to do.

In his book, *Waking the Tiger*, Stephen Levine explains that animals are routinely threatened in the wild, but are rarely left traumatized, because unlike humans, they naturally complete the cycle of shedding the residue of stress.[2] Levine suggests that humans have the natural capacity to do this too, but often don't allow it simply because we don't know how, or because doing so would be viewed as socially inappropriate. According to Levine, emotions may be unblocked and trauma healed through heightened awareness and somatic exercises. My body was instinctively expunging the past.

I also learned in my readings that by repressing and denying negative emotions, I hadn't been allowing myself to fully experience positive feelings either, because happiness and sadness are at opposite ends of the same spectrum. By blocking the pain, I'd been diluting the joy. Like darkness and light, one cannot exist or have meaning without the other, a concept known as duality. Understanding duality led me to perceive emotions as neither good nor bad, but as tools with which to work, heal, and grow. To open myself up to the whole range of emotions is to allow myself to be fully alive.

I read about and listened to CDs of Abraham-Hicks, offering an emotional guidance scale that ranges from joy, appreciation, empowerment, freedom, and love at the top; and fear, grief, depression, despair, and powerlessness at the bottom. To promote better feelings and a sense of peace, I would figure out what level I felt about an issue and choose a thought about it that took me higher up the scale. It didn't work to jump from a yucky bottom feeling all the way to a workout sensation instantly. The idea was to choose a believable thought that made me feel a little bit better and took me a few notches up the emotional scale, and then keep reaching.

Abraham-Hicks has a worldwide, sometimes over-zealous, cult-like following with seminars, workshops, retreats, and cruises. Although I never drank the Kool-Aid and became immersed in the philosophy, I did find a few of the concepts beneficial. That's all that was important to me.

I applied the attitude of "does it have value for me?" to everything from physical therapies to spiritual philosophies. It didn't matter if something could be proven scientifically, was backed by a huge following of believers, or was some far-out, never-heard-of, airy-fairy practice. What mattered was whether it worked for me. I was willing to reserve judgment, give anything a try, and see for myself.

As I began to express the pain I'd bottled up my whole life, I began to feel never-before-felt levels of joy and appreciation. Life became more vibrant. I know how corny it sounds, but I felt like I was in a toothpaste commercial with sunbeams bouncing off of my smile when I saw puffy white clouds floating in a brilliant blue sky. If a purring cat curled up on my lap, I was filled with warm fuzzies. I'd grin and giggle randomly at my own happy thoughts. When visiting, Ken asked more than once, "What 'ya smiling about? What's so funny?"

Along with expressing pent-up emotions, extending compassion and forgiveness to myself and others was a necessary step in my healing journey. Following the advice of several books, I performed guided meditations and sent long emails to Jimmie and Steve forgiving them for whatever I felt they needed to be forgiven, and asking for forgiveness for whatever they felt I needed to be forgiven in turn.

I wrote emails to family and friends apologizing for disrespecting our relationships by trying to kill myself, and for my behavior immediately following the injury when social controls weren't yet functioning in my brain. Although some people responded compassionately, others replied with "How could you?" I understood both.

Honest and open talks with my sons ensued, with me apologizing profusely for being ready to abandon them and throwing their lives into chaos. Although they were forgiving and expressed some anger, I expect that we're going to have many more talks as they confront wounds and give words to feelings in the future.

Forgiveness really is a gift that you give to yourself. Carolyn Myss, in *Why People Don't Heal and How They Can*, suggests that forgiveness frees up a person's energy necessary for healing. In *The Seekers Guide*, Elizabeth Lesser writes, "Humans are just inches away from paradise, but that last inch is as wide as an ocean. That inch is forgiveness."[3]

From your brain's perspective, forgiveness requires making a deliberate decision to move beyond feeling hurt or wronged by consciously shifting your perspective and attention, reframing thoughts, and pairing sad or disappointing memories with more positive thoughts. This practice, when done repeatedly over time, builds new neuronal pathways in your brain through neuroplasticity. In *A New Earth*, Eckhart Tolle proposes that forgiveness is just another word for non-reaction. Learning to forgive is teaching your brain to not react.

After decades of hoarding resentment, grudges, and hurt, I was a newbie to the practice of forgiveness, but better late than never. I started to feel lighter, as though I had set down weights I didn't even know I'd been lugging around for a long time.

*

The brain map completed before starting neurofeedback therapy showed brainwaves consistent with extreme anxiety, which I definitely felt then and in the past. In many of the books I was reading, meditation was suggested as a mental health tool to relieve stress and quiet the mind, and Dr Durbin recommended it to calm my brainwaves.

Ken, who'd practiced meditation for most of his adult life, told me that meditation was letting your thoughts settle like sediment in water. Huh? Lakota told me that meditation was observing your thoughts like watching a mouse hole for a mouse. What the heck? I'd always heard that meditating was observing your thoughts like clouds floating by in the sky. Yeah, yeah, yeah. While I understood that meditation was about clearing and settling the mind, I didn't have any idea how to do that. So, I did what I'd become so good at and scoured countless "how to" guides, watched instructional videos, and listened to guided meditations.

In the beginning, I meditated for 15 minutes three times a day, figuring that frequent sessions would settle my brainwaves more effectively than one long session. At first, I put pressure on myself to meditate "the right way" and to make something happen. I didn't know what exactly. Anything. Although I now know that this expectation is counter to the purpose of meditation, it was typical of me then, and of many who are just starting a meditation practice.

I discovered that there are many different flavors of meditation – some plain vanilla versions and others with exotic names like Zazen, Tonglen, and Dzogchen. Some meditation techniques are considered religious or spiritual practices, while some are deemed to be mental health tools. Regardless of the belief system or technique, most meditation methods have three components in common: focusing on something simple and non-thought provoking like the breath, a single word, or sound; consciously relaxing the body; and exercising an unattached awareness of the mind.

Until I found my niche, I explored meditating with my eyes open looking into space; staring at a candle flame; focusing on a single carpet thread; peering through my eyelashes; and with my eyes closed. Eventually, I settled on meditating with eyes closed and ambient music playing in the background. In my opinion, there's really no right way to meditate, within reason. What's right is whatever works for me that day. Trying to meditate is meditation as far as I'm concerned, and I count any time spent with the awareness and intent to practice as meditation. Meditation isn't about achieving anything or reaching some desired state. It's about getting to know yourself and working with your mind.

Exercising a detached awareness of the mind was ridiculously difficult for me at first, as it is for most people, but that's the biggest benefit of meditation. I read somewhere that during one 30 minute meditation, a person may have more than 300 thoughts. (That number seems low to me.) Building awareness of and less attachment to thoughts takes time, which is why meditation is called a practice.

I've been meditating for years now. On some days, my mind is like popcorn popping, and I'll find myself composing an email, reminding myself to pick up spinach at the grocery store, or diagnosing the crud in the dog's ear. After wondering, "How in the heck did I get here?" I let go of the thought and return to my breath.

The goal of meditation is to objectively observe thoughts and not identify with them. Eventually, this non-reactive, observant thinking transfers more and more into everyday life and becomes a way of being: mindfulness, instead of just an exercise on the meditation cushion. Mindfulness is about being fully present in the moment and aware of your thoughts, feelings, actions, and the world around you – and being aware of that awareness. The practice of mindfulness brings greater calmness, clarity, and insight in facing and accepting all experiences, even the uncomfortable ones, and using them to learn, grow, and deepen your strength and wisdom. Mindfulness is an internal compass giving you guidance by which to live. Adopting mindfulness was the single most beneficial change I made for my mental health and my life.

Water assumes the shape of the container into which it's poured. Like water, an untrained mind is molded by whatever random events arise. A trained mind maintains its form: calm, peaceful, and happy, regardless of what happens. Meditation and mindfulness allow a person to achieve this feat by observing their thoughts and emotions, rather than identifying with and reacting to them. It's like the difference in a person recognizing that they *feel* sad, not that they *are* sad.

The concept that I wasn't my thoughts or emotions was a radically new one for me. In the past, I believed that I was a horrible person because of some of the thoughts that crossed my mind. Although I still have shocking, not-so-nice, and wacky ideas – we all do – I don't define myself by them anymore. Through meditation I've learned to accept and release the ugly thoughts and negative feelings, rather than reject, repress, or identify with them, which some evidence suggests contributes to depression and sickness.

To me, meditation is training to consciously control the mind – not what originates in my mind, but my reaction to it – to consciously choose my thoughts about my thoughts. Although no one can expect to control the arbitrary thoughts that pop into their head, they can choose which ones to believe and put energy into. Herein lies the ability we all have to be happy and find peace.

While meditation can be a spiritual practice or mental health tool, or both, on a physical level, a person is altering their brain function by learning to change their response to their thoughts. Through neuroplasticity, regular meditation and mindfulness practice strengthens connections and expands circuits in the brain that are frequently used while weakening and shrinking those areas rarely engaged.

Ample research is currently being conducted to determine the effects of mindfulness and meditation on the brain, and initial results are promising. Studies have shown meditation to improve information processing, decision-making, memory formation, and the ability to maintain focus. A mindfulness practice can expand the hippocampus, responsible for learning and memory, and damaged first by Alzheimer's, and has been connected to lower rates of depression. Brain scans of meditators show more activity in parts of the brain associated with positive emotions and reduced activity in areas related to negative emotions. Regularly giving your brain a workout with meditation has been found to prevent the normal shrinkage of the brain that happens with age.

The benefits of meditation and mindfulness aren't limited to the brain. Meditation has been proven to strengthen the immune system, reduce blood pressure and risk of stroke, and minimize pain sensitivity. It's now known that a healthy emotional style and mental habits can be intentionally cultivated and learned like any other cognitive skill through mindfulness and meditation. It's powerful stuff!

My meditation practice was folded into what I called my "healing time", which I did every day for years. A comfy wicker chair by an east-facing window which captured the morning sun in my bedroom became my cozy healing corner. On nice days, if I turned the chair to face the window, I could run through my routine while basking in the sunshine.

WhenIfirstbeganmeditating,Icouldn'tnotthink.Becauseofthis, my healing sessions consisted of a series of mental exercises with very little time spent focusing on my breath and truly meditating.

After a bit of emotional freedom technique tapping, I ran through an extensive list of people to whom I sent love and light. Next, I completed a series of affirmations and visualizations dealing with whatever issues were concerning me at the time. Instead of worrying about something, I learned to deal with it in my meditation corner in a positive way. Only for about the last ten minutes did I try to clear my mind, observe my thoughts, and meditate. Over time, I gradually decreased the mental exercises and began to meditate for longer periods.

What I find so beneficial about meditation is that it gives me a specific time to calm my mind and focus inward, and provides an outlet to express emotion, question and analyze my thought processes and motivations, and try on different perspectives. Meditation is whatever I need it to be that day. It's the closest thing to a happy pill I've found. The truth is that meditation is damn near impossible for me to define because it's fluid, always morphing, and evolving. No matter what it is, it's always good for me.

*

My healing time also included visualization, beneficial make-believe, which leverages the mind-body connection, and the link between the visual brain and the involuntary nervous system. In visualization, the same process is at work as when you watch a scary movie. As the bad guy sneaks up on the pretty, unsuspecting lady and the music gets creepy, your heart races, your breathing becomes shallow, and the muscles in your neck tighten. Your body reacts even though your mind knows it's just pretend.

On brain scans, both imaginative thoughts and real-life physical and emotional states activate many of the same areas of the brain. From a neuroscientific perspective, imagining something and doing it aren't all that different. The thoughts, words, and images that run through your mind create constant changes in your body.

In his book, *The Brain That Changes Itself*, Norman Doidge describes an experiment in which two groups exercised a finger muscle for four weeks.[4] While one group actually did finger contractions, the other group just imagined doing them with a voice, like a coach, shouting for them to work harder. At the end of the study, the first group increased their muscular strength by 30 percent, while the visualization group increased their muscle strength by almost as much at 22 percent. Doidge explains that during the imaginary contractions, neurons responsible for movements fired, resulting in the added strength.

Doidge also describes experiments involving amputees with painful phantom limbs. After 12 weeks of therapy in which the amputees just imagined moving their missing limbs, the pain completely disappeared in half of the cases.

When I started visualizing, my mangled brain was in bad shape, but amazingly, almost everything I spent time seriously visualizing eventually came to be. Although the accomplishments didn't occur anywhere near quick enough for me, they did eventually happen. Because connectivity was a challenge for my brain, I imagined it making contact like an old-timey, telephone switchboard. My maternal grandmother was a switchboard operator at a residential hotel in the late 1960s. I would picture her sitting at the switchboard with the headset perched on her jet black, pin-curled hair, plugging wires for the incoming calls quickly into the holes for the requested rooms. Just as she connected the phone lines, I saw my brain making the necessary links to allow communication within my head.

As I healed, the images I visualized naturally evolved. After the switchboard, I envisioned the wooden cabinets holding the card catalogue filing system in the library at my elementary school and finished with the image of a computer doing a speedy Google search. On my way to the lake to run each day, I passed a house whose front yard had a large bed of well-established English ivy. I imagined the connections in my brain growing and intertwining like the densely tangled roots of that ivy.

I pictured my hand holding a pencil and writing, in elegant cursive, every letter of the alphabet and signing my name beautifully. In my head, I heard and saw my lips speaking fluidly and effortlessly with sharp, clear enunciation in a steady, strong voice. Because converting thoughts into words wasn't a seamless process, I'd visualize a gurgling brook, flowing over a pebbled streambed, to represent how easy, smooth, and natural speaking was. In my head, my speech wasn't impaired at all.

Visualization can be used in any situation. It's recognized as a mind-body therapy especially effective with stress-related health concerns, and has proven successful in bettering performance, changing behavior, and influencing an outcome. When you cut your finger, you don't have to tell your body step-by-step instructions to heal the wound. (Thank goodness!) The human body just miraculously and automatically has the inner wisdom and power to heal itself, and I believe that visualization allows a person to consciously direct this innate force.

*

Your body hears every thought you think and every word you say. The constant chatter running through your mind affirms your beliefs and attitudes, and is most often subconscious and largely critical or negatively rooted in emotional wounds, fears, and doubts. Becoming aware of and directing this mental energy to work for you, instead of against you, can positively impact your life.

As we grow up, we all learn beliefs and attitudes about ourselves, others, and the world around us, and learn how to conduct ourselves through the influence of family, religion, school, culture, and life experiences. For a while, we adopt these perceptions without ever questioning their authenticity or appropriateness for us as "just the way things are".

In her book, *The Four Levels of Healing*, Shakti Gawain shares a story to illustrate how subconscious beliefs can control our lives.[5]

In India, when training baby elephants, trainers begin by chaining one hind leg of the animal to a tree. The elephant becomes accustomed to the chain, and soon, it doesn't even try to break free. The trainer then reduces the size of the chain until all that's restraining the animal is a thin string. It's not the tiny string that holds the mighty elephant. It's their belief.

Gawain writes that our unconscious beliefs cause us to view the world through colored glasses without even realizing that we're wearing them. We believe the world is just that hue because it's what we've learned to believe, like the elephant. Because we interpret and interact with the world through these core beliefs, they tint every experience we have. We can become aware of this filter, noticing our thoughts and inner dialogue. Then we may choose to take the glasses off, and consciously see the world differently.

When first becoming aware of this inner voice, you may be surprised at just how harsh it is. Mine used to be a real witch. She constantly told me that I wasn't a good enough wife, girlfriend, mother, etc ... I couldn't possibly make it on my own. I needed a man. I wasn't smart enough or strong enough, blah, blah, blah. This bitch provided plenty of fuel for the anxiety, panic, and depression that led to my suicide attempt.

The first step to quieting the inner critic is to become cognizant of your thought patterns and core beliefs, especially those pesky ones that repeatedly pop into your head and govern your decisions and behavior. Notice which ones support you and which ones hold you back. Once you're aware of your limiting beliefs, you can make your mind your friend and supporter by consciously choosing to change the thoughts by using affirmations, visualizations, or thought reframing on the spot, during introspective time, or meditation.

Affirmations, or positive self-talk statements, can be used on their own to combat the inner critic, or as part of visualizations. My healing sessions included a lengthy list of affirmations, and although I didn't really believe the affirmative statements at first, they weren't so far out that they felt completely fake. In every case, my feelings evolved to match the affirmation over time, and each visualization had an accompanying affirmation. For example, in the connectivity visualization illustrated by the switchboard, card catalogue, and computer, the affirmation was, "My brain is well connected and can send and retrieve information quickly and efficiently."

*

It's well documented that directed thoughts, as with visualization and affirmations, can affect the body. Research has also demonstrated that human intention can even impact other living systems such as bacteria, mice, cats, and dogs. In one experiment, human thought influenced the direction in which fish swam.

We've all heard and probably even uttered the old quip, "I'll believe it when I see it!" What if – just what if – you had to believe it to see it? Reading the book, *The Intention Experiment*, by Lynn McTaggart, blew my mind and altered my perception of reality. She writes:

A sizable body of research exploring the nature of consciousness, carried on for more than thirty years in prestigious scientific institutions around the world, shows that thoughts are capable of affecting everything from the simplest machines to the most complex living beings. This evidence suggests that human thoughts and intentions are an actual physical "something" with astonishing power to change our world. Every thought we have is tangible energy with the power to transform. A thought is not only a thing; a thought is a thing that influences other things.[6]

Studies in quantum physics have shown that living things are constant transmitters and receivers of measurable energy. At the most basic level, thoughts are simply bundles of electromagnetic energy that can move beyond physical boundaries. According to McTaggart, "Intention appears to be something akin to a tuning fork, causing the tuning forks of other things in the universe to resonate at the same frequency."[7]

Picture two sticks stuck in the sand on the beach right at the edge of the ocean. A wave rolls in. Both sticks fall down. If you didn't know about the wave, you might think that one stick affected the other. In the nerdy world of quantum physics, this phenomenon is referred to as nonlocality. My technical explanation of nonlocality is the ability of one thingy to affect another thingy over any distance despite there being no exchange of energy. Just as scientifically, Einstein called it "spooky action at a distance". Nonlocality is real and has been scientifically verified by physicists since 1982.

The concept of nonlocality is the basis for some popular belief systems, such as The Law of Attraction. All too often though, the idea has been overly hyped, promising that anyone can get rich, find the person of their dreams, or get skinny effortlessly just by thinking the right thoughts, like a universal vending machine. While I don't believe it's anywhere near that simple or direct, let's assume for a minute that there's some truth to the basic premise of a thought's ability to influence other things.

If you're constantly worried and thinking about how you don't have enough money to cover all the bills, how are those thoughts going to influence your reality – if they do at all? If you worry unrelentingly about getting cancer and freak out at every little ache, pain, and bump, what kind of energy are those thoughts subjecting your body to? If money is tight, but you believe in your competence, trust in your ability to handle the situation, and focus on the abundance that's present in your life, how's this going to influence your body and world?

American culture practically condones worrying as being responsible and mature. When I began converting my anxious thought patterns, not stressing was so foreign to me that I felt like I was irresponsibly sticking my head in the sand. Although I don't advocate throwing caution to the wind and ignoring probable consequences with a "Who cares?" attitude, I found that not dwelling on or feeding my worrisome thoughts did a lot to help ease my anxiety and increase happiness.

I learned to recognize the negative, without giving it any more attention than necessary. Instead of worrying, I invested my energy into positive action in the direction I wanted to go, while not exerting unreasonable effort to force any one outcome. Eventually, I became able to stay open to and accepting of whatever materialized – which was, more often than not, not what I wanted or expected – and find the wisdom and benefit in it. There was always good to be found, even if something seemed bleak as hell and made absolutely no sense when first showing up, like my boy's visitation being stopped.

In any situation, my go-to question became, "How do I make this work for me?" I focused on the possibilities rather than the problems. Relieving my anxiety, increasing happiness, and accomplishing forward movement in my life determined where I put my energy and swayed my decisions. With this approach, I found that any situation could be "a success" and even unpleasant scenarios became more tolerable as I moved through them.

*

Mary Engelbreit said, "If you don't like something, change it; if you can't change it, change the way you think about it." An anonymous saying goes, "Life is like a kaleidoscope. Turn your head to a different angle to see it a whole new way." Both of these quotes refer to our ability to choose our perspective in any situation. Every spontaneous thought that pops into your head is subject to that subconscious, internal chatter colored by your conditioning. (Remember the elephant's string?) At any time, you have the power to say, "Hey, wait a minute! That belief doesn't work for me anymore. Let's look at it this way." Thought reframing, consciously becoming aware of thoughts and repositioning them, was a life-changer for me because it pulled me out of my depressive, negative thinking patterns.

What I found so effective about thought reframing is that I didn't have to strive to not have negative thoughts, nor did I feel the need to criticize myself for having them in the first place. Many cultural philosophies and religions are guilt-based, teaching that a person is bad and should feel shame for even having unsavory thoughts. But under no circumstances can a person ever control what thoughts come into their brain. We don't even generate these. The mind does on auto mode.

Don't believe it? Try predicting what your next thought is going to be. If you controlled them, you would know, right? Attempting to govern the origination of thoughts and berating yourself for not being able to do so is a self-defeating struggle. All anyone can ever take charge of is what they do with the thoughts that do arise. This knowledge empowered me with concrete and positive action I could take no matter how negative, inappropriate, or unhealthy my thoughts were, because I didn't have to judge them or me anymore.

Thought reframing can be a part of affirmations or visualization, or can be practiced on the spot. With repetition, through neuroplasticity, the practice has been proven to physically alter brain circuits. Like scratching poison ivy only makes it itch worse, the more you indulge anxious, negative, painful ruminations, the more frequent and persistent they become because your brain gets wired that way. In *Hardwiring Happiness*, Rick Hanson explains:

... [F]eeling stressed, worried, irritated, or hurt today makes you more vulnerable to feeling stressed, etc., tomorrow, which makes you really vulnerable the day after that. Negativity leads to more negativity in a very vicious cycle.[8]

We have brain circuits constantly scanning the environment for danger, ready to activate survival reflexes to keep us safe and these instincts have survived millions of years of evolution for a good reason: our protection. However, even though we aren't likely to have to escape being a saber-tooth tiger's dinner today, our brains still respond to common stressors as though they were life-threatening events. Robert M. Sapolsky, a Stanford University biologist, explains in a TED talk, *The Psychology of Stress*:

What stress is like for 99% of the beasts on this planet is three minutes of screaming terror on the savannah after which either it's over with or you're over with. We turn on the identical stress response for a thirty-year mortgage.[9]

Not all stress is bad though. Beneficial stress, called eustress, in the right amount, at the right time, can be motivating, invigorating, and productive even, such as the rush someone feels before making an important presentation or before competing in sports, for example. But chronic distress, the kind that makes you want to stomp on the accelerator and plow through the cars in front of you when stuck in traffic, has detrimental effects on the body. In his book, *Why Zebras Don't Get Ulcers*, Sapolsky writes:

Stress can wreak havoc on your metabolism, raise your blood pressure, burst your white blood cells, make you flatulent, ruin your sex life, and if that's not enough, possibly damage your brain.[10]

Jeffrey Schwartz, M.D., combined his interest in Buddhist philosophy with neuroanatomy research in the late 1990s to pioneer a therapeutic process of thought reframing. His four steps, as explained in detail in his book, Brain Lock, are relabel, reattribute, refocus, and revalue. They have been proven to rewire brains and change the behaviors of those with obsessive compulsive disorder (OCD).[11]

Although I was never formally diagnosed with OCD, I've definitely had the tendency all my life, which peaked right before the suicide attempt. After reading Schwartz's book, I put the four R's to work rewiring my brain. I typed up, printed out, and taped colorful reminders of the four steps to my computer, on the refrigerator, in my meditation corner, on the bathroom mirror, and even on the dashboard of my car. Every time one of those pesky, recurring thoughts that led to the depression, stalking, and suicide attempt reared its ugly head, I'd march through the four steps.

Like a reassuring parent to a child, I told myself, "Those are just signals in your brain taking the path of least resistance. You aren't going to think that way anymore!" My being hell-bent on not being a slave to my unconscious mind anymore led to an almost comical tug-o-war with myself. Over time, with dogged determination and religious repetition, the new me victoriously pulled the needy, obsessive me across the line into the mud puddle.

*

As already portrayed, I didn't have the highest regard for mental health counseling. Intermittently, for at least a decade before my divorce, I sat in many stylish offices, spilled my guts, paid good money, and didn't get much out of it. Although I may have felt better immediately, there wasn't any real, lasting change, and I ended up on antidepressants for years and still tried to commit suicide twice. I now realize that the whole process failed miserably, largely because of me.

In the winter of 2010, having stopped therapy and antidepressants two years earlier, I decided to see a mental health counselor in anticipation of going to court to seek removal of the supervision requirements for my children's visits. Although three years had passed since the restrictions were put into place right after the suicide attempt, I figured that I'd need a stamp of approval from a mental health professional that I was mentally healthy and not a threat to the children or myself. Jimmie's lawyer had repeatedly cited my preference for alternative therapies and dismissal of the Western medical system against me in court. I knew that it would shut up the other side and give the judicial system more confidence in me.

In my first session with Dr Hill, a psychotherapist, I confessed that I was only sitting on her couch because I needed her to be a witness for me in court. Although I didn't come right out and say it, I'm pretty sure she could tell that I thought the whole exercise was a waste of my time and money. By now, my ability to talk, although still not normal and effortless, had greatly improved, and I dumped out my story in all its ugly detail. I imagine that Dr Hill must have been thinking, "I've really got my work cut out for me with this one!"

I was pleased to find that Dr Hill had read many of the same books I had, and counseled in a mindful, enlightened manner. Finally, here was a mental health counselor from whom I could really learn something. When the student is ready, the teacher appears.

Dr Hill guided me through letting go of the kids emotionally and accepting our unusual living situation, while still being able to contribute to their lives as positively as I could, without placing a bunch of expectations on them or sacrificing my own happiness and goals. This process happened over years, in baby steps. My identity as "the mother" required a delicate extraction from my former identity that was all tangled in the "should" of society and the court. Shedding the mother role required that I form a new self-image, and the more life I breathed into the new me, the more I released my grip on the old Debbie.

Dr Hill advised me during the remaining legal battles with Jimmie and helped me to distance myself from him as much as I could emotionally and financially, while closing the deep emotional wounds from our life together. She helped me to understand that, even though the court rulings concerning the children weren't fair or reasonable, I'd invited the legal presence into my life through my own actions, and guided me to focus on improving my current situation while making sure that I never opened myself up similarly again.

Like a mother bird gently pushing a baby bird out of the nest, Dr Hill encouraged me to take the final steps in becoming independent and responsible for my own life and happiness. In the beginning, she'd call me at home and correspond via email in between our weekly sessions if I needed extra guidance and support, which I often did. I gradually learned to handle life on my own and rarely needed to contact her in between appointments anymore. Then, I reduced our sessions to every other week, and eventually to only once a month.

After three years of being my therapist, Dr Hill retired and it was her professional opinion that I didn't even need to start up with another counselor. I graduated! Oh, and she was a very strong expert witness for me in court.

Dr Hill practiced a form of talk therapy known as cognitive behavioral therapy (CBT). CBT is based on the premise that your thoughts and beliefs about yourself, others, and the world, directly affect your emotions and behaviors. Hence, if you change the way you think, you can alter your feelings and actions. CBT requires committing to and routinely implementing new thinking and behavior patterns. Unknowingly, I'd already been employing my own homegrown version of CBT with the practices in my mental health tool box.

CBT may take weeks, months, or even years of consciously employing new behaviors because it leverages the neuroplastic process, and studies have shown that CBT fosters permanent changes in the brain. In their book, *The Winner's Brain*, Jeff Brown and Mark Fenske tell of a study that found CBT more effective than antidepressants, and unlike medication, the benefits of CBT lasted after the therapy ended.[12] Adopting different thought and behavioral patterns recruits new neural networks that forge fresh connections and pathways in the brain.

CBT isn't a quick fix, but it does successfully rewire the brain over time. Fenske and Brown ask you to think about how long it took to acquire the behaviors you want to change in the first place. Good point. I'd spent four decades unconsciously carving pathways in my brain that sabotaged me at every turn, like trenches concealing enemy snipers. Because of the injury, my brain and I were finally becoming allies. I was learning to use it, instead of it using me.

CHAPTER 15

In a Cage With the Door Wide Open

"Too cool!" A rainbow of tropical fish dart about in synchronized clusters, while others huddle together in stationary groups as though one little swimmer is a comedian with some good material. Patches of coral and vegetation dot the lagoon floor, clearly visible through the crystal clear water. I inspect the pinkish coral, looking like mounds of brains, while the plants resembling eerie hands with too many long fingers wave at me, and the lacy fans sway back and forth with the current.

The cool water hugs my body. I can't believe it! I'm actually snorkeling in Hawaii. Even with my messed-up brain, life isn't so bad after all.

I'd flown to the west coast from North Carolina in early February 2008, seven months after the suicide attempt and brain injury, met up with Ken, and we flew to Hawaii. Packing for the trip, taking the cab to the airport, getting my luggage and myself on the plane, and navigating the airport maze to catch the connecting flight had me buzzing with anxiety and made my underarms wet.

Even before the brain injury, traveling alone would have put me on edge. Now, I was through-the-roof nervous, and worried thoughts raced through my mind. What if the cab driver wants to chat? Will he be able to understand my directions? Will I be able to figure out how to check-in and find the gate? Where did I put my ticket? Oh yeah, it's in my pocketbook. For the twentieth time, I check to make sure that my ticket is tucked right where it's supposed to be in the outside pocket.

Planning my traveling wardrobe carefully, I'd managed to cram everything I needed for one week and two different climates into a carry-on suitcase so I wouldn't have to check luggage, which was a good thing, but gave me something else to fret about. Will I be able to hoist the damn thing into the overhead bin? Hope nobody can smell my pits when I do that. Puhleez, don't let some weirdo be sitting in the seat beside me who's already taken up all the overhead space above our row.

Now, I know that I can halt this nervous chatter by coming into the present moment, but I didn't know that then. Fast forwarding through all the worst possible scenarios in my mind, I only made myself more on edge by the minute with each imagined catastrophe.

Everything about traveling was nerve-wracking for me, but I first had to get through airport security before I could stress about all of the other stuff to follow. As I'd learned to do with almost everything after the brain injury, I studied the people before me passing through the checkpoint. When it was my turn, I piled my purse and magazine in the blue plastic bin and positioned it and my suitcase on the moving belt just as I'd seen others do before me. Following their examples, I slipped off my shoes and stuck them in a container on the moving belt. "So far, so good," I exhaled.

The security attendant motioned for me to walk through the X-ray scanner. Beep! Beep! Beep! I'd set the alarm off. Shit. The guard then motioned for me to go back through the scanner mumbling something about my belt assuming that I knew what to do, only, I didn't have a clue. I hadn't seen anyone take their belt off.

I looked street smart, not like someone who never got out of the house, but because of the brain injury, everything was new to me. Of course, the security agent didn't know this. While the line impatiently shuffled behind me and after asking for clarification three times, the attendant finally explained, in step-by-step detail, that I needed to remove my belt and place it on the conveyor to be scanned.

This was exactly the type of incident of which I was terrified and tried my damnedest to avoid because I didn't want to draw attention to myself, or God forbid, have to speak to someone. In the early days after the brain injury, dread of these kinds of situations held me hostage in the house. I now realize that the people behind me in line just wanted me to hurry the hell up, and no one gave me a second thought beyond that. Even if they did, what did it matter? It didn't. Although I understand this now, back then I wanted to crawl under a rock.

When out in public after the injury, when my brain wasn't operating at full capacity, I often had that panicky feeling of a terrified five-year-old separated from her parents at the mall. Many times, I thought, "It'd be a lot easier if I wore a big bandage on my head or maybe a T-shirt that said 'Brain Injured'. At least then, people might have a little patience and understanding." The person that needed to have patience and understanding with me, was me.

At other times, I cheered myself on thinking, "You can do this." Although I found the whole brain-injured-woman-traveling-alone exercise incredibly intimidating, I also felt a liberating rush to be accomplishing these trivial tasks that people did every day without a second thought. It was tempting to remain safe in my house, but somehow I knew that I had to push through my fears to regain anything close to a normal life. And every little accomplishment I achieved on my own, whether it was flying across the country or taking the car in for an oil change, put me one step closer to that life.

Once I met up with Ken, we flew from Sacramento to Hawaii in first class. Although this wasn't typical of the old me, the post-brain-injury Debbie lived in the moment. Today, I wouldn't spend the extra cash to upgrade, but we thoroughly enjoyed the extra legroom, full meals and "free" drinks on the six-hour flight, and we especially liked the salt and pepper shakers in the shape of little airplanes.

Consulting a travel book to schedule our sightseeing, Ken proved to be a competent tour guide and looking for a more authentic experience of the island, he planned our excursions venturing off the touristy beaten paths. On our first full day, we set out in our rental car for Honomalino Bay, which promised good snorkeling in a picturesque setting. "A true gem of West Hawaii and rarely crowded," promised the guide book.

Upon parking at a public park and walking a little way to the bay, we were delighted to find a scene that looked just like a picture on a postcard. All that was missing was the, "Wish you were here!" Leaning palm trees loaded with coconuts flanked a black sand beach, leading up to azure water with gentle waves rolling onto the shore. Other than a small sailboat bobbing serenely in the middle of the bay, there were no signs of life anywhere. Quickly stripping down to our bathing suits, we donned our snorkeling gear and waded into the water.

At first we were content to swim around the bay, oohing and aahing at the sights under the surface. Having never snorkeled before and not as physically coordinated as I used to be, I took a while to get the hang of breathing though the tube while keeping my face planted in the water. After five minutes, I felt more comfortable with it, but kept checking to make sure Ken wasn't too far away.

I followed him along the right coast of the bay where it opened up to the ocean. Here the ocean floor was uneven, shallow in some places and much deeper in others, with large black lava rocks jutting up out of the water near the shore. The waves and current were much more forceful here.

Kicking some rocks under the water, my right fin slipped off and sunk to the bottom about ten feet below. Without the fin, I quickly discovered that I wasn't nearly as strong a swimmer, and the waves tossed me around mercilessly. At this point, just keeping my head above water with the waves continually pounding me was a struggle. As I gulped salty water, my heart thundered in my chest with the alarm I'd imagine an antelope feels when being chased by a lion. This was life or death.

Splashing around frantically, I managed to make it over to a group of rocks, and partially climb onto them, cutting my hands, feet, and legs in the process. Although perching here did provide respite from being pushed around by the water, the coral-covered rocks were slicing my skin upon contact.

Ken, who had been snorkeling nearby, noticed my distress, hurried to the nearest land, scrambled out of the water, and shouted at me to stay on the rock while he ran to get my sand shoes. Because it was a fairly long distance to where we'd dropped our clothes on the beach and was taking him a while to get to them, I decided to swim to the sailboat in the middle of the bay while he was running with his back to me. It felt like a better option than clinging to the razor sharp rocks.

After what seemed like the longest swim of my life, I reached the sailboat, managed to grab the top of the side of it, and squeaked out "help" several times, in between gasping for air. A thin scruffy-looking man with shoulder-length white hair wearing nothing but cut-off jeans came up on deck. He looked surprised to see a bleeding bikini-clad woman hanging from the side of his boat. For a few seconds, he had that "WTF?" look, like he couldn't decide if he was really seeing what he thought he was or if he'd just gotten hold of some potent smoke.

He quickly came to his senses, assessed the situation, and pulled me over the side of the sailboat onto the deck. Then, lowering a small wooden boat into the water, that I, less than gracefully plopped into, he rowed me ashore. My hippie hero!

Although I was out of breath and could barely talk understandably anyway, I managed to communicate a garbled but sincere "Thank you."

When I got to the beach, Ken was relieved, but not happy. He'd gone back to the rocks with my shoes only to find me gone. After frantically screaming my name and anxiously scanning the water, he spotted me hanging on the side of the sailboat.

"Do you have any idea how scared I was when I didn't see you on the rocks?" he asked.

"I'm sorry. They were slippery and cutting me. So, I took off for the boat."

"I'm just glad you're OK," he said, hugging me.

Not only did this close call shake me up pretty badly, but it was also a meaningful lesson that I didn't fully figure out until I returned home. Seven months earlier, I had tried to kill myself and was still undecided as to whether I wanted to live. I wanted to kill myself before, and now I was supposed to want to live, seriously mentally impaired, and sounding like I was drunk? I wasn't convinced.

I realized that instinctively, without all the drama of weighing the pros and cons in my head, something inside of me had just kicked into high gear and fought to live. I could've easily slipped under the water and finished what I'd started months earlier, but I didn't. I wanted to live. There wasn't any decision to be made.

This near drowning incident was a major turning point for me in my recovery. It showed me that my mind had been creating the sob stories about how unbearable life was, while my innate instinct, when faced with life or death, was to fight pretty damn hard to survive. For decades, I'd been doing a convincing snow job on myself and had been believing all of the depressing crap my mind conjured up. My head had been getting in the way of my spirit, whose natural essence was life itself.

After I had that realization, I started acting like I wanted to live. Instead of waiting around for a miracle to happen, I took responsibility for my recovery and my life, and started working to make a miracle happen. I tenaciously dedicated every day to rehabilitating and improving myself and my life. A few grains of black sand remained in my foot after one of the cuts healed to remind me of the valuable lesson I learned that day.

The trip to Hawaii proved to be a healing experience on several fronts. Ken, a compassionate and spiritual soul, encouraged me to talk about my feelings, past and present, with him. When visiting the island's volcanoes, he urged me to leave some of my pain and anger with the fiery mountains. We spent time in nature, explored botanical gardens, savored leisurely meals, rocked a reggae festival, napped on the beach, reminisced, and laughed.

Staying at a bed and breakfast on a coffee plantation, which served sumptuous breakfasts with the best coffee, of course, I found the trip nourishing to both my heart and soul. It was just what I needed at just the right time. And although I never braved snorkeling again, Ken did.

*

On the Hawaii trip and throughout my recovery, Ken was the one person, other than my mental health counselor, with whom I could express raw and uncensored emotions. He served as an empath, sharing my pain and sorrow, and helping me process it. Having a person with whom I could be emotionally naked without fear of judgment was invaluable and crucial to my healing.

There aren't many people who can just listen to and be with another person when they're in extreme pain without trying to deflect emotions, fix things, or offer solutions. I used to think that Ken was unsympathetic, detached, and somewhat uncaring, but now I can see that he was always nudging me to grow beyond my perspective of the victim. Most people want to shut down another person's emotion quickly due to their own discomfort with it.

Because I had already attempted suicide, my expressing emotion had to have scared the bejeebies out of others and probably had them wondering, "Does this mean she's going to try to kill herself again?"

Eckhart Tolle calls being able to be present with another's emotion as having "Presence." In his book, *A New Earth*, he tells of being present with a woman and calming her down in a situation that had her extremely agitated, but wasn't ultimately all that important in the overall picture. She wanted to know what he'd done to her. He explains:

Instead of asking what I had done to her, perhaps she should have asked what I had not done. I had not reacted, not confirmed the reality of her story, not fed her mind with more thought and her pain-body with more emotion. I had allowed her to experience whatever she was experiencing at that moment, and the power of allowing lies in noninterference, nondoing. Being present is always infinitely more powerful than anything one can say or do, although sometimes being present can give rise to words or actions ... The thinking mind cannot understand Presence and so will often misinterpret it. It will say that you are uncaring, distant, have no compassion, are not relating. The truth is, you are relating but at a level deeper than thought and emotion.[1]

In my childhood, I'd learned to conceal my true feelings and say what I thought other people wanted to hear in an effort to avoid a negative reaction. Because Ken was non-reactive, I could take baby steps towards being emotionally honest with him. As he had done my whole life, he refused to join me in a pity party or let me play my well-perfected victim role. Ken had been a teacher available to me, right in front of my eyes the whole time, but I couldn't see through the fog of my own judgments.

Ken is really my half-brother, but growing up in the same house, he has just always been "brother" to me. Because he's four years older than me, he was already away at college by the time I entered high school. Once he left for college, he never lived

248

at home again, so we didn't get to know each other as adults until after my brain injury.

Being boy-genius smart, Ken received a full Air Force ROTC scholarship to the Massachusetts Institute of Technology. Whereas I was always anxious and scared of the world, Ken exhibited a bold, if not sometimes exuberantly I, curiosity about it. Even as a teenager, he seemed more knowledgeable and worldly somehow than the rest of us, as if he belonged somewhere other than our small town in North Carolina. According to him, he "knew something else lay beyond the mind, something radiant and purposeful, and wasn't willing to accept that something as the God defined by our Baptist upbringing".

During his first year at college, 750 miles from home, Ken felt restless and lost, and like many freshmen, rebelled. Upon reading Aldous Huxley's book, *Doors of Perception*, which details Huxley's existential thoughts while tripping on mescaline, and experimenting with psychedelic drugs himself, Ken's expanded mind began to actively search for that elusive "something else".

Much to our parents' dismay, Ken dropped out of MIT, moved to Martha's Vineyard, started meditating, and followed a macrobiotic diet and lifestyle, centered on whole plant-based foods, selected and prepared to maintain the balance of life on the planet. While there, he started hanging out with disciples of Bhagwan Shree Rajneesh, an Indian mystic, guru, and spiritual teacher who gained an international following in the 1970s and 1980s. Rajneesh's teachings emphasized the importance of meditation, awareness, love, celebration, and humor. Because of his open attitude towards sexuality, the press dubbed him the "sex guru" and got a lot of headlines out of the collection of nearly 100 Rolls-Royce automobiles that his followers gave him.

Ken, who'd been experiencing frequent psychic episodes during this period of his life, sought out a spiritual teacher to help him understand these occurrences and offer guidance. At the time, he found Bhagwan to be "iconoclastic, eclectic, and not awash in dogma"; however, he now feels that Rajneesh was spiritually naïve and that his teachings brought harm to his life and the lives of others. As a Rajneeshee, Ken dyed his clothes orange, wore wooden beads, grew long hair and a Jesus beard, took infrequent showers, and trekked to India.

You can imagine how happy our parents were about all of this. I remember Ken giving Neil Young's song, *Old Man*, to our dad in an attempt to foster some understanding and try to bridge the gap between them a little bit. I think his gesture just made Dad scratch his head in confusion even more.

After a year of living in India and a serious bout of blood poisoning, Ken returned to the US and proceeded to move around from North Carolina, Florida, the Rajneeshpuram in Oregon, and an ashram outside of Boston over the next five years. He met, and fathered a daughter with, a young woman who had been attending the North Carolina School of the Arts as a dancer. She dropped out of school and became a Rajneeshee also. Another set of thrilled parents.

Over the next decade, the relationship ended, Ken settled in San Francisco and landed in the "real" world. As a young man, he experienced moderate material success in a globetrotting career configuring and installing custom, high-end video systems. After a decade in the field, he found himself burned out, lonely, and lost in what he considered to be a self-centered life, and badly in need of a sabbatical. Around that same time, Chris died, and Ken began following a spiritual leader who claims to be the living incarnated Buddha. After sitting with the enlightened being for ten days in meditation, Ken became a monk and lived with other like-minded souls in a spiritual community in northern California for three years. Upon leaving the monastery, Ken migrated to Mt Shasta, California, where he spent the next decade.

Mt Shasta is located at the very northern tip of California in between San Francisco and Portland. At an altitude of around 3,600 feet, the city of Mt Shasta is nestled at the foot of Mount

Shasta, the second highest volcano in the US The vibrant, spiritual heartbeat of Mt Shasta's small artsy community appealed to Ken, and the rustic beauty of the surrounding area offered him plenty of opportunities to hike, star gaze, photograph wildflowers, and connect with nature.

The summer after the boys and I moved to North Carolina, we visited Ken in Mt Shasta with my mother, for what my sons agree was the best trip ever. Parking our car at the base of the volcanic mountain, we hiked a short distance up until we reached snow and proceeded to pelt each other with snowballs, in our shorts and T-shirts. We explored mountains of black glass obsidian rock, formed by rapidly cooling lava, went spelunking in volcanic caverns, splashed in a waterfall, slept with spiders, and saw a bear. Better than Disneyland!

While Ken still lived a very different lifestyle by conventional standards, he had discovered a happy medium between his alternative world and the material world. Over time, he acquired a greater level of spiritual maturity, developed a strong sense of stewardship for the planet, and began to feel compelled to be of service to the world. This desire, along with his technical aptitude, eventually led him to a successful career in the renewable energy industry.

Ken has since moved off the mountain and into the Sierra Foothills of California. He owns a house in a surprisingly typical rural neighborhood, albeit, the house does have solar panels on the roof, and there's a compost bin in the garage and deer wandering around the back yard. There are also packs of wild turkeys roaming the streets.

Ken and I grew close in the years following my brain injury. I have so much more respect for the bravery he showed in pursuing a life free from the "shoulds" rather than the griping fear that I allowed to imprison me. Although he didn't do everything the "right" way by traditional, societal norms, he did what was right for him. I can't help but wonder what my life would've looked like if I'd been a little bit more like him.

While some may question his decision to drop out of MIT, I admire Ken's bravery in living an authentic, fearless life that didn't place material wealth at the pinnacle of success and happiness. I remember sitting in my pretentious Florida home, which looked like a Pottery Barn catalogue, feeling sorry for him while he was probably feeling the same way about me.

"You're a bird in a cage with the door wide open," he told me about the time I was living in that picture-perfect home. While I didn't completely grasp what he meant at the time, it turns out that he was so right.

CHAPTER 16

mess to masterpiece

I don't spend one second of one day begrudging the past, even though the journey has been ridiculously hard and excruciatingly painful at times. Although I most definitely wouldn't make the same decisions, I don't have regret. Without every single detail, no matter how ugly, Chris' sickness and death, marrying Jimmie and the take-no-prisoners war after splitting, being a co-dependent single mother, having the tabloid-worthy relationship with Steve, attempting suicide and giving myself a serious brain injury, and losing custody of my children, I wouldn't be the person I am today. One of Steve's favorite sayings was, "If you like where you are, you can't complain about how you got there." I now know that I am who I choose to be today, but I only know this because of the struggles of my past.

Because of neuroplasticity, this concept is more than just a pleasant platitude. It's a neurological truth as our brains are molded by our lives: our thoughts, experiences, and relationships, from the day we're born until the day we die. A field of study called epigenetics is even confirming that the influence of these variables is potent enough to determine how our genes express themselves.

In addition to altering your brain and genes, what doesn't kill you really can make you stronger. Studies have shown that many trauma survivors report positive changes and enhanced personal development in keeping with the idea of growth from hardship, a phenomenon known as post-traumatic growth (PTG), which can give meaning to all the misery.

Soon after my brain injury, when I was spending huge chunks of time feeling sorry for myself, sitting on the couch watching TV, I caught a show by comedian Josh Blue, who won The Last Comic Standing competition in 2006 and has cerebral palsy. Astonished, I watched Josh stand up on stage and run through his routine with a heavy lisp, a pronounced limp, and his right arm waving spastically, uncontrollably around him the whole time.

Instead of letting his impairments imprison and limit him, he had made a successful career making jokes about them. We feel comfortable laughing at him because he is so comfortable with and can laugh at himself. "People ask me if I get nervous before coming up on stage. I say 'Heck no, I've got this many people staring at me all day.'" I was amazed to see that he'd taken what would have been a huge deficit to almost anybody and turned it into a benefit.

I read about Bobby Henline, a war veteran who served four tours of duty in Iraq, and on the last tour, his Humvee was hit by an explosive device. The only survivor, Henline suffered burns on over 38% of his face and body, severely disfiguring him. Turning horror into humor and inspiration, Bobby, who has no hair, only a stub of one ear, and eyes that don't blink, performs for the public and troops, joking that he doesn't need a Halloween costume and that his last tour was a blast.

These individuals' stories of not only surviving hardship, but using it as the very stuff to thrive, inspired me and got me to thinking that maybe – just maybe – it was possible to turn my disaster around. Talking funny, not remembering my phone number, and having the penmanship of a kindergartener seemed like pretty small potatoes compared to these guys. Like their examples, I've been surprised to find over the years that my abnormal speech can actually be an asset, because it gives me credibility, as it's the only immediate evidence that my story is real. If it weren't for my impaired speech, it would be easy to look at me and say "Yeah, yeah, yeah, she's had a hard life."

Pain, trauma, and adversity can be weapons of self destruction or opportunities for growth, depending on how we respond to and use them. As cliché as it sounds, it really is up to us to determine whether the challenges we are faced with become stumbling blocks or stepping stones. Viktor Frankl, a neurologist, psychiatrist, holocaust survivor, and author, wrote in *Man's Search for Meaning*:

The way in which a man accepts his fate and all the suffering it entails, the way in which he takes up his cross, gives him ample opportunity — even under the most difficult circumstances — to add a deeper meaning to his life.[1]

By learning to work with the same types of situations that used to cause me such panic and pain, I can now find calm, joy, and trust in myself and the universe. It's not that I don't have any troubles anymore – far from it – but I don't let them traumatize me, hijack my life, and steal my peace of mind. After a few minutes, sometimes hours – OK, maybe even days – of the "Oh shit! I can't effing believe this" rush, I eventually take a deep breath, stop struggling, accept what is, and start trying to figure out how to navigate the situation for my benefit.

Acceptance of the reality that's before me is always the necessary first step. To accept, to stop struggling against what's actually here, isn't the same as condoning. Accepting is surrendering to the moment as it is. Not giving up.

A Chinese finger puzzle offers the perfect illustration of how struggling against "what is" can trap you. Two people stick their index fingers into the ends of the paper, accordion-like contraption. As they pull against each other to get their fingers out, the puzzle grips tighter. The solution to removing the fingers is to push them towards each other, relaxing and widening the ends of the puzzle. Similarly, when a person struggles and resists against their circumstances, they become more tangled up and imprisoned. Only by giving in and changing perspectives can a person begin to work with, instead of against, the events in their life.

Byron Katie writes in *Loving What Is*:

The only time we suffer is when we believe a thought that argues with what is. When the mind is perfectly clear, what is is what we want. If you want reality to be different than it is, you might as well try to teach a cat to bark. You can try and try, and in the end the cat will look up at you and say, "Meow." Wanting reality to be different than it is is hopeless. You can spend the rest of your life trying to teach a cat to bark.[2]

After accepting what is, I ask myself "How do I make this work for me?" This one little question shifts my perspective from that of a victim at the mercy of random circumstances to that of a conscious person engaging my power and choosing to work with what's in front of me for my best interest. This philosophy has become my secret for making lemonade out of lemons, and works every time.

Although my first inclination still might be to do some slick maneuvering to try to avoid events altogether, one of my wise friends will suggest a different approach, or when I'm ready, I'll remember to step back and try on a different perspective. Cooperating with reality, instead of fighting against it, allows me to return to calm because, no matter what shitstorm is swirling around me, I can always find peace in my thoughts. By shifting my mindset, I change my feelings, and in turn, my experience of what's before me.

Pain and suffering come from our attachment to our thoughts, which comprises the gap between our thoughts or expectations and the reality of what is. Again, in *Loving What Is*, Byron Katie explains:

A thought is harmless unless we believe it. It is not our thoughts, but the attachment to our thoughts, that causes suffering. Thoughts are like the breeze or the leaves on the trees or the raindrops falling. They appear like that and through inquiry we can make friends with them. Would you argue with a raindrop? Raindrops aren't personal and neither are thoughts.[3]

Katie advises us to meet our thoughts with understanding and inquiry, and proposes that behind every uncomfortable feeling is a thought that's not true for us. To change stressful, uncomfortable feelings, we must understand that our thoughts are causing them instead of looking outside of ourselves, blaming circumstances or people. After my initial "aack!" reaction, acceptance of what is closes the space between expectations and reality, and ends the pain, and only then can I begin to figure out the best way to navigate the situation. Enlightened individuals, I understand, may never even experience the initial alarm. With a shrug, a highly evolved mind might think, "Oh, now this." I'm not anywhere near there yet, but I'm much closer than I used to be.

I find it helpful to remind myself that just because events bring me pain or aren't what I expected or desired, doesn't mean that they can't turn out good. So many times, circumstances that I pegged initially as crummy turned out to be just fine – great even – when all was said and done. I've learned not to presume that I know what's "best" in any situation. What we like, want, and think we need won't always bring happiness, provide growth, or get us to our goals.

*

I've lived the majority of my life doing all the "right" things to achieve the "good life" I heard about growing up. To get to the promised land, I invested exorbitant effort into trying to avoid the big, ugly "bad things" I'd learned that I didn't want. Trying to avoid pain. Trying to avoid loneliness. Trying to avoid failure. With fear looming large, my decisions in life were all about what I didn't want instead of what I did want, and life became a frantic

257

obstacle course of avoiding rather than achieving. What I desired was secondary to what I feared, which meant I spent all my time dodging and reacting instead of taking positive action towards my aspirations or happiness.

Eventually, this strategy led to a numb, depressed existence culminating in a suicide attempt. If medals were handed out for avoidance behavior, I would've taken my place at the top of the podium. I stayed in my marriage for far too long, unhappy and severely limited because I was terrified of venturing out on my own. After summoning the guts to leave, I dived head first into another unhealthy relationship because I didn't want to be alone and feared losing what I believed were my most valuable assets: my looks. I thought that I'd better land and hang onto the best thing I could find right then before I went gray and everything sagged. Next, rather than face that breakup and more legal entanglements with the ex, I tried to kill myself. Oh yeah, I was quite the expert.

Surprisingly, avoidance can be an unrecognized motivating factor behind much of our lives. Instead of having a clear idea of our desires and making decisions accordingly, which may involve some risk and discomfort, too often we make fear-based decisions that limit us and our happiness. These choices may allow us to avoid that uncomfortable squirmy feeling, but they don't provide opportunity for real growth or forward movement. So, we stay safe. Comfortable. Stagnant.

Pema Chodron, in her book *Taking the Leap*, likens this to living in a cocoon. She writes:

We stay in our cocoon because we are afraid – we're afraid of the feelings and reactions that life is going to trigger in us. We're afraid of what might come at us. But if this avoidance strategy worked, then Buddha wouldn't have needed to teach us anything, because our attempts to escape pain, which all living beings instinctively resort to, would result in security, happiness and comfort, and there would be no problem.[4]

She advises us to see these uncomfortable, fearful situations as opportunities rather than obstacles. Chodron encourages us to "get comfortable with, begin to relax with, lean into whatever the experience may be", and tells us to drop the knee-jerk reactions and storylines, pause, and breathe. Be present. Be awake and aware. Be conscious and brutally honest with yourself about your intentions, reasons, and actions.

In the Heart of the Soul, Gary Zukav proposes that energy leaves the body, through thinking, speaking, and acting, as either fear and doubt or as love and trust.[5] According to Zukav, when energy exits as fear and doubt, the end result is always painful. (Just look at the events of my past life for proof.) Energy released as love and trust produces scenarios yielding the opposite: gratitude, contentment, and joy. (I'm hoping to prove this one true from here on out.) Zukav says that experiencing painful emotions is a sure sign that energy is being discharged as fear and doubt.

Fear is produced when your amygdala, a primitive part of the brain responsible for the fight or flight response, kicks in to ensure self-preservation. But in this day and age, when running into a life or death situation is highly unlikely on a daily basis, your amygdala doesn't need to be so vigilant. Mother Nature was kind enough to program the amygdala with certain fears at birth, and we pack on many more, learned from the world around us, the people in our lives, and our experiences. When we feel that pit-in-the-bottom-of-our-stomach afraid feeling, we need to make it a habit to ask ourselves if the fear is really warranted or if it's just an instinctual reaction to something unfamiliar and unknown. From your brain's perspective, to get over a fear, you have to expose yourself to it.

My amygdala has been on high alert most of my life. I've calmed it down with mindfulness practices and by consciously doing that which scares the heck out of me. Those around me have heard me say over and over, "I refuse to live a fear-based existence."

These days, if I'm scared of something, I'll usually take it on because I know there will be a sense of freedom and growth on the other side – and usually lots of laughs along the way.

Not long ago, I attended a social gathering by myself where I only knew one person well and a few people that I could call acquaintances, but barely. For some, this may not be any big deal. If you're one of these people, I'm in awe of you. With my speech impairment and social aversion, showing up solo was so damn hard for me. Even before the brain injury, I would have gladly rather had a root canal. Upon arriving at the event and not wanting to go inside, I sat in the car bargaining with myself. Would just making it to the parking lot be good enough? I already knew the answer to that.

Pulling on my big girl panties, I took a deep breath and a few more, and with constant positive self-talk and thought reframing, I went inside. Although I didn't stay long, can't say that I enjoyed it that much, and my amygdala was in turbo mode the whole time, I'm glad I didn't chicken out. Because I overruled my dread, I know that doing something similar will be easier the next time and even easier the time after that. By confronting and moving through fear, it subsides because the amygdala learns not to respond as if your life is on the line. Although the alarmed feeling may never disappear completely, it will lessen over time.

Living a fearless life doesn't mean recklessly throwing caution to the wind, because caution isn't the same as fear, and I have to be brutally honest with myself to know the difference sometimes. To consciously choose actions and thoughts that coincide with my desired growth and intentions, even if they are fear-producing, is always an option in every situation. Through these choices, I decide who I'm going to be. Dr Joe Vitale said, "You are the masterpiece of your own life; you are the Michelangelo of your experience. The David that you are sculpting is you." Your emotions and thoughts are your artist's tools.

I read somewhere that the more you love yourself, the less effect fear has on you. In an evolutionary process that took years, I moved out of my anxiety-ridden, fear-based existence, transcended my past, and began to experience compassion for myself. Because absolutely everything else good stems from self-love, learning to love myself was a cornerstone for creating the "new Debbie".

*

I've always considered myself a compassionate person and would have qualified as one of the biggest bleeding hearts around, but I was shocked to realize that I'd never included myself in my kindness. The same compassion that I gave so freely to others, I stingily withheld from myself. As Jack Kornfield said, "If your compassion does not include yourself, it is incomplete."

In our culture, compassion for others is highly valued. Although it's admirable to be supportive of a friend, kind to others, and help those in need, we tend to treat ourselves with a very different set of standards, where self-criticism is encouraged and even considered to be self-motivating. We beat ourselves up thinking that doing so will help us become better people and prevent us from making the same mistakes again, and being kind to oneself is often confused with narcissism. Self-compassion is about not having any judgment at all and about responding to yourself with kindness, caring, and understanding.

Studies have shown that self-compassion has mental health benefits, including fewer depressive thoughts and more optimistic ones, as well as overall greater happiness and life satisfaction. As opposed to self-esteem, self-compassion fosters a type of self-worth that isn't contingent on outcomes or social comparison, because the emphasis is on learning, rather than performance. When you extend kindness to yourself, life becomes about being healthy, happy, and reaching your highest potential, instead of being about competing, or feeling special or superior to everyone else. Self-compassion can be learned and is at the heart of mindfulness practices.

In a huge "aha moment", I realized that I'd always bent over backwards to be nice to everyone but me! I could forgive anyone for almost any heinous act, allowing me to keep my pretend world intact, but no justification was ever good enough for me not to live up to the ultra-high expectations I held for myself.

Using this perfectionism as fuel, I did accomplish some pretty amazing things. I put myself through college and graduated with honors. After 24 hours of back labor with no pain meds, I gave birth to a whopping nine pounder. I've managed to stay within a ten pound weight range my entire adult life. But placing unrealistic demands on myself also caused astronomical anxiety and provided ample ammunition for my low self-esteem. I never put that college degree to good use in an impressive career. I should have been a better mother to that baby. No matter what my weight, I never looked like the women in the magazines.

Because I didn't value or love myself, nothing I did was ever enough. That word, "enough", can lead to a boatload of suffering. What is "enough" anyway? The dictionary definition is, "adequate for the want or need; sufficient for the purpose or to satisfy desire". So enough is different for every person, in every case, and each individual gets to decide his or her own wants, needs, and desires, determining what enough is for them. Without changing anything but my perspective, I've recognized that I am enough, because I'm the one who defines what enough is for me.

With the brain injury, I was the most "not enough" I'd ever been. I had far fewer people and material things in my life than before; however, my meager circumstances became enough because I changed my definition of the word. "If I don't extend compassion to myself now, in this condition, as messed up as I am, how can I expect anyone else to?" I thought. By adjusting expectations and purposefully looking for abundance in my life, instead of focusing on what was lacking, less became more. Epicurus, the ancient Greek philosopher, wrote, "Not what we have, but what we enjoy constitutes our abundance."

While compassion and generosity are generally seen as positive attributes, I gave from a place of insecurity, low self-esteem, and a sense of lack, in an attempt to bolster my feelings about myself. That's giving to get, which is taking in the end. Like an unspoken insurance policy, I thought the more I gave to everybody, surely the more they would give back to me. Right? Wrong! I attracted people who were more than happy to take and take and keep on taking. Because I allowed this in my life, I ended up depleted and resentful, because I wasn't receiving anything in return or giving to myself.

A people pleaser of the worst kind, I tried to dodge others' displeasure at the cost of my own happiness. This mentality created a world in which I placed my happiness in the hands of others for them to crumple up and throw away, like a piece of trash. My people-pleasing tactics were really a veiled attempt to sway others' judgment of and reciprocation to me. When a school party needed organizing, baking, or decorating, I was your girl. When someone's kids needed to be watched, I was the go-to. You name it, I did it. However, I consistently neglected to take care of, give to, or help myself.

The flip side of people pleasing is resentment and hostility. Even if other people did respond graciously to my efforts, I didn't allow myself to receive their kindness, stockpiling animosity instead. I was numb to any consideration that did come my way, and compliments slid off of me like Teflon. In order to keep up my pleasant front, the bitterness I felt got buried and either erupted in angry outbursts or showed up as passive aggression. The people pleaser finds other people pleasers with whom they can vent, and I had one friend where playing the victim and spewing anger was about the only thing we had in common. Boy, we could have a pity party!

Having had way too much up-close and personal experience with narcissists in my life, I tried really hard to not be the least bit selfish, like them, which put me on my people-pleasing path in the first place. However, I've discovered that a little selfishness is healthy and absolutely essential to being happy. Even giving can be taken to an unhealthy extreme.

The Dalai Lama has this to say about selfishness:

It is important that when pursuing our own self-interest we should be "wise selfish" and not "foolish selfish." Being foolish selfish means pursuing our own interests in a narrow, shortsighted way. Being wise selfish means taking a broader view and recognizing that our own long-term individual interest lies in the welfare of everyone. Being wise selfish means being compassionate.[6]

I'm not a people pleaser anymore, and in fact, I'd bet that some would say I've gone too far in the other direction and have gotten a little too comfortable saying "no". First and foremost, I make myself the priority because I figured out that before having anything extra to offer someone freely, I have to give to myself. The brain injury taught me how to make my needs paramount because I absolutely had to, in order to recover. In every situation, I've learned that there is always a caring way to respond, which considers what is being asked of me, while factoring in my own needs and happiness. My answer doesn't have to be "yes" or "no", and is usually something in between.

I've learned to pay attention to many sources of wisdom to know what's right for me. We receive intelligence from all around us and many parts of our bodies, not just the brains in our heads. Knowing comes from our brains, our hearts, and even our guts. Intuitive intelligence has been validated by study after study.

Science is proving that our hearts are actually the first organ that experience the world. The heart perceives by interpreting incoming data, responding accordingly, and sending information to the brain for further processing. Over half of the cells in the heart are neural cells, clustered in ganglia and connected to the neural network of the body through axon-dendrites, just like in the brain. The heart is a specialized brain hooked into the central nervous system, making and releasing its own neurotransmitters, and the neurons in the heart have even been found to store memories.

We've all heard of a gut feeling. Well, the enteric nervous system consists of a network of some 100 million neurons (more than in the spinal cord) that line the gastrointestinal system. Although it can and does operate independently of the brain and spinal cord, the enteric nervous system also transmits and receives information from the autonomic nervous system, influencing physical and emotional states. Just like the brain in your head, the gut brain uses dopamine and serotonin, and other neurotransmitters, and as you might have guessed, is greatly affected by what we eat. Science is linking the enteric nervous system to many conditions, including stress, depression, autism, and even osteoporosis.

A person will greatly benefit from allowing their heart, head, and gut to contribute in directing their life and creating their reality. In Western cultures, we're often taught early on to rely solely on the brain in our heads and to not trust any other source of wisdom.

In the past, my bossy brain dominated the show, incessantly chattering nervous nonsense, freaking out, and barking orders. I'd severed my other channels of intelligence and didn't trust a message from my heart or gut, even if it could break through the firewall. When making decisions, I looked to others for advice or followed the "shoulds" of society. Through mindfulness practices, I've encouraged and increased my intuitive wisdom and now feel like I have wise friends in high places on-call 24/7 within my own being.

*

Daniel Siegel, professor of psychiatry at UCLA, executive director of the Mindsight Institute, and author, has coined the term "mindsight" to describe the human ability to observe and influence the flow of energy and information that makes up our own mental activity. Learned through mindfulness practices, mindsight is the ability of observation, careful discernment, and social and emotional intelligence.

In studies at UCLA using basic mindfulness techniques with preschoolers, researchers have successfully decreased bullying while increasing empathy and the ability to pause before acting. In preschoolers! In other studies, mindfulness techniques have been shown to actually change the executive functioning of the brains of adults with attention deficit disorders.[7]

Siegel uses the Triangle of Well-Being to illustrate optimal mental health. While it's a common belief that the mind is the activity of the brain, he proposes that that's only one part of it, with each point on the Triangle of Well-Being being an essential component of mental health. The first point is the physical brain and nervous system, the mechanisms by which energy and information flow. The second point, the sharing of information and energy, is our relationships with others. And the third point on the triangle is our mind, which is the process regulating the flow of information and energy.

Because of neuroplasticity, each point influences the others as the flow of energy and information moves in all directions around the triangle. The mind changes the structure of the brain and relationships. The brain changes the structure of the mind and relationships. Relationships change both. Understanding this dynamic can help mental health practitioners, educators, parents, partners, and individuals improve brains and lives.

Similarly, in his article *Good News: You Are Not Your Brain*[8], Deepak Chopra argues that although our thoughts and life experiences shape our brains and identities, we aren't our brains, and the brain isn't the mind. The author refers to humans as "conscious agents" with minds that shape reality, including "the reality of the brain".

While there's no question that people can become trapped by the wiring of their brains, as in depression, addiction, and phobias, he proposes that it's degrading to human potential to assume that the brain uses the human being, instead of vice versa, and doesn't provide an explanation for those who break free of bad habits, kick their addictions, or overcome depression. In these cases, he suggests that the mind takes control, shapes the brain, and the individual returns to the natural state of using their brain instead of the other way around. When the mind finds its true power, the results can include healing, inspiration, insight, self-awareness, discovery, curiosity, and quantum leaps in personal growth. "... [I]t would be a grave mistake, and a disservice to our humanity, to forget that the real glory of human existence is the mind, not the brain that serves it," concludes Chopra.

I've taken control of my mind, consciously directed my brain, and completely turned my attitude and life around. Starting at the lowest rungs on the mental health ladder, I've climbed to way above the normal line. I like the view much better from here – and to think it all happened because of a suicide attempt and brain injury. I'm happy, calm, optimistic, fulfilled, connected, and engaged in life. I told someone recently, "I don't feel like I'm searching for anything." That's a mighty nice feeling.

This peace comes at a time when my children live in another state and my friends and social interactions are few. I'm without a significant other and don't have any real plan for financial security as I head into my golden years. When spelled out like that, it doesn't sound too impressive, and the old me would be panicking about now, but the amazing thing is that I'm happy and not worried. Because I have faith and trust in myself and the universe, I know that I've got this, and I'm even curious to see how it all turns out.

Discovering the true power of my mind and learning to put it to work for me has not only allowed me to heal from a serious brain injury, but also to transform myself and my life from a mess to a masterpiece.

Anyone can do it. No brain injury required!

It may Not Look anything Like the Life you'd planned, But It can still Be Good

At more than a decade post-suicide attempt and brain injury, life has calmed way down, acquired a kind of comforting hum to it, and is eons away from what I thought it would look like at this age. We don't need to go into specifics, but let's just say I'm well past the half century mark at this point. And I'm happy to report that menopause was a breeze, and my hair miraculously still hasn't turned gray. It's a good thing too because I find myself stepping back into the big scary, exciting world – where most people are at 20 something.

Oh well, better late than never.

I've spent the last decade building a new me and a new life. The new me has some things in common with the old me. I still love cats. Currently, I'm down to four, and my old buddy Jack Russell left me over a year ago. The new me still loves pickles and red wine – usually not together – and two glasses is my max now. She is still on the thin side too, with really thick, unruly hair. But that's about all the similarities that readily come to mind.

The new me averages doing hot yoga about four times a week. In fact, after writing the book, I went on to open a hot yoga studio with some other passionate yogis and yoginis using a portion of the lump sum settlement I got from Jimmie. While I never felt confident enough in my memory or speech to get up in front of people and teach classes, I did perform most of the marketing and PR for the studio. After two years, it became evident to me that owning a yoga studio wasn't my future, and I sold it to one of the partners. I still go there and sweat.

The new me hardly ever puts on her make-up, brushes her hair, or wears the latest trend. My typical uniform is boots and jeans in the winter, and flip-flops and a sundress in the summer. I have to laugh at how somebody who used to be so concerned with her appearance shows up at yoga now in the same cat-hair-covered clothes that she wore the day before, bare-faced, with the age spots clearly showing, and hair hastily pulled back in a ponytail. If Chris could see me now, he'd cringe. The new me is OK with a messy house, black crud baked on the bottom of the oven, and a disheveled underwear drawer.

The post-brain injury me knows that these things don't really matter. And if they do to someone else, then that's their deal, not mine. And I don't give a flip. Seriously! I've got more important things to spend my time on.

I spent the first three years after the brain injury doing nothing but working on my healing. The next few years included a few healing therapies, lots of yoga and exercise, and huge chunks of time sitting at a computer recording the story you just read. Composing this book was a healing therapy of its own. It's as if putting all the hurt, drama, and emotion down on paper allowed me to expunge it. When I read it now, it feels like it happened to someone else. I mean intellectually, I know it was me, but I don't have one shred of the gut-wrenching pain and anger that once accompanied the memories. I don't know if it was the writing purge, my brain forging new pathways, countless hours of meditation and yoga, or just the years passing – probably a combination of them all – but something worked. Healing really is possible.

In fact, while I wouldn't want to go back to the person I was before the brain injury for a million dollars, I do, sometimes, miss the emotion of that life. I don't mean to romanticize it, but the exhilarating highs and rock bottom lows were addictive, seductive, and meaningful in their own way. If any of you out there have recovered from being an emotional mess like I was, do you know what I mean? Even though the pain and darkness were excruciating at times, it felt like I was really alive – alive in a bad horror movie, but alive. I guess I get nostalgic for the adrenaline rush.

Life these days is good. I'm happy and content, but it's a little flat compared to the lump-in-the-throat rollercoaster ride before. On a scale of one to ten, my happiness set point hovers somewhere around an eight. It takes something fairly extreme to move me off of that number very far in either direction.

However, I haven't achieved monk status yet. I proved to myself that I could still feel strong emotions when the neighbor's dog ate one of my cats. Surprisingly, I found myself screaming cuss words at the young man, who had put my cat in a garbage bag and threw him in the big, green, city garbage can, with his ID tag clearly visible, saying that he lived right across the street. Oh, yes! I can still go there.

To make a long, sad story short, more neighbors got involved, there was more yelling at different people, and nasty emails posted on the neighborhood board. I got really ugly and emotional. I have no doubt that I'm now "the crazy cat lady bitch" of the neighborhood. But that's OK. When I calmed down, which took a few weeks, I forgave myself and him, and found the lessons to be learned in the experience.

That's a big difference in the new me. When I have strong emotions now, I express them instead of stuffing them or being nice just to avoid conflict. I don't carry the anger and resentment around with me like I used to. I return to my baseline of calm pretty quickly. OK, that one took a while, and I'll admit that I still want to give that neighbor the finger every time I see him. But I don't.

*

The new me looks and acts normal (if there is such a thing.) Upon first meeting me, I don't think you would suspect that I have had a serious brain injury with some lasting impairments. In fact, I've been told as much by many people. However, if you spent any time with me on an ongoing basis, I have no doubt that you would scratch your head and think, "Something's not quite right with her."

I like to say that I'm similar to someone on the autism spectrum. The nuances of person-to-person interactions, politeness, and social norms elude and frustrate me, for the most part. I've learned the "acceptable" ways to behave and consciously have to remind and restrain myself. For example, I still have the very annoying post-brain injury trait of impulsively interrupting people when they're speaking. I know I do this. So, when I catch myself doing it, I consciously remind myself to listen and wait. And I still just cannot get the rhythm of speaking on the phone.

A lot of humor goes right over my head, but then some things I think are hilariously funny, and nobody else does. Before the brain injury, my math skills were weak. After, all I can say is, "Thank goodness for calculators!" I may have re-learned the multiplication tables after the injury, but I never used them, so now they're gone. My handwriting still looks like a fifth grader's, and I still type with a claw. I could go on.

But you know what? It's all good, and so much better than before.

The new me has the emotional intelligence skills she needs to make it on her own and be content in this life. I talked about many of those skills in this book: resilience, mental strength, self-esteem, self-compassion, and a tenacious, never-give-up drive. I won't say that I have what it takes "to be happy". I think happiness is fleeting, overrated, and a shallow, empty goal to aspire to. Life can be much deeper than just striving to be happy. I want to live a life of purpose, value, and meaning. If a little shallow happiness gets thrown in along the way, I won't complain.

I've spent years honing traits that allow me to be at peace with myself and the world – and while some days they are more readily available than others – I really do believe that these characteristics are part of my core now. Believe me, if I can learn and internalize this stuff, you can too.

As an extension of all my online brain activities and blog, I went on to start a website: The Best Brain Possible, and gave accounts of my experiences on the other major social media platforms around at the time. To my surprise, I've become regarded as an experiential mental health expert, and am asked to do podcasts and interviews along with neuroscientists and PhDs. As my online audiences grew, so did my social media marketing knowledge.

At the time of writing, I've just started a part-time job doing content creation and online marketing for a local university. It's my first "real" job post-brain injury, and in over two decades – since before the kids. I've been freelancing for a few years, which really means that I was spending a lot of time looking for work and making very little money when I found it.

While I'm competent and un-brain-injured in my own environment, I was very quickly reminded that I do still have some deficits. For the new employee orientation, seven of us met in the Human Resources office on the ground floor and went to the training room as a group. Later, when I had to go out to my car to retrieve the registration for a parking pass, I got in the elevator and pressed the down button. The elevator doors closed and immediately opened again with a loud ding. Let's try this again. Ding! Again. Ding! By now, I was getting that anxious, panicky, brain-injured feeling, and thinking, "I hope they can't hear that" in the training room just across the hall to the right.

At this point I had the bright idea to press a different floor. The building was only three stories. I just needed to do something – anything – to make the elevator move and quit dinging. So, I went to the third floor and got off when the doors opened. Now, I'm walking around the third floor lost with no idea where I am, or how to get to the car. Sure, if I had calmed down and used logic, I could have figured it out, but by now, my amygdala was running the show. I actually walked in an office with an open door and asked someone to help me. The kind soul took pity on the woman who could get so terribly lost in a three-story building.

It turned out that we had gone to the basement for training, not the second floor like I thought. While the experience was stressful and embarrassing at the time, I had to laugh and extend compassion and understanding to myself later. I was doing the best I could, and that's enough for me. Let's just hope my new employer is patient.

*

The new me hasn't had a romantic relationship since Steve. I find it amusing and ironic that I have a book with the word "sex" in the title. In fact, I'm going to have to learn to ride the bike again – or not. Sex is not important to me now, and I don't know if it will ever be. I've been known to quip, "If I never see another dick up close and personal in my life – I'm OK with that." And I am. I'm not advocating that this is healthy, or the right thing for anyone else. It's right for me, for right now.

I still love my solitude. I don't want to share my bathroom. I don't want to share my bed. I don't want to spend an inordinate amount of time shaving or primping. I also want to watch what I want on Netflix, and eat what I want to eat for dinner, when I want to eat it. After four decades of completely denying my own wants and needs, I'm still reveling in being a bit self-centered.

I think it's probably a natural reaction to veer to the other extreme. I do believe I'll find my way back to the middle one day. And if not, that's fine too.

*

I do share my house (but not my bathroom) these days with my oldest son, Collin. He moved in with me a couple of years ago, after graduating from college, and is now in graduate school for mental health counseling about an hour away. Yes, he said my suicide attempt influenced his choice of studies. Because he has an assistantship working in the department, he lives near school during the week, but comes home almost every weekend. It makes my heart happy to say that my house is his "home" once again.

I don't mind sharing my space with him or cooking foods that he especially likes, or altering my life in other ways to accommodate him. I have really appreciated having the chance to get to know him again as a young man, and to be able to parent and guide him in a way that I was not able to years ago. I taught him the wrong ways to react, emote, and behave. I feel very fortunate to have this opportunity to model better life skills for him.

And yes, we have had some of those heart-to-heart talks about what I did and how it affected him. I've seen the evidence of the deep wounds my actions made in him. I am terribly sorry that it all happened the way it did, and I would do it all differently if I could. But I can't. I can only extend compassion to myself and do things differently now.

Gabe has come out of all the mess remarkably unscathed. I like to think that maybe in those three years he came to visit me by himself every month, that we were both able to make some emotional repairs. He healed as I did. He is now a well-adjusted junior at a prestigious east-coast college. He is preparing for a career in environmental policy, and has interned for some green organizations in the DC area. He even meditates and runs. Collin does hot yoga and meditates.

I guess I have rubbed off on them a bit despite being separated for all those years – both good and bad. I'm curious to see what's ahead for all of us.

It sure doesn't look anything like the life I had planned, but it's still good.

If you found this book interesting ...
why not read this next?

Teacup in a Storm

Finding my Psychiatrist

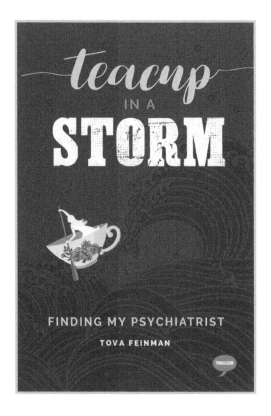

Wracked with trauma from childhood abuse,
Tova sought therapy to soothe her mind. However, it is
not as easy as simply finding a person to talk to ...

**If you found this book interesting ...
why not read this next?**

Shiny Happy Person

Finding the Sun Between
Clouds of Depression

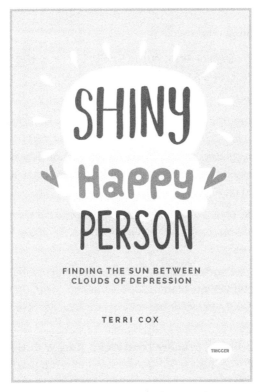

Shiny Happy Person is the story of one girl's inspirational
rise after a devastating mental breakdown that gave
her tormenting panic attacks, suicidal thoughts,
bouts of insomnia and crippling headaches.

END NOTES

Chapter Three

1   *Roots: The Saga of An American Family,* TV miniseries
    (ABC, April, 1977).

Chapter Four

1   **Quin Ping**. *The Relationship of Suicide Risk to Family History of
    Suicide and Psychiatric Disorders.* December, 2003,
    www.psychiatrictimes.com/addiction/relationship-suicide-
    risk-family-history-suicide-and-psychiatric-disorders,
    accessed on 4/17/18.

2   **Voracek, M. & Loibl, L.M.**. *Genetics of suicide: a systematic
    review of twin studies.* Wien Klin Wochenschr. 2007; 119
    (15-16): 463–75.

3   **Elizabeth Landau**. *Suicidal behavior may run in families.*
    CNN News Online, March, 2009, www.cnn.com/2009/
    HEALTH/03/24/suicide.hereditary.families/, accessed on
    11/15/15.

4   **Gerome Breen**, **Bradley Todd Webb**, **Amy W Butler**, **et al**.
    The American Journal Of Psychiatry. Volume 168 Issue 8,
    August, 2011, pp. 840–47, http://ajp.psychiatryonline.org/doi
    /abs/10.1176/appi.ajp. 2011.10091342, accessed on 11/15/15

Chapter Five

1 **Roger Ebert**. *Ted Talk: Remaking My Voice*. April, 2011,
   www.ted.com/talks/roger_ebert_remaking_my_voice.html.

2 **Roger Ebert**. *Finding My Own Voice.*
   Roger Ebert's Journal, August 12, 2009,
   www.rogerebert.com/rogers-journal/finding-my-own-voice.

3 **Eckhart Tolle**. *A New Earth: Awakening to Your Life's Purpose.*
   (London, England, Penguin, 2006), 56.

Chapter Six

1 **Daniel Oppenheimer**. *Alcohol Helps Brain Remember
   Says New Study*. April 12, 2011, http://web5.cns.utexas.edu/
   news/2011/04/alcohol-helps-the-brain-remember/.

2 **Pema Chodron**. *Pema Chodron – The Doorway
   to Freedom*. 2003, www.youtube.com/
   watch?v=P7dtLIXE5fU&list=PL4D822228DCC71E89.

Chapter Nine

1 **Michael Mason**. *Eulogy for Chris Hampton.*
   (writer, editor, producer, www.mikemason.net/work/resume.
   php). February, 1995.

Chapter Ten

1 **Suzane Northrup**. *The Séance Healing Messages From Beyond.*
   (New York, Dell Publishing, 1995), 169–99.

2 **Tracy Thorne**, Words and voice, music by Ben Watt,
   "Missing," ©1994 Atlantic Records.

Chapter Twelve

1 **Elizabeth Lesser**. *Broken Open: How Difficult Times Can Help
   Us Grow*. (New York, Villard Books, 2005), 115.

2 **Gary Zukav & Linda Francis**. *The Heart Of The Soul.*
   (New York, NY, Fireside Publishing, 2002), 237–46.

Chapter Thirteen

1 **Lynne McTaggart**. *The Intention Experiment.*
(New York, NY, Free Press, 2007).

2 **Norman Doidge**. *The Brain That Changes Itself.*
(New York, NY, The Penguin Group, 2007).

3 **Norman Doidge**. *The Brain That Changes Itself.*
(New York, NY, The Penguin Group, 2007), 316.

Chapter Fourteen

1 **Carolyn Myss** PhD. *Why People Don't Heal and How They Can.*
(New York, NY, Three Rivers Press, 1997), 28.

2 **Steven Levine**. *Waking the Tiger.*
(Berkley, CA, North Atlantic Books, 1997).

3 **Elizabeth Lesser**. *The Seeker's Guide.*
(New York, Villard Books, 1999), 362.

4 **Norman Doidge**. *The Brain That Changes Itself.*
(New York, NY, The Penguin Group, 2007), 204.

5 **Shakti Gawain**. *The Four Levels of Healing.*
(New York, NY, MJF Books, 1997), 30.

6 **Lynne McTaggart**. *The Intention Experiment.*
(New York, NY, Free Press, 2007), xxi.

7 **Lynne McTaggart**. *The Intention Experiment.*
(New York, NY, Free Press, 2007), xxix.

8 **Dr Rick Hanson**. *Hardwiring Happiness.*
(New York, NY, Harmony Books, 2013), 23.

9 **Robert Sapolsky**. *The Psychology of Stress*. March 20, 2012,
http://greatergood.berkeley.edu/gg_live/science_meaningful
_life_videos/speaker/robert_m._sapolsky/robert_m._sapolsky_
the_psychology_of_stress/.

10 **Robert Sapolsky**. *Why Zebras Don't Get Ulcers.*
(New York, NY, Holt Paperbacks, 1994), 384.

11 **Jeffrey Schwartz** MD. *Brain Lock.* (New York, New York, Harper Collins Publishers, 1997).

12 **Dr Jeff Browne & Mark Fenske**. *The Winner's Brain.* (Cambridge, MA, De Capo Press, 2011), 168.

Chapter Fifteen

1 **Eckhart Tolle**. *A New Earth: Awakening to Your Life's Purpose.* (London, England, Penguin, 2006), 176.

Chapter Sixteen

1 **Viktor Frankl**. *Man's Search For Meaning.* (Cutchogue, NY, Buccaneer Books, 1992), 76.

2 **Bryon Katie**. *Loving What Is.* (New York, NY, Three Rivers Press, 2002), 1–2.

3 **Bryon Katie**. *Loving What Is.* (New York, NY, Three Rivers Press, 2002), 5.

4 **Pema Chodron**. *Taking The Leap.* (Boston, MA, Shambhala Publications,2009), 17.

5 **Gary Zukav & Linda Francis**. *The Heart Of The Soul.* (New York, NY, Fireside Publishing, 2002), 51–55.

6 **Dalai Lama**. https://plus.google.com/+DalaiLama/posts/XfDYPFH6Jwb (March 2012).

7 **Dan Siegel**. *Dr Dan Siegel Inspire To Rewire.* http://drdansiegel.com/. (March 2012).

8 **Deepak Chopra**. *Good News: You Are Not Your Brain.* March 27, 2012, http://www.huffingtonpost.com/deepak-chopra/mind-brain_b_1379446.html.

And now that you don't have to be perfect, you can be good.

John Steinbeck, East Of Eden

the *Shaw* mind
FOUNDATION

Creating hope for children,
adults and families

Sign up to our charity, The Shaw Mind Foundation

www.shawmindfoundation.org

and keep in touch with us;
we would love to hear from you.

*We aim to bring to an end the suffering and despair caused
by mental health issues. Our goal is to make help and support
available for every single person in society, from all walks of
life. We will never stop offering hope. These are our promises.*

www.triggerpublishing.com

Trigger is a publishing house devoted to opening conversations about mental health. We tell the stories of people who have suffered from mental illnesses and recovered, so that others may learn from them.

Adam Shaw is a worldwide mental health advocate and philanthropist. Now in recovery from mental health issues, he is committed to helping others suffering from debilitating mental health issues through the global charity he co-founded, The Shaw Mind Foundation. www.shawmindfoundation.org

Lauren Callaghan (CPsychol, PGDipClinPsych, PgCert, MA (hons), LLB (hons), BA), born and educated in New Zealand, is an innovative industry-leading psychologist based in London, United Kingdom. Lauren has worked with children and young people, and their families, in a number of clinical settings providing evidence based treatments for a range of illnesses, including anxiety and obsessional problems. She was a psychologist at the specialist national treatment centres for severe obsessional problems in the UK and is renowned as an expert in the field of mental health, recognised for diagnosing and successfully treating OCD and anxiety related illnesses in particular. In addition to appearing as a treating clinician in the critically acclaimed and BAFTA award-winning documentary *Bedlam*, Lauren is a frequent guest speaker on mental health conditions in the media and at academic conferences. Lauren also acts as a guest lecturer and honorary researcher at the Institute of Psychiatry Kings College, UCL.

Please visit the link below:

www.triggerpublishing.com

Join us and follow us ...

@triggerpub

Search for us on Facebook

Please visit the author's website: **thebestbrainpossible.com**